*Pariswalks*

This is the
Henry Holt Walks Series,
which originated with
PARISWALKS *by Alison and Sonia Landes*
Other titles in the series include:

LONDONWALKS *by Anton Powell*
JERUSALEMWALKS *by Nitza Rosovsky*
FLORENCEWALKS *by Anne Holler*
ROMEWALKS *by Anya M. Shetterly*
VIENNAWALKS *by J. Sydney Jones*
VENICEWALKS *by Chas Carner and Alessandro Giannatasio*
RUSSIAWALKS *by David and Valeria Matlock*

# PARISWALKS

REVISED EDITION

## Alison and Sonia Landes

*Photographs by Anne Peretz*

*An Owl Book*

Henry Holt and Company • New York

Copyright © 1981, 1991 by Alison and Sonia Landes
Photographs copyright © 1981, 1991 by Anne Peretz
All rights reserved, including the right to reproduce
this book or portions thereof in any form.
Published by Henry Holt and Company, Inc.,
115 West 18th Street, New York, New York 10011.
Published in Canada by Fitzhenry & Whiteside Limited,
195 Allstate Parkway, Markham, Ontario L3R 4T8.

Library of Congress Cataloging-in-Publication Data
Landes, Alison.
Pariswalks / Alison & Sonia Landes ; photographs by Anne Peretz.—
1st Owl Book ed.
p.  cm.
"An Owl book."
Includes index.
ISBN 0-8050-1186-2
1. Paris (France)—Description—Tours. 2. Walking—
France—Paris—Guide-books. I. Landes, Sonia.
II. Peretz, Anne. III. Title.
DC707.L28 1991
914.4'36104839—dc20                                    90-43261
                                                            CIP

Henry Holt books are available at special discounts for bulk
purchases for sales promotions, premiums, fund-raising, or educational use. Special editions or book excerpts can also be created to
specification.
For details contact:
Special Sales Director, Henry Holt and Company, Inc.,
115 West 18th Street, New York, New York 10011.

First published by New Republic Books in 1975.

First Owl Book Edition—1981
Revised Edition—1991

Designed by Claire Naylon Vaccaro

Printed in the United States of America
Recognizing the importance of preserving the written word,
Henry Holt and Company, Inc., by policy, prints all of its
first editions on acid-free paper. ∞
1  3  5  7  9  10  8  6  4  2

To David, *père de famille*

# Contents

# Acknowledgments

We would like to thank all our friends who came to visit, and who were willingly or unwillingly dragged out into the streets of Paris to test our walks with us, and all those who read the manuscript, for their encouragement and helpful advice. We have received many wonderful letters from readers and walkers, with valuable information and suggestions. One person to whom we are most indebted is Jacques Hillairet, author of the *Dictionnaire Historique des Rues de Paris*, the bible for all who want to know the history of Paris street by street. An exceptional note of gratitude and admiration for Theresa Burns, our editor. Not only is she always there to give us sound advice when we call, she cares deeply about the Walks Series. We thank her for that. *Un grand merci* to our spouses, David and Nicholas, for their moral support, and to David for reading every word we wrote with a discerning eye.

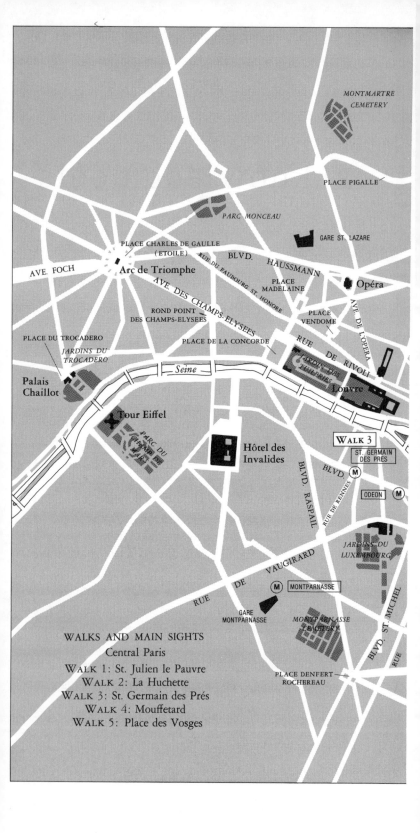

MONTMARTRE CEMETERY

PLACE PIGALLE

PARC MONCEAU

GARE ST. LAZARE

PLACE CHARLES DE GAULLE (ETOILE)

BLVD. HAUSSMANN

AVE. FOCH

Arc de Triomphe

RUE DU FAUBOURG ST. HONORE

PLACE MADELAINE

Opéra

AVE. DES CHAMPS-ELYSEES

ROND POINT DES CHAMPS-ELYSEES

PLACE VENDOME

AVE. DE L'OPERA

PLACE DU TROCADERO

PLACE DE LA CONCORDE

RUE DE RIVOLI

JARDINS DU TROCADERO

Seine

JARDIN DES TUILERIES

Louvre

Palais Chaillot

Tour Eiffel

PARC DU CHAMP DE MARS

Hôtel des Invalides

WALK 3

ST. GERMAIN DES PRES

BLVD. BLVD. RASPAIL

RUE DE RENNES

ODEON

JARDINS DU LUXEMBOURG

RUE DE VAUGIRARD

MONTPARNASSE

GARE MONTPARNASSE

MONTPARNASSE CEMETERY

BLVD. ST. MICHEL

RUE

WALKS AND MAIN SIGHTS
Central Paris

WALK 1: St. Julien le Pauvre
WALK 2: La Huchette
WALK 3: St. Germain des Prés
WALK 4: Mouffetard
WALK 5: Place des Vosges

PLACE DENFERT ROCHEREAU

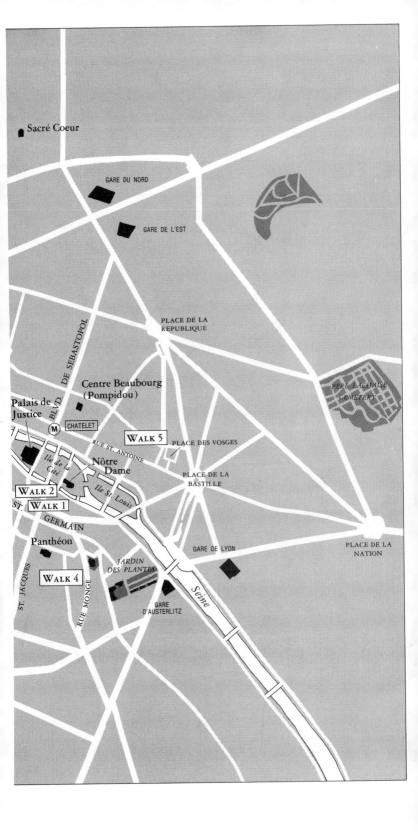

# Introduction

In this book we offer you step-by-step tours of five of the oldest and most fascinating neighborhoods of Paris. On the Left Bank: St Julien le Pauvre, La Huchette, St Germain des Prés, and Mouffetard. On the Right Bank: the Place des Vosges and some of its surroundings.

The two-and-a-half-hour walks, which cover an area of approximately five blocks each, will make you a connoisseur of these neighborhoods. What is hidden to the casual observer becomes the key to Paris. Through the signs and stories of the past, the architectural details, and the life of today, the city unveils itself. The acquisition of this knowledge makes you a friend and possessor of the *quartier* forever.

We feel that this represents a significantly different approach to travel. The typical visitor to Paris, relying on conventional guidebooks, does his best to make the most of his time by taking in the tourist "musts." He may not be able to match Art Buchwald's "five-minute Louvre," but he gives it a quick going-over between the Arc de Triomphe and the Eiffel Tower. He does "Paris by Night"

1

and takes the bus tour to Versailles. All of these things are, as the Michelin guide puts it, worth the trip, but neither separately nor together do they constitute a visit to Paris.

Today Buchwald's tour would take longer. As you will see from reading this book, the French take great pride in their public buildings and monuments. Under the direction of Prime Ministers Pompidou and Mitterrand no less than seven major historic structures have been built. Each is remarkably innovative and controversial: the Pompidou Center, the Picasso Museum, the new Opéra, the pyramids of the Louvre, the Musée D'Orsay, La Villette Science and Technology Museum and its geode amphitheater (a must for children), and La Défense.

Even guides that aim to help visitors get to know a place by walking the ground take them from one point to another so quickly that they can obtain at best a passerby's impressions.

There is another strategy to visiting a city—what we call close-up tourism. We want to make you feel, even if for only a short time, a part of Paris; to be someone who gets to know a piece of the city intimately, house by house, shop by shop. We have chosen for the purpose *quartiers* where many of the streets are still the narrow, irregular, meandering paths of medieval and early modern times. These five neighborhoods have, for the most part, been preserved by the accidents of history, though continually threatened by the hammers and shovels of urban planners and boulevard builders.

Although these neighborhoods have been spared the demolition and monument building that have transformed most of old Paris, that has not stopped them from changing over time, but they have done so at a different rhythm. They are not fossils but living, active microcosms of Paris. The visitor who looks at them with a careful, unhurried eye can peel off layer after layer of the past and read them like a live archaeological dig. By comparison, much of Paris is a construct of the nineteenth and twentieth centuries. These other, newer neighborhoods have their own interest, but there is a homogeneity and imitation about them that exclude the spontaneity and ability to surprise of the older city.

No matter how often we researched our walks, we never failed to make new discoveries, even for this, the fifth edition. When we are in Paris we walk with visitors from all countries, student groups from junior high school to college, and French friends, all of whom shared our excitement and, to our surprise and delight, found things we had not yet noticed. One friend said she would never walk down a street in the same way again. We expect this to happen to you, and we would be pleased to hear about your discoveries.

On these walks you may sit, stand, snack, lunch, or dine. Eating places have been carefully chosen for their interest as well as their cuisine. The walks are free. They are designed to be comfortable, nonstrenuous, and fun. Most of the people in these areas know us well and if you show them the guide they will be happy to speak to you, and our maps and pictures should guide you without difficulty. At the end of the "Information and Advice" section, on pages 21 and 22, we have included a chronology of important historical events. There are lists of hotels, restaurants, and shops at the end of the book. It is wise to read each walk before setting out, in order to plan your day more effectively. We advise morning walking because mail and other deliveries are made then and courtyard doors remain open. You will not be disturbing anyone by looking quietly at courtyards or through glass doors at entries. To enter, just push the button that looks like a doorbell or the main button on the keypad; to exit, push the matching button inside the doors.

A few words about how we came to do this book. One summer before leaving to spend the year in Paris, we (mother, Sonia; daughter, Alison) decided that since we were already a sort of agency for advice about the city, we ought to put our advice in writing. We felt eminently qualified: we had lived in Paris on and off for a total of five years; the children went to school there; one of them was even born there. We had first gone as a family in 1948 because David, the *père de famille*, was working on his Ph.D. in French history. That was when Pierrette Coadou, a wonderful Breton lady, came to live with us, and she has helped keep the French feeling alive in the household ever since. That was the beginning; since then the pleasures of Paris and friends, David's research and this guide, have taken us back innumerable times.

Everyone was surprised that a mother and daughter were able to work together easily and successfully. We were asked questions such as "Do you still talk to each other?" "Who did the writing?" "Who did the research?" and so on. Yes, we still talk all the time, and we shared all the work. Although our styles differ—one is more friendly and will talk to anyone, one is a stickler for accuracy in every statement—we have continued in all the succeeding revised editions to combine our efforts by dint of give and take, and lots of laughing.

# Information
# and Advice

## HOTELS

We are pleased to report that hotels in France represent one of the better buys in Europe. The deluxe hotels are stunning, the first-class ones superb, and the moderately priced hotels not only are very comfortable but have such a distinctive style that you will find yourself planning to return to the same one over and over again. Whatever hotel you choose, ask for a room on the courtyard. Paris is a busy city and wakes up early, so you want to get away from the noise. Taxes and service, 15 percent, and breakfast, may be included. Check on these arrangements beforehand. Breakfast is continental, which means *café au lait*, tea, or chocolate, and croissants (if you're lucky) or a roll and butter and jam. The French don't eat American-style breakfasts, and only hotels with kitchens could oblige you. It is wise, anyway, to adjust your eating habits to the country you are visiting.

The old horror stories about antiquated French plumbing are no longer true. On the contrary, when the

French do a modern bathroom they go to excess and cover the walls from top to bottom with inch-square pastel tiles. The ever-present bidet serves not only its intended purpose but is also useful for rinsing out a few things, keeping bottles warm or cold, or soaking tired feet.

Make the most of your hotel by getting the staff to help you in all kinds of ways. The person at the desk is the one to speak to. He or she will take messages, give you directions, look after your luggage, mail your letters, and help you make telephone calls. The larger hotels have a concierge at a separate desk. In addition to the regular services a concierge will arrange for theater tickets, transportation, and might even wrap a package and mail it home. A concierge who has helped you in some special way deserves a special tip when you leave. (We give details of some hotels on pages 256–57).

# TRANSPORTATION

There are five ways to get around Paris; each has its advantages and drawbacks. The first and best method is, of course, on your own two feet. People-watching, window-shopping—in short, real contact with the city— are only for pedestrians. Wear your most comfortable shoes. Stick to the crossings and cross with the light; Paris traffic is unending. Taxicabs are another method of transportation; they are no longer easy to hail, and when you are within 100 meters (a little more than 100 yards) of a taxi stand they are forbidden to pick you up except at the stand. Taxis, unfortunately, take only three people, all in the backseat, for everyone's protection. (We have wondered, however, if that regulation was passed to accommodate drivers' dogs in the front seat.)

The rates vary with the time and place. In Paris, from 6 A.M. to 10 P.M., the driver should use tariff A; from 10 P.M. to 6 A.M., tariff B. In the suburbs, even if part of the ride is in Paris, the driver should use tariff B from 6 A.M. to 10 P.M. and tariff C from 10 P.M. to 6 A.M. The tariff will also change coming or going to the airport; the boundary is the Boulevard Périphérique. Taxis use tariff B on Sundays and holidays. Not every driver is honest, and tourists are easy victims. The most common trick is the long, unnecessary detour, which can be guarded against by following the route with a map so that you have some idea where you're going. It is also a good idea to mention the denomination of any large bill used in payment at the time you hand it over. (It's a good idea in shops as well.) Take the time to count your change. We stress the hazards, but there are compensations. Taxis in Paris are inexpensive. A ride right across Paris, even in traffic, rarely exceeds twelve dollars. To call a taxi the best two numbers are 42-02-42-02 and 42-03-99-99. There will be about a 20-franc charge for the call on the meter when it arrives.

Private (or rented) cars are also a possibility, but unless you know Paris well, we would not suggest using them. In addition to navigating unknown one-way systems, there is the special hazard of the French system of priority for the car on the right. It reaches absurd proportions in large traffic circles like the Etoile (where the Arc de Triomphe is located). Rumor has it that some inexperienced drivers have been trapped there for hours, unable to get across the streams of incoming cars.

Parking is almost impossible in Paris except in underground paying garages. The French, however, will leave their cars anywhere, blocking your car or even your doorstep. The French police retaliate with parking fines ranging from $40 to $150, towing it away, or by fastening a *sabot*, or "boot" to the wheel of an illegally parked car. This *sabot* is like our boot that prevents movement and can be removed only by the police, who collect a fine on the spot. If this happens to you, just pay up. Avoid getting involved in anything official with the police or the government.

The best way to cover long distances in Paris is to take either buses or the *métro*. The advantage of the bus is that you can see where you are going. You can run into traffic, although on many of the larger, busier streets a separate lane has been set aside for the exclusive use of buses and taxis. There are bus maps available; in any case your hotel concierge or a policeman will be able to help you. Bus stops are round red-and-yellow signs fixed about five feet above the ground, and list the numbers of all the buses stopping at that point. Be sure to flag down the numbered bus you want, or it won't stop for you. On each bus pole there is also a plate (about four feet above ground) listing the names of every stop along the route. This listing is divided into *sections*, and if your ride is longer than two full *sections*, your fare will be two tickets (the maximum) instead of one. The plate shows by a red line the distance you can travel for one ticket. You use second-class *métro* tickets or buy tickets on the bus (this costs much more). You are required to punch your ticket yourself, in a machine placed near the door for that purpose. Do this, and then hang on to your ticket(s), because there are occasional *contrôles*, when officials check their validity. Some buses stop running around 9:30 P.M. Night and Sunday service is irregular. The plate at the bus stop will tell you this as well.

The Paris *métro* is a marvelous invention. It covers almost every square inch of Paris with speed and efficiency. Buy a booklet, or *carnet*, of ten tickets; if it hasn't gone up again, second class is 31 francs. Try first class for better upholstery on the seats and a smaller crowd at rush hour. Most *métro* stations also sell a weekly tourist pass and a monthly pass, a *carte orange*, that permits unlimited travel on the buses and the *métro*. The price varies depending on whether you buy first class or second class and whether you need a *carte* for Paris only or Paris and the suburbs. You must have a small picture of yourself which is affixed to your pass when you buy it.

The *métro* has become fully automatic now, and there are no longer old men and women sitting at the entrance to clip your ticket. Now there are barriers that swallow your ticket at the front, read the magnetic tape to be sure you're using a valid ticket, and spit it out as you pass through. The barrier won't release to let you through until you have taken your ticket again. As on the bus, hang on to your ticket, for the *contrôleur* may come by to check.

Finding your way is not at all difficult. The *métro* walls are covered with maps, some of which even light up your route electrically when you press the button for your destination. Find where you are and the stop that you wish to get to; then trace the route, picking out the terminal stops, which will be the name of your *direction* on each line. For example, if you are at Opéra, and want to get to St Germain des Prés, you would go four stops to Châtelet in the *direction* of Mairie d'Ivry. There you would change, following the signs that read *correspondance* (*sortie* means "exit") until you find the signs for *direction* Porte d'Orléans. On this line you would go four stops to St Germain des Prés. Everything is clearly marked, and even though in some stations you may feel you've covered a mile of hallways and staircases, do not despair. The Châtelet station has become so large that it has been connected to the Les Halles station, and some trains now stop twice in this huge network of corridors and *correspondances*. When you are finally on the *quai* and the train pulls into the station, lift the latch of the doors and slide them open—they are not automatic. When you want to get out of the train, do the same. The *métros* run until 12:30 or 1 A.M., depending on the line, and are, for the most part, safe.

We must caution you, however, about pickpockets. They are most often found at Opéra and Chaussée d'Antin. The pickpockets are extremely professional and can enter a *métro* carriage, lift your wallet, and leave in the time it takes for the doors to shut. Another method is for a crowd of children, nine or ten years old, to surround you, spill something on you, or trip you up, and—in the ensuing scuffle—take your wallet. Don't be polite; scream like mad. Less common but potentially more dangerous is the motorcycle snatch, perfected in Italy. This takes place on the street as a boy on a motorbike swoops by and grabs your bag. If you are carrying a shoulderbag slung diagonally across your chest you can be dragged along too. Our advice: be observant and carry your money, credit cards, and passport in separate places. That way, if something happens, you won't lose everything.

If you are staying in Paris for a week or longer you might invest in the invaluable *Paris par Arrondissement*, which is available at news kiosks and bookstores. Paris is divided into twenty *arrondissements*, called simply the first (*première*, or *1ère*), the second (*deuxième*, or *2e*), and so on. (The *arrondissement* numbers begin at the Place de la Concorde and spiral round the city.) The book contains detailed maps of each *arrondissement*, lists of the important buildings or sites, museums, hospitals, churches, police stations, post offices, and the days for the outdoor markets, or *marchés*. A *métro* map and schematic drawings of the bus routes are also included.

# RESTAURANTS

Restaurant-going in Paris is a fine art, and entire books are devoted to the subject. Restaurants serve lunch from 12 or 12:30 P.M. until after 2 P.M. Dinner is never served before 7 P.M., and the fancier the restaurant, the later it fills. Meals are often copious, comprising at least three courses, sometimes as many as seven. Take your time and make it an evening—never expect to eat before going to a concert or the movies. The chef and your stomach expect you to give the food the same attention it got when it was prepared.

Knowing how to order and what to expect is often difficult. In this regard, it is a wise idea to check the menu and prices displayed, by law, outside the restaurant. This may save you from surprises and embarrassment. (Beauty salons, hairdressers, and barber shops are also required to display prices.) You should consider the possibility of ordering the *menu conseillé* (literally, the "recommended menu"), which usually takes the form of a *prix fixe* (set price) meal, with service, and sometimes wine, included. These meals are offered at the behest of the government, to make tourism easier on the pocket, and they almost always represent a saving. You must specify to the waiter in advance that you are ordering from the special menu. Not every restaurateur or waiter serves from the *menu conseillé* with the same good will that accompanies à la carte dishes, but persist and enjoy your meal. Don't be afraid to ask what something is or what the waiter would recommend. If you take his advice, he will be flattered, and your service will be even more careful. This is particularly true of better restaurants. The same advice goes for the wine waiter (*sommelier*). Unless you know your wines well and you are already paying a substantial sum for an exquisite meal, don't worry over the wine list. Tell the sommelier what you're eating and roughly what you would like to pay for wine and let him choose. If you are in a cheaper restaurant eating a standard French meal and you are not fussy, you can ask for house wine. A *carafe* is a liter, a *demie* is a half-liter, and a *quart* is a quarter-liter. If you don't like wine, or you find that you fall asleep for two hours in the afternoon when you imbibe at lunch, stick to the mineral waters, naturally bubbly Perrier, or plain sweet water like Evian, Vitel, or Contrexéville. The French depend on bottled water to ease their digestion and keep their weight down. (It is difficult to judge the truth of these claims. Half of our French friends are trim and eat with pleasure, the other half have the famous French malady, liver trouble, *mal au foie*.)

Other things to avoid are spirits before dinner; they dull your taste buds, as does smoking at table, which bothers the other diners. (Some of France's great chefs have been known to ban guests so indifferent to fine cuisine as to smoke during the meal.) The French drink an apéritif before dinner; we recommend a kir, a combination of dry white wine and crème de cassis.

You will be given bread in a restaurant but no butter, except with certain foods such as oysters (served with rye bread and butter) or radishes. If you really want it, ask for it. The bread is for soaking up sauces, and it is not considered crude to break off a piece and do so. You may begin the meal with a mixed salad, but lettuce salad is always served after the main course; it is not mixed with any other vegetables and is served with an oil and vinegar dressing. When you order a steak (*entrecôte, bifteck, tournedos,* or *filet mignon*), *saignant* means "rare," that is, dark red, and *à point* (literally "just right") is the reddish-pink color we usually associate with rare meat. In winter choose a *pot-au-feu* or *cassoulet.*

If you order a *café* after your meal, you will get a demi-tasse of strong black coffee. You'll find the French never put milk in their coffee once they've had their *café au lait* at breakfast; request it if you wish. It is called *un crème*. If French coffee keeps you awake, ask for the decaffeinated coffee that is now served in most restaurants.

Sitting at a sidewalk café is a perfect pleasure in Paris. They are everywhere and of every sort. The cafés on the big streets are best for people-watching, but a cup of coffee will be twice the usual price. Remember that you are really paying for your chair, and if you choose, you can sit in most cafés with your one cup of coffee for hours and read, write, watch, and feel French. (We wouldn't recommend this, though, at the heavy-traffic, high-turnover places. They expect you to order a new drink every so often, especially at busy times.) The small, dark, corner café is the local hangout. The customers know the owner; there is frequently a pinball machine with a few men sitting around and gossiping. They will eye you suspiciously as you enter, but in a few days you can become a "regular" if you wish. Drinks are cheaper at the bar than at the tables, but remember to leave a small tip for bar service. (At the tables it is always included in the bill.) Almost every café will serve some food, ranging from breakfast croissants to sandwiches, French "hot dogs" with melted cheese, or *croque-monsieur* (toasted cheese and ham sandwich), omelettes, and simple meat meals. The best cafés have small kitchens and serve some excellent *plats-du-jour* ("today's specials").

A red lozenge-shaped sign over the door of a café designates it a *tabac*, which means you can buy cigarettes, matches, *métro* tickets in a *carnet*, and stamps (the café owner, however, can rarely tell you how much postage you need); and you can mail your letter in the pale yellow mailbox right outside the door. Cafés are important for another reason; they almost always have toilets. A nice café should have decent toilets, or WCs. (There are now high-tech pay *toilettes* on the streets of Paris, which disinfect automatically after each use. The old *vespasiennes*—Clochemerle-type urinals for men only—are now gone.)

# TIPPING

How much to tip around Paris? First, never let yourself be forced into more than you want to give. If you get bad service, respond in kind. Because travelers are wiser and more careful with their money these days, most restaurants, cafés, and hotels place an automatic 15 percent service charge on the bill. If you have any doubts about whether or not your bill includes service, ask, *"Service compris?"* If the service is included, you may round up, but this is not compulsory.

Taxis—10 percent is generous
Lavatory attendants—1 franc
Waiters—15 percent is already included, but you may leave the small change if you like
Cafés—the tip is included for table service; at the counter leave some change
Cloakroom attendants—5 francs per person
Tour guides—5 francs as you leave

Porters—there is a set price per piece of baggage, approximately 5 francs

Hairdressers—10 percent

Theater and cinema ushers—1 franc per person in a cinema, and 2 francs in a theater

# TELEPHONES

The most expensive way to phone home from Paris is to call from your hotel room. If the call goes through the switchboard the hotel will impose a surcharge often amounting to more than the cost of the call. Some of the larger hotels have joined AT&T's Teleplan, which limits these surcharges to a reasonable level. Other hotels have direct dial phones and add a percentage fee to each message unit used for any call regardless of distance. It is less expensive to call from a public telephone, a *cabine*, either on the street (it may be hard to find a working one) or in a post office. The call can be dialed directly: dial 19 to reach the international lines, wait for the tone, then dial 33 plus the number in the United States.

Most public telephones now work on a Telecard system. You must purchase a credit card–size card at either a *tabac* or a post office, valid for a certain number of message units depending on how much you pay. This is inserted into the phone, which then reads the magnetic stripe and deducts your allowance as you speak. You will see a readout of what you have so you can know how many units remain. You'll need a lot of units for an international call.

Several points to bear in mind: the French do not have a minimum period for long-distance calls, thus a ten-second call to the States is inexpensive. Local calls in Paris cost 1 franc. If no one answers, you will not be charged. If, however, you get a busy signal, hang up instantly or there will be no return. Tremendous advances have been made in the French phone system thanks in part to the nonprofit lobbying group, the brainchild of Jean-François and Marie-Madeleine Berry, the Association of Users of the Telephone and Telecommunications (AFUTT). Much shorter installation delays, lower phone rates and modern equipment are some of the improvements.

# SHOPPING

Be brave and buy some of those French clothes you have always wanted. With luck, you will love what you buy and wear it with pleasure. We do, however, have a few words of warning. Prices are high and sales are much less frequent. Salespeople have been known to expect you to buy the first thing you try on. Simply let them understand you'll make up your own mind, thank you. Don't allow yourself to make an unwilling purchase.

We have included a size chart for men and women but, since the French tend to be smaller and thinner than Americans, when in doubt, try the larger size.

## Women's Sizes

| Dresses | | | Sweaters | | Shoes | | |
|---|---|---|---|---|---|---|---|
| U.S. | UK | FR. | U.S./UK | FR. | U.S. | UK | FR. |
| 8 | 10 | 38 | 32 | 38 | 6 | 4½ | 34 |
| 10 | 12 | 40 | 34 | 40 | 6½ | 5 | 35 |
| 12 | 14 | 42 | 36 | 42 | 7 | 5½ | 36 |
| 14 | 16 | 44 | 38 | 44 | 7½ | 6 | 37 |
| 16 | 18 | 46 | 40 | 46 | 8 | 6½ | 38 |
| 18 | 20 | 48 | 42 | 48 | 8½ | 7 | 39 |
| | | | | | 9 | 7½ | 40 |

## Men's Sizes

| Suits | | Shirts | | Shoes | | |
|---|---|---|---|---|---|---|
| U.S./UK | FR. | U.S./UK | FR. | U.S. | UK | FR. |
| 34 | 34 | 14 | 36 | 8 | 7$^1/_2$ | 41 |
| 35 | 36 | 14$^1/_2$ | 37 | 8$^1/_2$ | 8 | 42 |
| 36 | 38 | 15 | 38 | 9$^1/_2$ | 9 | 43 |
| 37 | 40 | 15$^1/_2$ | 39 | 10$^1/_2$ | 10 | 44 |
| 38 | 42 | 16 | 40 | 11 | 10$^1/_2$ | 45 |
| 39 | 44 | 16$^1/_2$ | 41 | 12 | 11$^1/_2$ | 46 |
| 40 | 46 | 17 | 42 | 12$^1/_2$ | 12 | 47 |
| 42 | 48 | | | | | |

If you are determined to buy French clothes but can't seem to cope with the shop assistants, we recommend Au Printemps or the Galeries Lafayette. These stores carry everything and are located behind the Opéra at the Chaussée d'Antin *métro* stop. If you make a combined purchase of 1200F or more, and you have your passport with you, you can buy the item tax free. Ask the cashiers about the TVA, and if you are buying enough, they will fill out a customs form and give you an addressed envelope for their store. When you arrive at French customs at the airport or the border, you must give them the forms and show them your purchase, so keep them available. They will then stamp everything, and a few weeks after the store has received the forms your money will be refunded by mail or credited to your credit card account. Visa (Carte Bleue) will pay for almost anything in France. Be sure to arrive at the airport with enough time to do this; you may not be alone at the customs desk.

We feel the following items represent good value: stationery items, including appointment books and notebooks, leather goods, wallets, briefcases, shoes, bags, and anything from a Prisunic, Monoprix, Uniprix, or the other stores of that type all over France. Be sure to have a look at the children's clothes. Sale time is the last two weeks of June in most stores. If you're not trying to save money, have fun—try the small shops you pass as you walk around the city.

Food shopping in Paris is a pleasure, although prices are usually higher. Whereas Americans spend a modest proportion of their wages on food, the French spend around 40 percent.

Never touch the fruit or vegetables unless no one is looking; it's a cardinal sin. If you are not in Paris long enough to get to know the merchants, you just have to take a chance on getting good produce.

Carry your own shopping bag. If you are in a deli-catessen *(charcuterie)* and buy runny salads, ask for plastic bags. About the *charcuterie*—the food is usually as good as it looks. One of the best ways to lunch in Paris is to buy cold meats and salads from the *charcuterie*, cheese from the dairy store *(crèmerie)*, bread from the bakery *(boulangerie)*, and wine from the wine merchant *(marchand de vins)* and make a messy, joyful picnic in your hotel room or on the nearest park bench. (The grass is almost always off-limits, *interdit.*) There are also little groceries *(alimentation générale)* where you can buy all of these and more, but their standards are not those of the specialty shops, and they are not less expensive. They do save walking, but why would you want to do that? You can buy a hot lunch *(plats cuisinés)* from almost any *charcuterie*. For maximum pleasure and economy, never travel without knives, forks, plates, napkins, cups, and a corkscrew. French bread has no preservatives and will not be edible the next day, or even that night if you buy it in the morning. It is still the best buy in France. The prices of fancy breads like wood-fire, whole wheat, or viennoise (a soft white bread) will vary—as do the prices of pastries, from shop to shop—but only slightly.

Food stores are open from 8 or 9 A.M. until around 1:30 P.M., then closed until 4 or 5 o'clock, and then open again in the evening until 7 or 8 P.M. You could starve in

Paris looking for food in the intervening afternoon hours if it were not for stores like Monoprix and Prisunic. These are reasonably priced minisupermarkets open all day from Monday to Saturday. Most shops are closed on Mondays, except for the grocery chain of Felix Potin. In August the problem of closed shops and restaurants will be greatly aggravated, as is the difficulty of finding medical help: no self-respecting Frenchman stays in Paris that month, just when all the tourists are there. Late spring and early autumn are the best times to visit. On the other hand, the city is yours in August.

## WHAT'S HAPPENING

The best source of what is going on is *This Week in Paris* (*Pariscope* or *L'Officiel des Spectacles* in French), sold at any newsstand. It gives you all the information on plays, exhibits, tours, concerts, museums, lectures, restaurants, strip shows, films, cabarets, TV programs, and everything else happening in Paris and the suburbs, with the dates, hours, and prices. Films are almost always subtitled, not dubbed, and there are student rates except on Saturday and Sunday.

## NEWSPAPERS

The *International Herald Tribune* ranks with the best English-language papers. It is small, generally eight pages, so space is at a premium. Not only do the editors keep the news articles brief and tight, but they also show superb judgment in picking the important stories. In addition, the features are first-rate—the columnists (a wide range of political opinion), the sports news, the financial page (invaluable for its exchange rates and the market quotations), the arts, entertainment, comics, and auction coverage. The *International Herald Tribune* is not cheap.

It costs about one dollar, but most agree that it is indispensable. Also read *Passion*, an American magazine about Paris.

French newspapers are different. Their journalistic tradition does not require them to explain a story or provide background, so if you haven't been keeping up with the news you may not be able to understand what all the fuss is about. Nor do they cultivate an ideal of objective news reporting; instead, many important news stories are opinion pieces, almost editorials. *Le Monde*, the newspaper of the French intellectual and professional elite, is probably the only newspaper in the world that is prepared to devote long pages, for several days running, to the economy and society of Sri Lanka or Paraguay. Its worldwide coverage is more complete than anything offered in the United States, and it is a salutary experience for the American traveler to read *Le Monde* and see the world as others see it. The slant is left-liberal. Also on the left, but much livelier, is *Libération*, affectionately called "Libé." For a conservative bent, try *Le Figaro*, whose weekly *Figaro Magazine* has become the organ of a new, almost radical Right. Sports fans have *L'Equipe* (much on French league soccer, rugby, and basketball, and highly chauvinistic reports on French performances in international competition). For good photography, read the weekly *Paris-Match*; and the equivalents of *Time* and *Newsweek* (available in European editions) are *L'Express* (left of center) and *Le Point* (right of center).

# HELP

In a medical emergency call the American Hospital of Paris at no. 63 Boulevard Victor Hugo, Neuilly, telephone 47-47-53-00. The staff speak English, and many of the doctors are American or American-trained. If you intend to remain in Paris for a long time, you may wish to get an identification card from the hospital and carry it with you in case of accident. (Or make your own. State your name, address, nationality, and that in case of accident you wish to be taken to the American Hospital.) The emergency number on the telephone is 17, but this will connect you to the police, who rarely understand English.

If it is impossible to get to the hospital, call a French doctor. They make house calls as a matter of course. Ask a French friend, the American Hospital, or your hotel for the name of a doctor. There is no guarantee, of course, that you will be able to communicate with him when he comes. We advise using SOS doctors at 47-07-77-77. These are doctors in radio-controlled cars with medical and pharmaceutical equipment. They have an excellent reputation.

For common minor problems, like an upset stomach, pharmacies in France give simple medical advice. Beware, however, of their recommendations; a French idiosyncrasy is the use of suppositories, not pills. You may want to bring your favorite remedy from home.

If your local pharmacy is closed, there will be details of the nearest open one displayed on the door. The following pharmacies are open at odd hours:

RIGHT BANK
Drugstore Publicis, no. 133 Avenue des Champs-Elysées, 8e (tel. 47-20-94-40), and Rond Point de Champs-Elysées, both open 9 A.M.–2 A.M.

Pharmacie les Champs-Elysées, 84 Avenue des Champs-Elysées (tel. 45-62-02-41), open 24 hours.

Pharmacie de la Muette, no. 11 Chaussée de la Muette, 16e (tel. 42-88-21-69), daily 8:30 A.M.–10 P.M.

LEFT BANK
Drugstore Publicis, no. 149 Boulevard St Germain, 7e (tel. 42-22-92-50), daily 9 A.M.–2A.M.

Pharmacie des Arts, no. 106 Boulevard Montparnasse, 14e (tel. 43-26-56-20), daily 8:30 A.M.–midnight.

If you have lost your passport or are in some trouble, the American Embassy is located at 2 Avenue Gabriel (tel. 42-96-12-02).

There are certain tourist centers in Paris where English is spoken:

Charles de Gaulle Airport, Information (tel. 48-62-22-80 and 48-62-12-12). Terminal Maillot (buses for Charles de Gaulle Airport) (tel. 47-58-20-18). Orly Airport Information (tel. 46-87-12-34 and 48-53-12-34). Terminal Invalides (buses for Orly Airport) (tel. 45-50-32-30).

## BRIEF CHRONOLOGY

| | |
|---|---|
| BC 52 | Roman invasion of Lutetia |
| AD 360 | City received the name of Paris |
| 481–511 | Reign of Clovis; makes Paris the capital |
| 511–58 | Reign of Childebert, son of Clovis |
| 885 | Norman invasion of the capital |
| 1000 | Church of St Germain des Prés begun |
| 1180–1223 | Reign of Philippe Auguste |
| 1226–1270 | Reign of Saint Louis. Sorbonne founded |
| 1380–1422 | Reign of Charles VI |
| 1420s | Paris under English occupation |
| 1547–59 | Reign of Henri II and Catherine de Medicis |
| 1574–89 | Reign of Henri III, their son |
| 1589–1610 | Reign of Henri IV, married to *chère* Margot, his cousin Marguerite de Valois, sister of Henri III, then in 1600 to Marie de Médicis |
| 1605 | Place des Vosges started |
| 1610–43 | Reign of Louis XIII, following murder of Henri IV by a mad cleric. Place des Vosges inaugurated April 5, 6, and 7, 1612. Richelieu was Louis's first minister from 1624 to 1642 |

| | |
|---|---|
| 1643–1715 | Reign of Louis XIV (*le Roi Soleil*: "the Sun King"). His eight children by Mme de Montespan were tutored by Mme de Maintenon, whom Louis secretly married in 1684 |
| 1715–74 | Reign of Louis XV |
| 1774–92 | Reign of Louis XVI, with Marie Antoinette |
| 1789–99 | French Revolution. Revolutionary government guillotined Louis and Marie Antoinette at the Place de la Concorde |
| 1793–94 | The Terror. In 421 days, 2,669 people condemned and executed. Robespierre, Revolutionary leader and member of Committee of Public Safety, was chiefly responsible |
| 1795–99 | Directory |
| 1799–1804 | Consulate under Napoleon Bonaparte |
| 1804–14 | Empire, with Napoleon as emperor |
| 1852–70 | Reign of Napoleon III. Georges Haussmann was his city planner |
| 1910 | Great Paris flood |
| 1914–18 | World War I |
| 1939–45 | World War II. German Occupation from 1940 |
| 1968 | *Evènements de mai*—"events of May": serious student riots in Paris |
| 1972 | Malraux law decrees Paris buildings must be cleaned |
| 1980–1990 | A decade of historical building in Paris |
| 1981 | François Mitterrand begins his first term as President of the French Republic |
| 1992 | The date of the realization of the European Economic Community. Common market becomes a single unit. All internal borders lapse |

# Walk · 1

## St Julien le Pauvre

"*Shakespeare and Co. Kilometer Zero Paris.*"

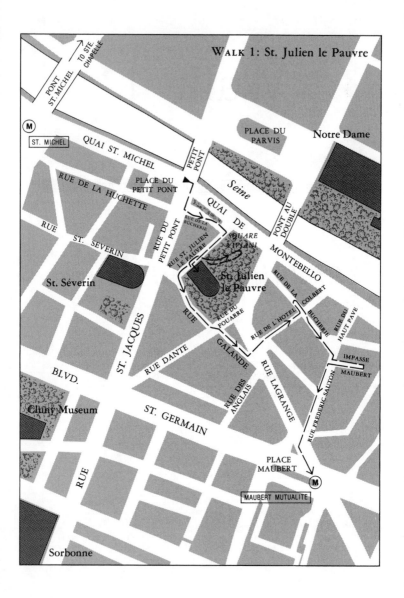

WALK 1: St. Julien le Pauvre

PONT ST. MICHEL

TO STE. CHAPELLE

(M) ST. MICHEL

QUAI ST. MICHEL

PLACE DU PARVIS

Notre Dame

RUE DE LA HUCHETTE

PLACE DU PETIT PONT

PETIT PONT

Seine

RUE ST. SEVERIN

RUE

RUE DU PETIT PONT

QUAI DE LA BUCHERIE

QUAI DE

PONT AU DOUBLE

St. Séverin

RUE ST. JULIEN LE PAUVRE

SQUARE VIVIANI

MONTEBELLO

St. Julien le Pauvre

RUE DE LA COLBERT

RUE DU HAUT PAVE

ST. JACQUES

RUE DU FOUARRE

RUE DE L'HOTEL

BUCHERIE

RUE GALANDE

IMPASSE MAUBERT

BLVD.

RUE DANTE

RUE DES ANGLAIS

RUE LAGRANGE

RUE FREDERIC SAUTON

Cluny Museum

ST. GERMAIN

RUE

PLACE MAUBERT

(M)

MAUBERT MUTUALITE

Sorbonne

**Starting Point:** The corner of the Petit Pont and the Quai de Montebello
**Métro:** St Michel
**Buses:** 24, 27, 47, 63, 86, 87

Here you are in the heart of Paris, looking at Notre Dame on the Ile de la Cité, where the Parisii, the tribe for whom the city was named, originally settled long before Caesar came here in 50 BC. At that time there were eight or nine islands in this region of the Seine; now there are only two—this one and, behind it, the Ile St Louis.

The Place du Parvis, the square in front of Notre Dame, is the official center of France; stone markers along the French roadside mark the kilometers to this spot. This walk will not take you farther than "0 kilometers Paris," but there is much to see.

The Seine in prehistoric times was a wide, slow-flowing river more than a hundred feet higher than it is today. The river meandered all over the area between Mont-Sainte-Geneviève to the south (take a look about five blocks down and you will see the hill) and Mont-martre, one mile away to the north.

Even Parisians forget the river was so wide, but in 1910 an extraordinary flood in the month of January reminded them of the tributaries of the Seine still flowing underground; the subterranean waters welled to the surface and swept the city. From the present course of the river to the Place de l'Opéra and from the Gare St Lazare to the suburbs of the north, the secret Seine came up from hiding and took possession of the city once again.

Postcards depicting the flood show men and women rowing around Paris at the level of street signs. A great many important historical records were lost, including those of some of the major libraries and banks of the city. Deep cellars in this area are still cemented in mud from the flood, and excavations constantly unearth buried architecture and artifacts.

For ancient Paris this sprawling river, whose waters were sweet and clean enough to drink, was a boon. Because of it, the Parisii felt safe from surprise attacks; an enemy would have to cross large stretches of swamp to reach the island. The river was also an excellent highway for trade, as it still is today. By Gallic times the Seine had already dug its present channel, but the banks to either side, especially the Right Bank, remained swampy and uninhabitable. The first part of the mainland to be settled was the south or Left Bank, where the ground rose more sharply than on the marshy Right Bank (called the Marais, or "swamp"—see Walk 5). If you look up the Rue du Petit Pont with your back to the bridge, you will see, about two hundred yards away and beyond what is now the Rue des Ecoles, the College of France on the left side, and the observatory tower of the Sorbonne on the right. Two thousand years ago Roman baths stood on these sites—the Romans occupied Gaul, including Paris, for over four hundred years—for it was on this hill that the ancient residents finally got far enough above the waterline to build important structures. The remains of the baths still exist under the College of France; other ruins close by, unearthed as recently as 1946, can be seen in the garden of the Cluny Museum. The area between this high waterline and the river, the area you are visiting today, was settled much later.

The site of the present church of St Séverin, the back of which you can see down the Rue du Petit-Pont on the right, was a small dry hillock where a hermit chose to settle in the fifth century. Later, as the Seine continued to dig itself a deeper channel, the area between high ground and the river filled with houses and narrow paths.

Even as late as the Middle Ages, the street level was thirty feet (two stories) lower than it is today. This is why three levels of cellar still exist in the seventeenth-century buildings you see in the area. Until the middle of the nineteenth century the streets and alleys of the *quartier* ran steeply down to the river's edge. The present ground-floor shops (the café Le Notre Dame and Optique, for example) are on what was once the first floor of these buildings. Notice the thirty-foot embankment that rises from the Seine; where that stands, houses once stood.

The first bridge connecting the Ile de la Cité to the mainland, the present Petit Pont, was built here because at this point the island is closest to the Left Bank. A little fortress, Le Petit Châtelet, which doubled as tollhouse, stood at the end of the bridge on the spot where you are now. It was the custom then, as it is today on some bridges, to pay a toll in order to pass in and out of the city. Another, larger, fortress, Le Grand Châtelet, stood on the right bank of this part of the Seine at the Pont St Michel. Both these bastions were used as prisons during the French Revolution. With the help of underground passageways to many points in the vicinity, prison affairs could easily be carried on in secret.

The Petit Pont was not only a passageway; two- and three-story houses and shops lined either side, making it the busiest street in town. In the Middle Ages the picturesque aspect of this bridge, really a street thrown across the river, was enlivened by philosophers offering their intellectual wares, by jugglers, singers, and dog and bear trainers. During the day it was a paradise for cutpurses, at night for cutthroats.

This bridge has been rebuilt after fire, flood, and attack more times than the French care to count. Fire was the most common cause of destruction, until the eighteenth century, when the bridge was finally rebuilt in stone.

In the Middle Ages people believed that bodies drowned in the Seine could be located by setting afloat in the river a votive candle on a wooden disc and noting where it stopped or went out. It was doubly important to find drowned bodies before the authorities did, because a huge fee of 101 *écus*, the equivalent of a year's pay for a manual laborer, is said to have been charged for the delivery of a loved one from the morgue at the Châtelet. One version of a story told about this bridge and its fires has it that a poor old widow whose son had drowned had set a candle afloat in hopes of finding his body. The candle floated close to a straw-laden barge, setting it on fire. The barge touched the wooden scaffolding of a pillar of the bridge, and from there the flames spread on to the bridge itself. In three days the raging fire destroyed the bridge and the houses on it.

If you like, climb down the steps on the island side of the channel near the Petit Pont or on the Left Bank toward the Pont au Double, and look at the Seine close up. You will be in the company of fishermen who catch live, though small, fish; of *clochards*, "tramps" who find this spot slightly warmer and more private for sleeping than the streets; and of lovers of all ages expressing various degrees of affection.

The Quai de Montebello, the street that runs along the riverside in front of you and is packed with cars (we say this with absolute confidence after having watched the street over an entire year at all hours of the day and night), was built by Baron Georges Haussmann. He was the famous city planner of Napoleon III who (in the 1850s and 1860s) built most of the avenues and boulevards that have fortunately and unfortunately saved Paris for the automobile.

Cross the *quai* with the light (watch for turning cars). The small strip of park before you was once covered by the Petit Châtelet; later, there was an annex of the Hôtel Dieu hospital here. The park was finally cleared in the early 1920s. This little park with benches and the park of St Julien le Pauvre to your left (with your back to the river) are the only pieces of green along the Seine, the only spots in Paris as far downstream as the Eiffel Tower that the French have allowed to lie fallow. This pocket-sized park, which once belonged to vagrants and *boules* (bocci) players, has now been redesigned and modernized.

## Place du Petit-Pont

The street that leads out from the bridge is called the Place du Petit-Pont. At the next crossing its name changes to the Rue du Petit-Pont. In both places, the street is the same width. If you look very hard at the buildings on either side of the Rue du Petit-Pont, you will probably be able to work out why the *rue* is as wide as the *place*. The apartment houses on the left side of the street were built in the seventeenth century; they are straight buildings with slim rectangular windows, free of ornamentation except for iron grillwork on the windows. On the right side of the street, nineteenth-century buildings (heavy with curves, carvings, protuberances, and balconies) stand on ground cleared when the street was widened and rebuilt two hundred years later, in 1857.

The Rue du Petit-Pont lasts one short block, when it becomes the Rue St Jacques. From prehistoric times this road, which climbs straight up the gentle hill in front of you, was the main road from Paris to the south. When the Romans first came to Lutetia, which was what Paris was then called, they came this way. Soon after, they transformed the dirt road into a paved road nine meters (29 feet) wide. Two huge stones from this construction were found in 1926 below the surface; you will see them later in the *parvis* of St Julien le Pauvre (see page 44). Elephant remains have also turned up, which will give you an appreciation of how the Romans thought big and built big, and why we still speak with admiration and awe of Roman roads.

As early as 1230 the Rue St Jacques was given its present name because the famous pilgrimage to the shrine of Saint James (Saint Jacques) of Compostela traveled south along this road. Santiago (Spanish for Saint James) de Compostela, a city near the Atlantic coast of Spain, was rich in scallop shells, *coquilles*, which the pilgrims were quick to gather and bring back as proof of their voyage and their devotion. They displayed the shells whenever and wherever possible, and as a result they have come to be a common symbol even to this day. Shell Oil uses the name to represent their role as a refueling stop for us on our American pilgrimages; we eat *coquilles* St. Jacques, and shell designs are common as a decoration on buildings and churches, and in wood on furniture.

### Rue de la Bûcherie

Turn left into the Rue de la Bûcherie, the street facing the small park, pass the café, **Le Petit-Pont**, a good place for a light lunch and a most pleasant spot on a sunny day, and stop at the restaurant **La Bûcherie**. A *bûcherie* is a storehouse for wood. It was on this street that barges loaded with logs for heating deposited their goods. This restaurant remembers its past, not only in its name, but with a wood fire, which burns continuously on a hearth in the center of the room. It was, and still is, a hangout for actors and politicians, though the celebrities themselves change. The restaurant is expensive but the quality is always high. If you choose not to dine here, peer in at the window to look at the back wall. It is covered with a tapestry woven for the restaurant by the famous reviver of the ancient art and modern tapestry-maker, Lurçat. He used to live upstairs and wove this wall of tapestry in lieu of paying rent. In France art and food are closely linked and in view of this M. Bosque engages an art advisor to help decorate his walls. Paintings by Miró and Jean Hélion (the ex-husband of Peggy Guggenheim) are among the collection.

The house next door, **no. 39**, is most amazing. The houses we have been looking at are mostly seventeenth-century; this one was built in the early sixteenth. It is a small two-story wooden structure, the kind that was typical five hundred years ago and can still be seen in towns like Riquewihr in Alsace, or Conques in southern France, but has almost vanished from most European cities. The building once served as an inn and was hidden from sight for most of its long history. **Le Petit Châtelet**, as the inn was called—after the fortress it stood behind, and to whose employees it gave meat and drink over the centuries—was tucked away until 1909, when the ground was cleared between the Rue de la Bûcherie and the river. This building had been closed for many years, but fortunately Chantal Silly, the owner of another restaurant around the corner, restored it and opened a fine restaurant. She is not, however, cleaning out the twelfth-century *caves* (cellars) under the building because of the enormous time and money required.

The little building is architecturally interesting for several reasons. Almost no wooden structures in Paris have survived; the big enemy has been fire, as evidenced from the history of the Petit Pont. Note the large dormer windows that jut out from the steep roofline and the smaller windows on the attic floor above. Look at the exposed side of the building on its right, and you will see coming out from the exterior wall the ends of the framing beams used in its construction hundreds of years ago. These are the wooden joists one sometimes sees as exposed rafters in a ceiling.

*Rue de la Bûcherie*

Now look at the exposed side of the half-timbered remains of the building on the left. There you will see one of only three open staircases, *escaliers à claire voie*, left in Paris. This was the typical staircase of the sixteenth century; it was replaced in the seventeenth by the closed *escalier à vis*. We will wind up and down one of these corkscrew staircases in this walk.

Immediately to the left is **Shakespeare and Company**. You will get a hint of the uniqueness within from the notice board and its amusing announcements without. George Whitman, the owner (and a distant cousin of Walt) doesn't try very hard to sell books; he just likes people who like to read. The ground floor is mainly devoted to books-for-sale of all kinds—old, new, all in English. Whitman recently bought the house next door and

keeps his own library and antiquarian books there. The
walls are covered with books he does not sell, and this
is where one gets a feeling of Whitman's unusual person-
ality. If you nose around long enough and look interested,
Whitman might invite you to tea. The shop itself is a
treasure trove of books and of people. The front room
was once a stone courtyard into which Whitman has set
fragments of marble friezes, tiled borders, and brass
plaques, one of which might be a portrait of Walt Whitman himself. The narrow one-way staircase at the very
back of the store leads to a maze of book-lined rooms
filled with chairs and couches. You can read the books
in these rooms, meet people, and even take a nap if you
wish.

More than a bookseller, Whitman takes in travelers,

especially serious writers—a vanishing breed, he feels. If an author notifies him ahead of time, he or she may be fortunate enough to stay in one of Whitman's rooms free or in exchange for working in the shop for a week or so, until other quarters are found.

Shakespeare and Company has always promoted the literary avant-garde. When the publishing house of the same name was originally founded by Sylvia Beach, it was the only house that would publish James Joyce's *Ulysses*. Now Whitman gives young writers a chance to be heard at poetry readings (in his library every Monday night at eight) and to be published in his review.

Give this store some browsing time. It is generally open from noon to midnight, or one to one. If you want a souvenir of Paris, buy a book and get it stamped here. The inscription around the head of William reads, "Shakespeare and Co. Kilometer Zero Paris."

## Rue St Julien le Pauvre

Go around the corner to the right into the Rue St Julien le Pauvre. **Nos. 4-8** on your right are all owned by the same people. The **Esmeralda Hotel**, no. 4, is a hotel named for Victor Hugo's heroine in *The Hunchback of Notre Dame*. The hotel has recently achieved some fame in another book, *Linnea in Monet's Garden*, a children's book by Christina Björk and Lena Anderson. For connoisseurs of the neighborhood, the details in the book's watercolors will be impressively authentic. The owner of the Esmeralda is, herself, a character for a book. She came to Paris from the provinces and thought that the city was especially beautiful from the Seine. She and her husband went into partnership with a financial backer and with one decrepit boat started the **Bateaux Mouches**. On the first day out the boat malfunctioned, going only in circles. Today, however, it is a hugely successful tourist attraction, though she has no connection to it as a result of her divorce. She never intended to run a hotel but somehow acquired it. It had only one bath and was occupied by women who had lived there for forty years and scarcely paid rent. She had to wait for changes in the law before she could evict them, restore the building's seventeenth-century details, and put in all the bathrooms a hotel must have. Today the small rooms are each uniquely decorated with antiques and will fulfill all your dreams of a truly "Left Bank" experience of Paris. Book well in advance.

Notice the soft-beige stone building, **no. 10** and, in particular, the ground-floor apartment's elegant windows, which are taller than the others. If you count the panes on each story you will see that the number of panes decreases and the windows get smaller as you go up. At the very top the tiny mansard windows (named after their inventor, the architect François Mansart), which peep out from the sloping roof, are reduced to one small pane. The taller windows of the ground floor mean, of course, higher ceilings, a mark of distinction still dear to the French, especially in old, nonstandardized apartments.

The exterior decoration tells the same story. Thus, the iron railings on the protruding sills of the two balconies on this first floor are finer than those on the floor above, after which there are no more balconies or grillwork at all. Look at other examples of handwrought iron decoration on nineteenth-century houses as well as those of the seventeenth century as you walk around the city.

It is clear that the first floor above the street was once the coveted apartment (*appartement noble*). The ground floor, called the *rez de chaussée*, which means "even with the road" was reserved for the concierge's one or two rooms, the courtyards, and the rubbish. The wealthy nobles and bankers stepped up one flight; the middle-class professionals and shopkeepers climbed two or three; the servants and workers trudged to the top. Apartment buildings, therefore, in all but the poorest neighborhoods were microcosms of French society.

The advent of the elevator, however, turned this arrangement upside down and made possible the one-class high-rise building. Today the servants' rooms—often used as workshops or extra bedrooms, sleep-in servants being hard to come by—are located on the ground floor alongside the concierge; the apartments cost more the higher you go; and the prize residence is a sunlit, glass-enclosed, terraced retreat at the top, as far as possible from the city's noise and dirt. There are relatively few of these newer apartment buildings on the Left Bank, but the next time you visit the bourgeois neighborhoods of western Paris (the eighth, sixteenth, and seventh *arrondissements*), take a look at the imposing, prosperous buildings with cut-stone façades, and follow the lines of balconies up to the elegant penthouses at the top.

**Les Colonies** at **no. 10** is a new restaurant under the same ownership as the Indonesian one that used to be here. Despite the name, the menu is mainly French and medium priced.

A very important person lives upstairs in the house at **no. 12**: the architect Claude Frémin. He is responsible for some of the most remarkable restorations in the area, including this house and the Auberge des Deux Signes around the corner on the Rue Galande, which you'll see later. Frémin's latest project has been the restoration of the street: the wide brick pavements have returned it to its original medieval width.

At **no. 14** is the **Tea Caddy**, one of the nicest tea shops in Paris. Particularly on cool days, a stop in this cozy shop is wonderful. Light meals (mainly eggs in various forms), pastries made on the premises, and a wide variety of teas are served. The Tea Caddy was founded in 1928 by Miss Kinklin, an English governess to a Rothschild offspring. The tea shop which she had always dreamed of was their retirement gift to her.

The Tea Caddy was formerly the stables of the building next door. The entrance of no. 14 is an impressive stone gateway with massive wooden doors. Look above at the pediment where Themis, the Greek goddess of "justice in all its relations to men," sits. She is represented as a dignified and commanding prophetess holding the scales of justice, surrounded by olive branches of peace; a cherub holds an hourglass. The symbolism of this sculpture was carefully chosen in the early seventeenth century when this gateway was added to the official residence of Isaac Laffémas, prefect of police of the Châtelet under Cardinal Richelieu. The prefect was, among other things, the king's prosecutor, and we have cause to wonder how wisely he used those scales. While he and his family lived comfortably above ground, three levels of cellars below were used as a prison. (The cellars date from the fourteenth century and were originally used to house the monks from the church of St Julien le Pauvre across the street.) This prison eventually fell into disuse in the seventeenth century, but 150 years later, in 1793, the Revolution created such an overflow of prisoners in the Petit and Grand châtelets and everywhere else that these cells were restored to use. We have it on good authority that instruments of torture, real ones, now rusted, still exist in the lowest basement. Hélène, an excellent hairdresser (and good friend to many in the *quartier*) whose salon was just down the street, saw them when she and her husband were on the track of a damaged water pipe: a rack and a devilish seat with a hole in it to allow the heat from boiling oil to cook a bound and helpless victim. In the name of justice, of course.

The house has been converted into apartments whose owners keep the door locked. This is unfortunate because the interior restoration was beautifully done and is a perfect example of how modern additions and restoration can enhance the original fifteenth-century structure. Look over the wall at the façade of the building. It is merely façade. Concealed underneath this *trompe l' oeil* of plaster cut to look like stone is a fifteenth-century half-timbered wall.

Visit the odd church of **St Julien le Pauvre**. Before you is a truncated edifice with a lopsided pediment crowning

*Themis, the Greek goddess of Justice,*
*at No. 14 Rue St Julien le Pauvre*

a flat, improvised façade, the remains of a thirteenth-century pillar, and an iron-caged well flanking the front portal. There is much to tell about Saint Julien himself, and you may wish to sit inside the church (cool in summer, warm in winter) and read his story, which supposedly took place in the first century.

Julien, the son of a noble family, was an avid hunter. One day he was having excellent luck in the forest: he had killed a doe and her baby and was about to shoot the stag when the animal turned and spoke to him. "How darest thou kill my family and pursue me, thou who wilt one day kill thine own father and mother?" Julien was staggered by these words and swore a sacred oath that he would never hunt again. Also, to prevent the fulfillment of the prediction, he left his parents' castle and went off to serve the king.

In the course of his duty Julien traveled to distant lands, where he fought so valiantly that the king knighted him and rewarded him with a castle and the hand in marriage of the widow of a rich lord. The couple lived together very happily, except for Julien's irrepressible passion for the hunt. One morning his wife encouraged him to go into the forest, saying that he had abstained long enough and, besides, it could in no way affect his parents. Julien succumbed and set out to hunt. But though he imagined game in every thicket he could kill nothing.

In Julien's absence an old and travel-weary couple arrived at his castle. His wife took them in and, as they conversed, discovered they were Julien's parents, who had searched for him everywhere since his unexplained departure. She welcomed them heartily and invited them to stay, offering them her own bed.

When Julien returned from the hunt, tired and frustrated, he went straight to the bedroom to rest. Opening the door he perceived two figures in his bed and flew into a rage. "This is the reason my wife encouraged me to hunt," he said to himself, and he drew his sword and slew the sleeping figures. At that his wife came to tell him the good news of his parents' arrival. When Julien realized what he had done, he wept bitterly: "What will become of me, most unfortunate man? It is my dear parents I have killed. I have fulfilled the promise of the stag on the very day that I broke my vow never to hunt again. I will enjoy no rest until I know God has accepted my repentance."

With these words he resolved to abandon his estate and fortune in order to do penance. His wife would not let him leave alone, and so the two settled on the shores of a large river, ferrying people across the water and offering them lodgings in the small guest house that they built on this spot.

One bleak winter night, when Julien had gone to bed exhausted, there was a knock at the door. A hideous stranger, half-frozen and half-dead, stood there asking first for hospitality and then to be rowed across the river. Julien brought him into his own bed and treated him with care. Later, as he was ferrying him across the river, the stranger who had looked so hideous moments before was suddenly transformed into a radiant angel. He said, "Julien, the Lord sent me to tell thee that thy repentance hath been accepted and that thy wife and thyself will soon be able to rest in God."

His story is depicted in a remarkable fourteenth-century stone relief, which is now fixed on to the façade of a modern cinema around the corner at no. 42 Rue Galande, which we shall see later.

Not only was the large river where Julien and his wife settled the Seine, but the site of their house later became the junction of the two main Roman roads from Paris to the south: the Rue St Jacques led to Orléans, and the Rue Galande led to Lyons and Italy. Actual proof of the existence of an oratory and hostelry on this spot dates from the sixth century, when Bishop Gregory of Tours visited the area and the church of St Julien in particular. Records have been found stating that Gregory gave a midnight mass here in 587.

Both the hostelry and oratory were destroyed in 866 by the Norman invaders. The church was rebuilt much later, between 1170 and 1240. Much of that structure remains today, making St Julien the oldest church in Paris. (Although Notre Dame was started a few years earlier, 1163, it was not completed until 1330. Parts of the church of St Germain des Prés—the bell tower, the bases of two towers, and part of the nave—are older, but at the time it was built it was outside the city walls, so it doesn't count for strict antiquarians.) St Julien le Pauvre is a poor church in comparison with the other two. It has neither bell tower nor transept, but it does have lots of pillars.

What the church lacks in appearance it makes up in colorful history. The original center of learning in Paris was Notre Dame in the Ile de la Cité, and it was Peter Abélard, the famous (and notorious) theologian-philosopher, who broke with established doctrine there at the beginning of the twelfth century and led a massive student exodus to St Julien le Pauvre on the Left Bank. Three thousand rebels went along with him, thereby creating what became known as the Latin Quarter, that is, the quarter of Latin-speaking clerics.

St Julien le Pauvre became the official seat of the newly chartered University of Paris and enjoyed the privilege of being the site of the election of the *rector magnificus* and of a sermon every two years restating the rights of students and teachers. The church grew rich and built a network of underground cells to house more than a hundred monks. In time, however, the center of instruction shifted south, and by 1449 the monks had been reduced to a lonely three.

In 1524 the church was almost destroyed; the next year it was decided never to hold elections there again. Students, unhappy over the election of a new rector, proceeded to break chairs, windows, furniture, and statues, forcing the church to close. With closure came neglect: an appraiser in 1640 noted that the rain and weather penetrated the building "as if it were open countryside."

43

This is why the present entrance stands far back from the original front of the church, which stood about where the street runs now. The whole entrance hall was on the point of collapse and had to be removed in the middle of the seventeenth century. All that's left are the ravaged thirteenth-century pillar with thin colonettes above, on the left side, and the twelfth-century flowering well, on the right. Beside the well lies a huge slab of stone that dates from the fourth century but was unearthed only in 1926. These stones formed part of the famous Roman road that became the Rue St Jacques.

After its long period of abandonment, the church and its land were ceded in 1655 to the Hôtel Dieu, the city hospital. The hospital restored the remains of the church sufficiently for it to serve as its chapel. During the French Revolution, however, more than a hundred years later, the chapel, along with so many other churches, was shut down. (That was very unfortunate, because hospital care in those days was to be avoided like the plague; prayer was said to account for much of what healing did take place.) St Julien continued to suffer ignominy and was used alternatively as a salt storehouse, as fairgrounds for wool merchants, and as a flour granary. Photographs from the nineteenth century show barrels of goods piled on the *parvis*, the terrace in front of the entrance. Houses and stores leaned against the church, glad to use its wall as one of their own.

Sometime after the Hôtel Dieu took over St Julien and its property, it built two wide three-story annexes on the Left Bank facing the river, between the Petit Pont and the Pont au Double. These massive additions blocked a view of the river and darkened the streets in this area. Photographs taken from the front of the church looking toward the Seine show a street that looks like a dead end. The buildings were finally taken down in 1877, when the hospital confined itself to its historic location on the Ile de la Cité next to Notre Dame. The city fathers decided then that no structure would ever again be built on this

*Well and road stone in the parvis of St Julien le Pauvre*

spot. That is why we are fortunate enough today to have two green pockets on the banks of the Seine on the Quai de Montebello.

It was one thing to demolish these squat sick wards; it was quite another to tear down St Julien itself. That intention seems scarcely credible, but in fact an extension of the Rue Monge (what is now the Rue Lagrange) was planned that would have cut into this area and gone right

through the church to the Rue St Jacques. At the last minute, as is so often the case when it comes to saving historical monuments, the plans were revoked, and St Julien and the small neighborhood remained intact.

Look at the uncomplicated interior of the church. You may be surprised to see a rood screen (iconostasis) with three doors and six rows of icons in front of the altar. There is a simple explanation for these unexpected objects: in 1889 the unused church was given by the arch-diocese of Paris to the Eastern Catholic community, the Melchites. The service, sung in Greek, can be heard on Sunday mornings.

Most striking is the tremendous number of twelfth-century columns, especially in such a small area. The capitals, like those in Notre Dame, are decorated with leaf and fern patterns, except for one on the right-hand side nearest the screen. Four harpies—birdlike women with wings—peer down at you, warning perhaps of the wages of sin. Storytelling on capitals is typical of the earlier Romanesque style of architecture. Notice also the large arabesque iron music stand to your left that faces the screen.

Outside again (with your back to the church entrance), look to your left at the back of a seventeenth-century building covered with fake timbering, nailed on twenty years ago to give an appearance of great age, as though three hundred years were not enough. (Contrast this with the genuine article, Le Petit Châtelet, on the Rue de la Bûcherie.) The blood-red door belongs to **Caveau des Oubliettes**, an underground cabaret installed in what was once a prison. *Oubliettes*, from the French word meaning "to forget," were cells where prisoners were put away and left there, solitary holes with nothing but a grate above for food to go in and waste to go out. Turnover of occupants was rapid. The waiters, garbed in medieval costume, will show you old prison holes with fingernail messages scratched by the dying, a guillotine, a chastity belt, and barbaric instruments of torture. But it would seem that the proprietors have allowed themselves some poetic license in these matters. In fact, the cells of the Caveau were used not for prisoners but for monks, while the real *oubliettes* are those we spoke about on the right side of the Rue St Julien le Pauvre (below the Tea Caddy, no. 14). The Caveau is fun, especially if your French is good enough to follow the words of the entertainers. If not, there are always the gestures. The Caveau is open every night from nine to two in the morning (tel. 43-54-94-97).

. . .

Before turning into the Rue Galande go into the garden next to St Julien. This is the **Square Viviani**, the loveliest park on the banks of the Seine. Eight hundred years ago it was the scene of boisterous, bustling student activity. Later it became the site of one of the annexes of the Hôtel Dieu. Forty years ago it was the untenanted backyard of St Julien. Today it is an oasis amid the concrete, stone, and asphalt of some of the busiest streets in Paris. You will find tired tourists and passersby, couples, mothers and children, and an occasional vagrant. Ordinarily, the French do not allow anyone to walk or play on the grass. But you can in the Square Viviani, because everyone is more relaxed in this part of town.

Paris is filled with parks and small squares, but this one has more to offer than most. It has the great distinction of affording from its benches what may well be the finest view of Notre Dame. After peering through the trees and changing your seat several times, turn and look at pieces of Notre Dame in the park itself. Those odd fragments of broken statuary, worn down by time and weather, were once a part of the cathedral. When pieces of sculpture decorating the church decay beyond recognition, they are moved to parks and replaced by whole new copies made in restoration workshops behind Notre Dame.

What passes for the oldest tree in Paris stands in this park, but not without the help of stone buttresses. The acacia (really a false acacia—*Robinia pseudoacacia*), which still blooms every spring (a miracle of tenacity), was planted in 1680 by a Mr. Robin who brought it from Guyana. Two kinds of prop hold it up: the modern straight-lined, buttresslike crutch, and the older imitation trunk of ridged stone.

Continue walking around the church until you reach a sealed window. Directly behind this window in the apse of St Julien, in a lower garden, you will find a well. This was once a mystical well that supposedly cured the crippled and the sick. The window in the apse of the church was turned into a door for easy access to the well. One day the church decided to give the water away free. Suddenly it cured no one. The door was walled over.

Cross the square to what is now the **Rue Lagrange** (named after the great mathematician and astronomer who helped invent the metric system during the French Revolution), which starts at the *quai* and then bends toward the Place Maubert. The part from the *quai* to the bend, adjacent to the park, has swallowed what was once the Rue du Fouarre, of which only a little leg is left, connecting the Rue Lagrange and the Rue Dante. In the Middle Ages this was a narrow way, lined solid with student housing, and its animation and intellectual activity made it one of the most famous streets in Europe. Classes were held in the open air—the students sitting on the ground and not on benches—so that, as a bull of Pope Urban V in 1366 put it, "occasion for haughty pride be kept away from youth." The ground was always filthy and often damp, so the students spread straw to sit on. The Old French word for straw is *feurre* or *fouarre* (compare the English word *forage*); hence the name of the street, originally named the Rue des Ecoliers after the students. Classes were taught by such notables as Abélard and Albertus Magnus; and, later on, Dante—whose street begins where the present Rue du Fouarre ends—studied here. Dante refers to the *vico degli strami* (literally, "the road of straws") in his *Paradiso* (10:137) and speaks of the violent discussions he shared in and listened to there.

When the Rue du Fouarre was in effect the campus of the University of Paris, the students lived in dormitories called colleges in the Square Viviani. Each one represented a different "nation" and constituted collectively the College of Nations. In the thirteenth century these were Normandy, Picardy, France, and England. In time these proliferated, and all European and even some Asian countries were represented in Paris. Thousands of students and hangers-on filled this area. Vagabonds sleeping on the students' beds during the day and high life among the students and their clashes with the citizens gave the street a bad reputation. In 1358 Charles V was forced to chain the street at both ends to keep it closed at night. Today the old road is a wide thoroughfare, and the rush of cars crossing from the Left Bank to the Ile de la Cité is continuous.

## Rue Galande

Recross the park, where the colleges stood, and leave it by the gate through which you entered. Go left, past the church, to the corner of the Rue Galande and the Rue St Julien le Pauvre. This place marks the beginning of the road that led to Lyons and Rome. In 1202 the street took the name Garlande, later Galande, after the name of a family who owned a large enclosure of land here. This was the road that students and teachers took to go from the Ile, or from St Julien, to the Rue du Fouarre, and it remained as important as that little road. In 1672 the street was widened to all of 8 meters (26 feet) and became one of the best addresses in Paris, a place where families of the nobility lived. After the Revolution, though, things went downhill, and by 1900 the guidebooks were advertising Galande as one of the seamiest streets in the city. Much restoration, some of the best in the area, has taken place on this street, and we will be able to visit several of these magically transformed buildings.

Find the two tiny houses squeezed in against already existing walls. (Watch for rooms or houses tucked in between existing walls or roofs; it is an economical way to build.) **No. 75** is a wooden house, a rarity, above a private garage, a greater rarity. **No. 77** is a french-fry place from which you can carry off your lunch and eat in the Square Viviani.

The **Trois Mailletz** at **no. 56** Rue Galande has a long history. The stonemasons who were building Notre Dame came here for drinks and food. After World War II it became known for its jazz clubs and the torture instruments in the *oubliettes* in the cellar (the same cellar as 14 Rue St Julien le Pauvre).

In the early 1980s the club was sold to a group of young people who remodeled the building and threw out the torture instruments. When they couldn't pay the rent, they too were thrown out. Today there is an excellent fifties-style classic jazz club on the spot, with food and music until 3:00 A.M.

At the door of **no. 52** a stone pillar has been uncovered. Curious caryatids adorn the corners of every window of this house, front and back. The neighbors say the figure is Quasimodo. This is the entrance of Les Oubliettes, the building with the false timbering.

Inside the pleasant courtyard of **no. 48** there are two publishing houses. The former tenant was a furniture restorer, Alain de Lavalade. In the process of relaying the stones in this courtyard, M. de Lavalade made two discoveries—the first is an oval stone, which is an entry to the underground cellar. The second is a square stone under the planter on the left. Under this stone there is a corkscrew staircase descending to the first basement. In the right lower wall of his workroom M. de Lavalade uncovered a washbasin. This wall was once part of a chapel and the washbasin was used to dispose of the wine in the communion cup. More about this chapel when we discuss **no. 46** next door.

**Cybele** at **no. 65 bis** is a gallery, bookstore, and archaeological treasure trove. The paintings are modern, featured in changing exhibits in the restored, vaulted twelfth-century cellar, while upstairs there is a fine collection of books on the ancient civilizations of Egypt, Greece, and Rome and authentic archaeological artifacts in a restored seventeenth-century building.

No. 65, now restored, was built in the sixteenth century and was occupied by the noble family of Châtillon. The restoration here was undertaken by the City of Paris.

The residents moved out during the work period but were given the option to return to this now-magnificent building. The rents are low and the tenants have the right to pass on their apartments to their children.

Above the doorway, notice the recently uncovered head of a woman surrounded by garlands of roses and oak leaves. We were the first to get a glimpse of her—one day as we were studying the building something fell at our feet from above the doorway. It was a totally black piece of nineteenth-century plaster, which had covered over the original sixteenth-century stone garland carving. Not as exciting as uncovering Eve at the Cathedral of Autun, but on our scale, still pretty terrific. Compare this head with that above the doorway of the building to the left. Similar garlands, of acorn and oak, appear above the first-floor windows, rolling waves above the next bank of windows, and rosettes above the next. Garlands of flowers are a fitting decoration for this street, Rue Galande. The two-windowed semi-circular gabled roof is crowned by a double ledge extending from the roofline. This sort of gable-front house, with a roof at right angles to the street, was declared illegal in the sixteenth century because rainwater collected between the buildings. From that time on, the roofline had to be parallel to the street so that the rain would drain into gutters instead of falling on passersby. About thirty gable-front houses still exist in Paris, one farther down a street that we will pass later on. The stone sculpture of garlands and an urn above the entry was uncovered by the restoration work on the building.

**Nos. 61** and **59** look like one building on the outside but hold surprises on the inside; these were not revealed to us until we had walked the street dozens of times. The flowing tresses of the lovely Art Nouveau lady crown the entrance to both buildings here. No. 59 was, as it says in the stone, built in 1910, and it and **no. 57** are examples of the brick construction that Paris has used for low-cost houses. (Rich and not-so-rich Parisians insist on build-

*Two friezes on the Rue Galande*

ings with cut-stone façades.) Notice that the building is set back about ten inches from its neighbor. This is an example of the fond hope the city had of moving back the building line in order to widen the street. As each building was torn down, its replacement had to be set back a prescribed distance. Fortunately, few buildings do come down in Paris, and that explains the ins and outs of Paris sidewalks.

Except for the woman's head, this part of the building is not exceptional. The door here is usually open; if not, open it and walk in. The hall is divided in two; the left side leads to apartments, but down the corridor on the right side you will find an iron-grille door, which opens to an old and beautifully restored house, **no. 61**.

The stairway and stairwell beyond the iron grille are an example of the care taken to bring the building back to its original shape. When Martin Granel and his family bought the place, it was almost impossible to get inside. The wall to the right of the staircase bellied out so far that the pillar of the house on the ground floor had to be

reset. The brick and wood stairs were redone with old wood that came from the South of France. The banister behind the pillar dates from the time of Louis XIII. (Doors, paneling, and rafters were also brought from the south to complete the interior of the house.) Every piece has been fitted and finished with great care.

The courtyard to the left of the staircase is filled with curious sights. The stones on the ground come from a former printing establishment next door, and the black print and designs are barely legible, though in reverse, on the portions of the floor that are not frequently walked on. There is a stone fountain and lots of greenery. A once-open staircase, now enclosed behind a wide expanse of beautiful windows, looks down on the courtyard. We were fortunate enough to be able to roam the house from the top to the bottom. Each landing and corner, and there were many, was used to good advantage. Old armoire doors concealed the washer and dryer. Velvet hangings enclosed a bedroom.

In 1198 some of this land on the odd-numbered side of the Rue Galande was given to the Jews for a burial ground. It had once served as such in Gallo-Roman times, from AD 270 to 360. In the twelfth century, Jews were returning from a sixteen-year exile imposed by King Philippe Auguste, one of the many that they suffered in different countries during those years of crusading fervor and intolerance. They came back, of course, to their old neighborhoods at the Petit Pont and the Rue de la Harpe, where they already had a cemetery, though it was no longer available to them. In any event, when Philippe III became king in 1270, he declared that the Jews of Paris could have only one synagogue and only one cemetery, so the one on Rue Galande was given up. Then in 1311, another king, Philippe le Bel, expelled the Jews once again, and closed the other cemetery as well. The absence of any traces of tombstones suggests that the Galande ground may have been used by Jews of modest means; the engraved tombstones found in 1849, however, under no. 79 Boulevard St Germain, have been a source of complicated and passionate Hebraic studies.

**No. 46,** the **Auberge des Deux Signes,** is not only one of the best restaurants in the area but also a masterpiece of discovery and restoration. We shall tell the story of this building as we heard it from the owners, M. and Mme Dhulster. M. Dhulster's father, who came from Auvergne, had a coal and wood business, which he combined, as was customary, with a restaurant-bar to serve the hearty needs of his workers. The zinc counter (one French word for bar is *le zinc*) that once served them is gone. In those days, even more than now, coal and wood haulers got very thirsty. Because there was no central heating, each flat needed its own fuel; because there were no lifts, haulers had to climb a lot of stairs to deliver these goods.

The coal and wood business has given way to the restored restaurant. Read about the interior first, and then enter the restaurant, book in hand, during the quiet periods between meals, and whoever is there will let you roam around or help you find your way. Better yet, take lunch or dinner there and make a tour part of the experience.

The uncovering and restoration of no. 46 began when the municipality planned to realign the street and remove part of the building, which dates from the sixteenth century. Because the construction of the house was superior to that of many around it, the owners received permission to let it stand and to restore it. Among their most successful efforts was the cleaning of coat after coat of plaster from the large beige stone pillars in front. These are now separated by sections of plate glass, but earlier these spaces were filled with many smaller panes, and originally there may have been only shutters, open for trade in the daytime, closed at night.

The big surprises lay hidden in the back of the house where construction from the fourteenth century had been covered. Not afraid of hard work, Dhulster decided in

1962 to dig out a lower level of his basement. (Like all the basements in the area this had been flooded and filled with mud in 1910, and undoubtedly by previous inundations as well.) A few steps down, he began to unearth vaulted arches built six hundred years ago. With the help of his son, Dhulster carried out twelve thousand coal sacks of dirt and gravel over a period of two years, finally revealing a large vaulted room that had served as a dormitory for a hundred monks from St Julien le Pauvre. All of this was done without official permission. When the Dhulsters finally told the proper city officials, the latter yielded to the spectacular evidence, authorized the work, and saw to it that the crumbled arches were reinforced by the most modern techniques and the use of pre-stressed concrete.

In 1969, while the family was redoing the bedrooms on the second and third floors in the back part of the house, a pick hit some iron and the unveiling of an entire fifteenth-century Gothic window began. Part of St Julien le Pauvre, the Chapel of St Blaise for masons and carpenters, once stood here. It was demolished in 1770, obviously not completely, and in 1812 a house was built over and around it. This window, a stone *pignon ogival* or "pointed gable," had to be completely dismantled (each piece weighed about five hundred pounds) because the floor and ceiling rafters attached to it had pulled it out of shape. The enormous yet fragile puzzle was then pieced together and returned to its original position. Jacques Chirac, Mayor of Paris, awarded M. Dhulster the National Order of Merit for the realization of this building.

Before you leave the vaulted window, look to your left on the ground. Here is a well that once stood outside this church window in a tiny alley. Not only is its border in perfect condition but it still has water in it, beautifully limpid. Dhulster let himself down this deep well and, as usual, made another discovery. Some of the stones move on pivots; that means there is still another buried cellar, farther down.

Be sure to see the stone spiral staircase down to the basement, and the beautifully finished wooden one from the ground floor to the first. Notice the modern skylight and the fantastic greenery growing from it down into the restaurant, above the round table laden with beautiful breads and tarts. If all this isn't enough to find in one place, reserve a table at night with a view of Notre Dame. The service and food are superb: elegant but not pretentious, provincial but not peasanty.

Outside on the wall of **no. 42** find the sculptured stone rectangle depicting St Julien and his wife rowing their charge across the river. It is the oldest standard in Paris, originally above the entrance to the church and mentioned as early as 1380. When the front portal of St Julien le Pauvre was taken down in the seventeenth century, the sculpture found its way here. Later on, when this building was gutted to install a modern cinema (one of a great many built in the fifth and sixth *arrondissements* in the early 1970s), the frieze was carefully boxed over, protected, built around, and finally uncovered.

At the corner to the right, at **no. 4 Rue Dante**, is the **Librairie Gourmande.** This is one of only three cookbook stores in Paris. The proprietor was a bookseller *(bouquiniste)* on the Seine for over thirty years. She obviously needed more space—the walls, tables, and even the floor are covered with books old and new. The valuable ones are in a glass case at the back of the store. Turn left from the corner of Rue Galande to **La Fourmi Allée,** a bookstore named for the winged ant who spreads her wings after her cramped work, at **no. 8 Rue de Fouarre.** Only books written by women or about women are sold here. Take tea and a light lunch as you read. Note the wonderful collection of teapots in this feminist store.

Continue down the Rue Galande across the Rue du Fouarre on your left and the Rue Dante on your right. (These are really a single street that changes names at this point.) At **no. 31** you can see a fine example of a medieval gabled roof. Notice the room tucked in between the sloping gabled roof and the straight wall of the house next door. The restoration of this building, like most restorations here, took place only a few years ago under the careful surveillance of the Monuments Historiques, a group that watches over all historic renovations in Paris. Claude Frémin, the architect, has hopes of restoring the gabled rooftops to the entire street.

## Rue de l'Hôtel Colbert

Across the Rue Lagrange on the Rue de l'Hôtel Colbert is the **Hippopotamus**, where at all hours of the day you can get grilled steak or hamburger without the roll. On the other corner be sure to look at the plaster which has been neatly chipped away to show you the original stones underneath. Walk down a bit, past the first two windows, and you will come to a rounded one, probably once an entrance. If you have the good fortune to find the curtain pulled back, look in and you will see an extraordinary blend of old and new—a huge stone fireplace to the left, a modern sunken kitchen to the back, a spiral staircase to the right. A few steps farther, and you can enter the apartment building (remember that you might have to press a button in order to be admitted and again to leave) and look through an iron grille to an interior garden. Tall French windows look out on to a raised grassy section dotted with trees.

At **no. 12** is the restaurant **La Cour Colbert**, once a house used by the homeless as *un asile de nuit* (shelter), where they slept "on the rope." A rope was stretched across the room and for a *sou* men could rest on it. When the allotted time was up, the rope was released, and all the men fell to the floor. Today the restaurant here serves excellent classic French cuisine ranging from reasonable to fairly expensive.

The **Hôtel le Colbert, no. 7**, is a superb recent copy from a seventeenth-century plan found in the archives of the Ecole des Beaux Arts. This is an elegant but personal small hotel and a lovely place to stay. A new *salon de thé* decorated with large, upholstered chairs perfect for relaxing after a long day of Pariswalking and a breakfast room in the vaulted cellar were to have their grand opening one week after we were there. The rooms have all been redone, including an apartment under the eaves with a skylit view of Notre Dame and the rooftops of Paris that just might fulfill your most romantic dreams.

Look across the street at the corner building. Near the number plate on the wall, **no. 8,** you will find an old name of the street cut into the stone, Rue des Rats, the "street of rats." An old resident assures us the name was fitting, that rats abounded just a short time ago. The name of the street was originally the Rue d'Arras because a college from the diocese of Arras was founded here (in 1320). A poet rhymed it with *rats,* and it wasn't long before the new name took hold and was inscribed as such when street names were cut in stone. In 1829 the inhabitants of the street petitioned for something more elegant, which the city authorities took from the title of an important *hôtel* (that is, a private house) that once stood on the street. Why that house was called the Hôtel le Colbert, no one knows, for Colbert never lived there. In any event, the original building was demolished when the Rue Lagrange was cut through in 1887.

The wall into which this street sign has been carved is the side of the old Faculty of Medicine. Look up at the round decorated window, called a bull's-eye (*oeil-de-boeuf*), and try to see into the room inside. This part of the building is the Amphithéâtre Winslow, built in 1744. This three-story room is well worth trying to see, though you may need an excuse to get in. The floor of the amphitheater is beautifully done in rosewood, oak, and teak, and the tiers of balconies look on to a huge center pillar that holds up the cupola like a mushroom stem. It is said that this room was used for medical demonstrations; now the balconies house a library collection. The entrance to the Faculty of Medicine is around the corner to the left on the Rue de la Bûcherie. When you get there, notice the ironwork on a 1909 grille inside the courtyard on the right-hand wall.

The Faculty of Medicine was created by King Philippe VI in 1331. Before this, in the Middle Ages, only monks had studied medicine, necessarily limiting medical care to one sex. (Given the ignorance of the medical profession, the women were lucky to be neglected.) In 1131, however, an ordinance forbade men of the church to study medicine, a prohibition confirmed in 1163 by the Council of Tours and thereafter enforced by excommunication. Thus, there were no trained doctors in France until 1220, when several small schools were opened; they subsequently merged into this Faculty of Medicine over a hundred years later. At first, classes were held with the other schools on the Rue du Fouarre, and exams were given in the masters' houses. It was not until 1472 that the present buildings were started. They were subsequently enlarged on several occasions and flourished until the Revolution, when the Faculty of Medicine, like all the other schools, was abolished. In 1808 the buildings passed into private hands, and in the next century knew a wide variety of uses: a laundry, an inn, an apartment building, even a brothel. In 1909 the structures were finally rescued and restored and classified by the city as historic monuments. They now house the School of Administration of the City of Paris.

In Jacques Hillairet's *Dictionnaire Historique des Rues de Paris*, there is a marvelous description of the kind of medicine that was taught by this school in the fourteenth and fifteenth centuries:

> The prescribed remedies were, for a long time, limited to a choice of three: laxatives, enemas, and bleeding. It was in this tradition that Charles Bouvard, Louis XIII's doctor, administered to the king in one year: 47 bleedings, 212 enemas, and

215 purgatives, total: 474 treatments, after which the doctor was ennobled. Richelieu submitted in the same year to 54 bleedings and 202 purgations. As to Ambroise Paré, he bled 27 times in four days a 28-year-old young man, that is, a bloodletting every 4 hours for 4 days, and in 1609 Le Moyne took 225 pints of blood in 15 months from a young girl.

There were, however, other treatments: a treatise of medicine that appeared in 1539 affirms that the blood of a hare cures gallstones; the droppings of mice, bladder stones; the excrement of dogs, sore throats; boiled wood louse, scrofula. It is also written that lung of fox washed in wine cures asthma; earthworms washed in white wine, jaundice; kittens, finely chopped with a goose and salt, gout; the excrement of a red-headed man, weak eyes. The wax from your ears applied to the nostrils promotes sleep; and Montaigne wrote that a man's saliva will kill a serpent. In 1540 André Fournier, professor at the School of Medicine, gave this recipe to make hair grow again: Boil 300 slugs, skim off the grease, add three tablespoons of olive oil and one tablespoon of honey, and anoint your skull with the mixture. One of his colleagues in this same period recommended the following rememdy to get rid of fleas: Take the heads of many red herrings, tie them with a string, place this in the mattress, and they will flee.

## Rue de la Bûcherie

As you retrace your steps down the Rue de la Bûcherie, don't miss **no. 9, Tapisseries de la Bûcherie**, the showroom for the exquisite tapestry creations of Melpoint. Inquire about courses for tourists and look into the historic courtyard.

**Galerie Urubamba** at **no. 4** was formerly a kosher butcher's. Find the marble slabs that served as counters and the meat hooks above the window. Today, it has a fascinating collection of North and South American Indian arts, fabulous feathered headdresses, and silver-and-turquoise jewelry.

## Rue Frédéric Sauton

You are now at the intersection of the Rue de la Bûcherie and the Rue Frédéric Sauton (on the right) and the Rue du Haut Pavé (on the left, or river, side). This apartment building on the left-hand side, between the Rue de la Bûcherie and the *quai*, shows the kind of reclamation and restoration that is taking place throughout the area—beautiful work for a privileged few. It costs a lot of money to buy land in the heart of old Paris, relocate tenants, then gut the buildings and redo the interiors from scratch. But then, people are prepared to pay a great deal to live across the river from Notre Dame.

**Rouvray**, at **no. 1** Rue Frédéric Sauton, was one of the first shops to brighten up this once dark and dreary street. It is run by an American, Diane Armand Delille, who is a connoisseur of American patchwork quilts; and it is the center for this art in Europe. Rouvray offers classes, equipment, and books for instruction. An exhibition of their quilts often tours France.

## Impasse Maubert

Next door is the entrance to the Impasse Maubert. There is a private house on the right, in a small garden. Today, for privacy, they have put up a tall fence, but in the past this charming, light-filled house was visible. A picture of the house at the time of purchase shows nothing but the side of a wall; the house was completely covered by houses against it and over it. The dead end

63

was blocked with shacks and sheds of every sort. It took imagination, daring, and lots of work and time to renovate the building. It was on this same spot that one of the first "colleges" in Paris stood: in 1206 a college of Constantinople, conveniently close to Place Maubert and the Rue du Fouarre, was created for Greek students.

Return to the Rue Frédéric Sauton, now barred to the automobile. At **no. 5** is **l'Objet Trouvé**, run by a Frenchwoman who speaks excellent English. This shop sells Indian *objets d'art* and imports Turkish kilim carpets. Because Nelly Lauer travels frequently to India to pick her merchandise, the shop carries unusual exotica. She designs and assembles her moderately priced jewelry made from antique pieces. She puts together two exhibitions a year. This is a nice place to buy yourself a present.

The **Tortue Electrique** at **no. 7** is a toy shop specializing in antique and unusual toys. The mock-turtle in the store is its mascot. The book collection contains contemporary works on the theme of games, as well as iconography and documentation related to the concept of play. This is a grown-up toy shop. The Tortue Electrique (Electric Turtle) is the name of an early, well-known game.

This new building replaced a jumble of old buildings around a large courtyard. One section used to house a famous Czech puppet theater that played wonderful fairy tales with the help of a devoted audience.

At the back of the courtyard of **no. 19,** a long subterranean passageway leads to no. 16 on the street behind, Rue Maître Albert. If you can get access to it, you will see prison cells on either side.

At **no. 25** Frédéric Sauton is a Michelin one-star restaurant, **Dodin-Bouffant**. Dodin-Bouffant, a fictional character in *La Vie et les amours de Dodin-Bouffant* by Marcel Rouff, was an extravagent gourmet and may well have been the source for the elegant stew of the same name. The originator and chef, Jacques Manière, is one of the glamorous people of Paris. He is good-looking, speaks beautifully, and is a philosopher about *haute*

*cuisine*. He asked if we wished to see the *caves*. We thought we'd see bottles of wine, but instead we saw *viviers*, "holding tanks," filled with live shellfish. We swallowed a plump oyster and had the tang of the sea in our mouths for the rest of the day. The headwaiter, M. Cartier, now runs the restaurant.

Down a few steps at **no. 29** is a large Vietnamese grocery store, **Thanh Binh**. In front, women sell packages of meat from cardboard cartons and piles of fresh herbs. Inside, the shop is tightly packed with a bewildering assortment of exotic foods, fruits, and ready-to-eat rice and meat steamed in banana leaves, tapioca in grape leaves, and shrimp muffins. Language is a problem here.

You are now in the **Place Maubert**, where there is a large open market every Tuesday. In the thirteenth century the square was famous for its outdoor classes; the philosopher Albertus Magnus lectured here on Aristotle.

If you are energetic enough at this point, visit one or more of the spectacular monuments in the area, such as Notre Dame, La Sainte-Chapelle, the Sorbonne, or the Cluny Museum, all within easy walking distance.

# Walk · 2

## La Huchette

*Voici la Rue de la Huchette,*
*Mais prends bien garde à*
  *ta pochette.*

This is the Rue de la Huchette,
But better watch out for your
  wallet.

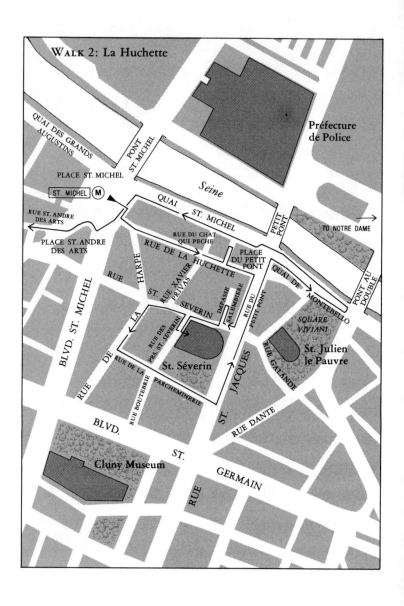

WALK 2: La Huchette

Préfecture de Police

QUAI DES GRANDS AUGUSTINS

PONT ST. MICHEL

PLACE ST. MICHEL

ST. MICHEL Ⓜ

Seine

RUE ST. ANDRE DES ARTS

QUAI ST. MICHEL

PETIT PONT

TO NOTRE DAME

PLACE ST. ANDRE DES ARTS

RUE DU CHAT QUI PECHE

RUE DE LA HUCHETTE

PLACE DU PETIT PONT

PONT AU DOUBLE

BLVD. ST. MICHEL

RUE LA HARPE

RUE XAVIER PRIVAS

ST. SEVERIN

IMPASSE SALEMBIERE

RUE DU PETIT PONT

QUAI DE MONTEBELLO

SQUARE VIVIANI

RUE DE

RUE DES PRS. ST. SEVERIN

St. Séverin

RUE GALANDE

St. Julien le Pauvre

RUE BOUTEBRIE

RUE DE LA PARCHEMINERIE

ST. JACQUES

BLVD.

RUE DANTE

Cluny Museum

ST.

GERMAIN

RUE

**Starting Point:** Place St Michel
**Métro:** St Michel
**Buses:** 21, 24, 27, 38, 47, 58, 63, 70, 81, 86
(within three blocks of Place St Michel)

## *Rue de la Huchette*

When you leave the Boulevard St Michel and turn left into the Rue de la Huchette to the point where the street narrows, imagine yourself back in the crowded and dirty Middle Ages. This neighborhood of tangled streets and narrow houses looks in many ways the same as it did hundreds of years ago. Aside from the land, which then sloped down to the water's edge instead of rising to the level of the present embankments of the Seine, this quarter is the same maze it was in the twelfth century, although the houses date from the seventeenth.

Baron Georges Haussmann, Napoleon III's famous city planner, cut wide swaths of boulevards (St Germain, St Michel, St Jacques) all around this neighborhood but barely touched the interior. He did, however, widen the western entrance to Huchette, which is why the houses from St Michel to the Hôtel Mont Blanc are nineteenth century.

Just before you enter the old Rue de la Huchette you

will see, to the left, the **Hôtel Mont Blanc**. The hotel has had its ups and downs, going from a country-style inn to badly run-down. Now it is on the upswing again. Half of the ground floor has been sold and converted into a half-French, half-Greek restaurant, pleasant but not what the neighborhood needs. The hotel is very reasonably priced and all the rooms have just been redone and include direct-dial phones and double windows. The former owners had fixed up the vaulted cellar as a breakfast room, with some etchings of the history of the Petit Pont. Look at these closely (there are two more in the lobby) to see how the river looked before it was diked up. The lobby also has an article about how a two-thousand-year-old bracelet was discovered during excavations in the nearby Caveau Huchette. There is speculation that a huge treasure, including a five-hundred-pound gold cross, is buried under these buildings, hidden during the French Revolution.

To the right of the door, against the wall that juts out and narrows the street, you will see a plaque commemorating an event from World War II. Before the Allies entered Paris, street fighting broke out all over this area. There were barricades at each end of Huchette. Just across the Seine, Parisians liberated the Prefecture of Police from Nazi control and used the spot as a vantage point for shots at the enemy. One of the tragedies of the fighting on the Rue de la Huchette was recorded on this tablet: "Here fell Jean Albert Vouillard, dead in the course of duty, killed by the Gestapo the 17th of May, 1944, at 20 hours. Rainbow." "Rainbow" was the name of his cell of Resistance fighters. The bullets that were sprayed into the wall have been plastered over.

The irony here is that the width of the street at the top is the unfinished work of Haussmann. His intention was to widen all these narrow pathways so that revolutionaries would be unable to barricade the streets as they did in the Revolution. At the end of the German occupation during the Second World War, however, it was the Resistance fighters' ability to do this that permitted them to defend Paris against the Germans.

Across the street at **no. 23** you will find the smallest theater in Paris. It performs only Ionesco—*The Bald Soprano* and *The Lesson*—the same plays since the mid-fifties. The theater holds eighty-five persons, seated straight across the room, and has no aisle. If you visit after three in the afternoon, try the door to the box office, then smile at the lady who sells the tickets, open the inside door, accustom your eyes to the dark, and get a glimpse of this tiny theater. At one point the son of the founder wanted to turn this into yet another restaurant (!) but he fortunately was stopped by the government and so the theater continues in its thirty-third year. Attend a performance if you can; Ionesco's French is easy to understand, and the plays are pure fun. The intermission is almost as good as the play; this street is really a night street. Turn to the right for some Tunisian delights before going back to see the rest of the play.

In the fourteenth and fifteenth centuries Huchette was called the Rue de Rôtisseurs, the "street of roasters." Whole sheep and oxen were turned on spits over open wood fires, and beggars held up their bread to soak up the smoke and smell. A papal delegate called it "verily stupendous." Today Greek restaurants have returned the street to its old activity, and the roasting goes on. Starting at 11 A.M. the lambs and pigs turn and crackle on the spits. The sight takes some getting used to. The stacks of kebabs, ready for the grill, wait for your order. Read the posted menu carefully before entering any of the restaurants; the à la carte menu costs mount speedily. However, some couscous restaurants (the smaller the better) will serve you dinner very cheaply.

Today nearly every shop is a Greek restaurant, and the street is losing the attractive diversity it once had. A few years ago the street was evenly split between the Arabs and the Greeks, with a sprinkling of French holdouts. Now the Arab population has left for Belleville, a

*World War II commemorative tablet on the Rue Huchette*

depressed area in the northeast of Paris. There were bombings on the Rue de la Huchette, two in Tunisian restaurants and a later one in a Greek restaurant. Whether this was caused by disputes over prime real estate, or some other reason, we cannot say. The residents of the neighborhood are not happy with the changes. There isn't a single French food shop and only one bakery sells *baguettes* alongside the ethnic pastries.

## Xavier Privas

You are now at the crossing of Xavier Privas and Huchette. Xavier Privas was the name of a singer from Montmartre who was famous in the 1920s, and although that is not particularly interesting, the previous names for the street are. At first this part, from Huchette to St Séverin (to your right), was known as Sac à Lie, "bag of lees." Lees are the dregs of wine, which, when dried, were used to prepare and clean leather hides and parchment. That was in the days when streets were known by their activities. Since few people could read, written street names were not displayed until 1729. With time and the disappearance of the sacks of lees, the street name changed from "Sac à Lie" to "Squalie" and it was finally engraved into **no. 19** up the street as "Zacharie" in the seventeenth century, and there it remained for almost three hundred years.

The part of the street that runs from Huchette to the *quai* used to run down, not up, to the Seine and was filled with the life and business of fishing scows, which were moored at the bottom of the street. Owing to many unpleasant incidents and general filth, the street was gated in during the first half of the seventeenth century. Recently it rivaled its medieval reputation, when the Paris sanitation men went on strike. You will notice that there are no entry doors on this small section of the street between Huchette and the river. No one's territory, so everyone dumped. One morning the pile reached over six feet, and the army was forced to come down and shovel away the mountain of rubbish.

As for incidents, the street has not lost its old vigor. At any and all hours of the night one can hear shouts and screams and songs. One night when militants were trying to mount a demonstration, the riot police ploughed up this street, six abreast and eight deep, driving young and old before them like chaff in the wind.

Each morning, however, the paths (no more cars since January 1973) take on the most picturesque and old-fashioned appearance. The shop- and innkeepers are outside in their white aprons washing their windows and their walks; the residents stop and talk or hurry about with their baskets of bread and meat. Huchette once boasted a butcher, a baker, and even a candle-maker; in fact, Xavier Privas from the Rue de la Huchette to the *quai* was once called the "street of three candle-makers."

Look across Huchette at **no. 14**, a five-windows-wide seventeenth-century building. The ironwork of the balconies is handwrought, made to order for the owner. He had his initials, D. C., laced into the decoration except for two windows, on the first floor, which say Y very clearly. There is still another Y to be found. You can see it on the stone space between the two windows—a framed circle with a graceful Y incised in its center. What is it all about? Shoppers 250 years ago understood. The letter Y (called a Greek *i* in French: *i grec*, pronounced "ē-grek") advertised the wares of the shop below. This shop was a *mercerie*, a haberdashery—selling needles and sewing materials. There was also an important article of clothing sold here: a lace or garter that tied a man's breeches to his leggings. The tie was a *lie* (as in the word *liaison*), and breeches were *gregues*. One of La Fontaine's rabbits has a pair; in a moment of danger he *"tire ses gregues"* ("hitches up his breeches") and runs away. When you put the tie and the breeches together (the *lies* and the *gregues*) you hear *l'i grec*. Now look once more at the incised Y on the wall between the windows—it looks like a garter. There are more of these amusing plays on words, called *calembours* (a "rebus") left in Paris, one close by on St Séverin. Among the best of them was a sign with six circles, 0s, which when spoken (sēzō) sounded like *ciseaux*, "scissors." It represented a scissors and knife shop on Rue Dragon.

## Rue du Chat qui Pêche

Look down the alley to the left at one of the most nondescript but oft-described streets in Paris, the Rue du Chat qui Pêche, the "street of the fishing cat." It took its name from a sign that hung above a shop, no doubt a fish shop, though no source actually says it was. Before the street took its present name, it was called the Rue des Etuves, the "street of steam baths." There were half a dozen such streets and alleys in the Paris of the late thirteenth century, and some twenty-six bathing establishments. Every morning the crier was out on the street calling to prospective clients: *"Li bains sont chaut, c'est sanz mentir!"* ("The baths are hot—no fooling!") They were hot in more ways than one. Many of them provided mixed bathing and supplementary services; as one preacher warned his flock: "Ladies, do not go to the baths, and don't do you-know-what there." The combination of clerical disfavor and public harassment reduced the number of these establishments to two by the early seventeenth century. The result was a malodorous population. Those who could afford to, doused themselves with perfume. The others . . . well, people's noses must have been tougher then.

This narrowest street in Paris was, contrary to what you might expect, wider in the sixteenth century. The six-foot-wide alley with its gutter of water (and urine) running down its middle looks and smells like a medieval street.

Walk up the alley away from Huchette; the alley suddenly widens, brightens, and then opens on to the Seine and, to the right, to a surprise view of Notre Dame. In the sixteenth century this street, like Xavier Privas, tumbled down into the Seine. It too was gated in at night, though no sign of the gate can be seen in the stone.

Return to the Rue de la Huchette. No. 12, on the corner of Huchette and Chat qui Pêche, was built at a later date than its neighbor and is the reason why Chat qui Pêche is narrower today than it once was. **No. 10** next door is the "corner" house where Bonaparte lived in his poorer days in a room at the back, facing the Seine. He was reputedly dying of hunger when Paul Barras, later important in the Directory (1795–99), gave him a chance to show his mettle; Bonaparte began his rise to glory when, with a "whiff of grapeshot," he dispersed the Paris mob in front of the church of St Roch. Jacques Hillairet, in his superb dictionary, summarizes Bonaparte's career in a change of address: "From this point on, fortune smiled on him. When he resided once again on the banks of the Seine, it was, in 1800, at the Tuileries."

Notice the absence on Huchette of wide doorways (*portes cochères*) that were built to allow a horse and car-

*Rue du Chat qui Pêche*

riage and later an automobile to enter a courtyard. Huchette was never a luxury street. The doors are narrow, and the halls lead back deep inside to reach the one staircase that serves both front and back of the house. Long and narrow buildings were common in the seventeenth century because street-front property was so costly. Open any of the doors, and if a restaurant kitchen hasn't filled the space, you will have a long, dark walk to the courtyard and stairs.

**Galerie du Scorpion** at **no. 9** is a Moroccan shop of rugs, clothes, handmade curiosities, and jewelry.

At **no. 5**, the **Caveau de la Huchette,** dedicated to the jazz of 1925, calls itself "the celebrated cabaret of jazz where one dances." It is open every night from 9:30 P.M.

to 2 A.M., Saturday until 3 A.M. Officially, the Caveau is open only to students, but friends of ours long past their student days spent a night of nostalgia there dancing the "lindy" to tremendous applause from the young connoisseurs who frequent the club. This is a good place for singles. Although the French dance style is different from ours, you'll have fun. There is a low cover charge, but no drink minimum.

The building that houses the Caveau dates from the sixteenth century and was connected by secret passageways to the Petit Châtelet, then a prison at the Petit Pont. According to a publicity flysheet put out by the proprietors, the Templars, a Catholic religious order, used the cellar as a secret meeting place in the late thirteenth century. Their riches were so great King Philippe IV felt the need to suppress them in order to relieve them of their wealth. It was the curse laid by the Templars on the king and his descendants that Maurice Druon took as the theme of his series of historical novels, *Les Rois Maudits (The Accursed Kings)*.

In 1772 the Freemasons met here in secret. Then, during the Revolution, these cellars and subcellars served as tribunal, prison, and place of execution. The process was swift. A deep well in the lowest level is said to have washed away all traces of this summary "justice." It was in one of the back rooms of this hotel that Elliot Paul started his nostalgic, intimate account of life in the Rue de la Huchette, *The Last Time I Saw Paris*. (The title is taken from the song of the same name, which recalled the happiness and sweetness of Paris before the German occupation.)

During World War II secret Resistance cells found their natural home here, while outspoken patriots filled the cafés. Jacques Yonnet, in his strange and haunting book, *Enchantement sur Paris*, describes the street as one of the ignition points of the occupied city. Perhaps "Rainbow" met here.

**No. 4** is a large seventeenth-century building, originally with three *portes cochères*, that was redecorated in the eighteenth century. Typical of this kind of face-lifting was the placing of masks on the façade. Here, fortunately, someone has preserved an old sign, *à la Hure d'Or* ("at the golden boar snout"—designating a *charcuterie* perhaps?) dated 1729. Look above the awning for the sign. Today, there is a club called Le Prestige. The restaurant on the corner changes hands almost every year.

Leave the narrow Rue de la Huchette and enter the **Rue du Petit-Pont,** which becomes **Rue St Jacques.** To the left is the *quai*, the Petit Pont, and Notre Dame; to the right is a long avenue that stretches south toward Orléans and, for the pilgrims who went on France's most popular pilgrimage of the Middle Ages, on to Santiago de Compostela in Spain. The building on the south corner of the Rue du Petit-Pont and the Rue de la Huchette looks like a seventeenth-century structure but was actually built from scratch in 1979.

Face the Seine and cross the street to the north corner. Close to the ground you will find a plaque commemorating bravery in World War II. It tells of two anonymous civilians and one soldier, Jean Dussarps, who were killed defending the little fort on the street. Below that, honor is paid to Madame Béatrice Briant, who was the leader of a group of voluntary fighters against the Germans.

Walk south to **no. 6** Rue du Petit-Pont, where an old and elegant grocery finally closed after holding out for more than fifty years. Part of the space, however, was taken over by members of the family who would have liked, if possible, to keep the grocery. Their souvenir shop, **Reflets de Lutéce**, reflects the same care and quality, offering interesting and original merchandise at very reasonable prices.

## *Rue St Séverin*

Walk away from the Seine, down the Rue du Petit-Pont, and right again into the Rue St Séverin. Countless nineteenth-century descriptions of this street and its neighbors all sound the same theme:

> And you wonder, remembering that these streets were full of cut-throat alleys, just how any Parisian managed to reach even middle age. I never pass here without seeing some long-lost villain lying in wait ready to pounce out on some unsteady wayfarer.

> All these streets, as I say, are picturesque and dirty.

> Between Cluny and the river is a network of very old, squalid, and very interesting streets.

To some degree the same comments can still be made. If you happen to walk here in the early morning when the crowd has gone home (whenever that may be) and the rubbish remains, you would be tempted to use the same adjectives. *Clochards*, male and female, sleep against walls or in doorways. Half of the food from the restaurants seems to have landed in the gutter. But at 7:30 the street cleaners arrive, and a new day begins.

The street was widened in 1678. If you look at the massive Gothic church on the left, it is not difficult to see why the houses on the other side of the street were chosen for removal. The present houses, therefore, date from the late seventeenth century.

The **Latin Mandarin** at **no. 4** is a small restaurant with a minute kitchen in the back. The restaurant may once have been a hall or a courtyard. It was started by a tiny lady, Mme Duc, who ran the restaurant with the help of her ten children. Her husband worked elsewhere, as

*Rue St Séverin*

an accountant. Vietnamese women often run small restaurants and food shops. You rarely see Vietnamese men
in the neighborhood; they're off working elsewhere. On
the other hand, you rarely see North African or Greek
women; they are at home, cooking. The present owner
is a close friend of Mme Duc. He offers the same fare
with some new dishes of his own.

Impasse Salembière, now **Impasse Eliane Drivon,** is
a closed alleyway. Once it was an open street, notorious
for its piles of rubbish and sleeping *clochards*, who found
it a haven. Now that the doors are locked at night, the
alley is immaculate. Try the *porte* button, open the door,
and take a look. Notice how the walls of the buildings

almost touch each other up above, typical of many medieval streets. Look at the old street name cut in stone above the street sign: Rue [blank] Séverin.

The stationery store that used to be at no. 6 has sold out to yet another restaurant and moved into the narrow hall of **no. 8**; the presses were moved to the courtyard. Behind this courtyard is a hidden building, reputedly fifteenth-century. To see it, go next door, past the Chinese restaurant into **no. 10,** down the long hall, up a few stairs, and along a short corridor. Look over the wall to your right. One section of **no. 6** has been restored in wood, unusual for Paris.

*The cloister of St Séverin*

Notice a very low, narrow seventeenth-century door to **no. 12.** Push open this small, heavily carved door to a centuries-old entry that boasts rafters in the ceiling, exposed building stones on the walls, a wrought-iron gate too heavy to budge, and an iron stair rail followed by a funny hand-carved wooden one.

Turn now and look at the **church of St Séverin.** In the sixth century, when everyone else lived on the Ile de la Cité, a hermit named Séverin found a patch of dry ground in the swampland across the river and settled there. The site was ideal for a hermit—separated from society but close enough to receive visitors. (Contrary to popular belief, the main aim of a hermit was not to cut himself off from humanity, but to induce it to beat a path to his solitary door.) Séverin must have received many, for at his death his reputation as a good man was so widespread that an oratory was built in his memory and called St Séverin. From that early date onwards, several churches have been built and destroyed on this site— once by fire, once by a Viking invasion—but all have been named for the hermit Saint Séverin.

The present church represents a combination of styles that stretches across the centuries from the thirteenth to the twentieth. There was never enough money to complete the building at any one time, so the work went on and on, and still does. Before the nineteenth century, architects and builders felt no compulsion to preserve or restore original forms. No age or style was sacred. All construction was "of the day." As a result the church has a parade of arches that tells the story of Gothic architecture from its primitive beginnings to its last flamboyant manifestations.

After you have looked at the massive exterior, which has recently been cleaned, transforming the building's appearance, enter the church, take a seat in one of the back rows, and take in the whole of the structure. Then look up the right-hand aisle. The three pillars closest to the entrance are early-thirteenth-century Gothic and are among the few remains of the previous church, which was destroyed by fire. The two arches between them, though broken (or pointed), are almost round, as in the earlier Romanesque style. The pillars are short, cut by capitals halfway up their length. On the wall above the arches and above the columns is a simple cloverleaf pattern, sculpted in stone. Look now at the next four pillars, done two centuries later. They are tall and straight, and the arches meet at a tighter angle. The goal of Gothic architecture was to reach higher and higher into open space. Notice the arcs that radiate outward from the stone trefoils on the wall above these arches. The small semicircles turn on themselves to make new ones, and the effect is that of a flame, from which we get the term *flamboyant*. All of this is still controlled, however, in contrast to the late flamboyant pillars behind the altar.

But look first at the pillars and arches surrounding the altar. Study the stonework carefully, and you will notice that the basic structure of the arches is the same as that of the fifteenth-century ones just described. Why, then, do they look so different? It's a seventeenth-century story. The famous and capricious cousin of Louis XIV, known as La Grande Mademoiselle, got into a dispute with the curé of St Sulpice, her neighborhood church, and decided to change parishes. To show her pleasure with the one and annoyance with the other, she bestowed her gifts and her idea of fashion on the church of St Séverin. The priest dared not, or at least did not, refuse. In the spirit of the Renaissance, La Grande Mademoiselle wrapped the pillars in red marble and rounded off the archways with the same red marble. There is more of the same stone in the shape of an altar now in a side chapel on the left. Formerly it was placed in the center to match its surroundings. The lady was busy elsewhere as well. If you look at the bottoms of the early flamboyant pillars of the fifteenth century (nos. 4–7, counting from the entrance), you can see the remains of fluting, which was added to the simple pillars. They are now being restored to their original shape, and by the time you visit, there may be no trace of these alterations. Almost every time we visited, we found further work in progress.

Now let us go to the flamboyant pillars behind the altar. Try—very hard—to find the sexton and ask him to turn on the lights of the apse. The effect is astonishing and marvelous. This spot is often called the Palm Grove; the pillars do look like trees spiraling up into palms overhead. The central twisted pillar is the prime example of French flamboyant Gothic. The spirals begin at the bottom and palm out above into so complex a network that it is almost impossible to trace their path. The grove has been called "a sanctuary of serenity," but we find this particular pillar anything but calm. It is known as Dante's pillar; he is reputed to have leaned against it often. The fact that Dante lived two centuries before the pillar was built did not stop the nineteenth-century chroniclers of old Paris from linking it to him!

Now, as you face the entrance, follow the outside aisle behind Dante's pillar around to the left (back toward the entrance) until you come upon a stout pillar capped by a magnificent broad-shouldered man holding up the arch and reading out a message. Half of this pillar was built in the fourteenth century and the other half in the fifteenth. It would have been simple to complete the pillar as it was begun, but here is proof that emulation of the past or any idea of unity of style was totally absent from the thinking of the time. And so it stands, fourteenth and fifteenth centuries both embodied in one pillar.

Continue up this side aisle toward the entrance and on the wall to your left you will find one of the best collections of votive tablets in Paris. This was the parish church for the Latin Quarter, and grateful students covered the walls with plaques that gave thanks to God for success in exams. If you have trouble finding these plaques, it may be because they have been removed. The sexton told us "they" planned to remove them because gratitude was "no longer *à la mode.*"

Cross over to the other side aisle (on the left side walking away from the entrance), and in the first chapel you will find a red porphyry marble altar. Professor Raoul Gaduyer, a venerable theologian-sociologist who knew every stone in this church, spent hours explaining and telling us stories. At the red altar, however, he hesitated, smiled, then hesitated again. We waited patiently for the smile to reappear and the story to begin. This large porphyry altar was another of the gifts of La Grande Mademoiselle. But the antiheroine of this story was Louis's mistress, Madame de Montespan. During her long liaison with the king she was concerned about his attentions to other, younger women. In her anxiety and despair she finally contrived to get the priest (Heaven help him!) of St Séverin to say a black mass on the red altar to ensure Louis's fidelity. The tender hearts of two unfortunate turtle doves served as the unholy instruments of her black magic. Bad enough, but her magical exploits continued (and here we are discussing only her black masses, not her poisoning of some of Louis's other mistresses). Another mass was said elsewhere in Paris with the same thought in mind—Louis and his love. That time the red altar was supplanted by a smaller and softer one, the naked body of Madame de Montespan. But the chalice would not stand upright, either because of her curves or her trembling. The solution was to place it securely between her thighs. All of this, as you can imagine, was done in great secrecy. Private records were kept, however, and these have recently turned up in the archives of the Prefecture of Police.

Continue down this side aisle to the chapel where the modern windows begin. The sixteenth-century painting on the wall to the right of the windows was uncovered in 1968, when the modern stained-glass windows were installed. The painting is a Last Judgment. The words on the right call up all saintly souls, men and women, to Heaven. On the left (sinister) side, however, are those damned to eternal Hell—all of them women, beaten on their way by devils, all of them men. An interesting testimony to the artist-priest's view of the roles of the two sexes.

Look at the nonrepresentational stained-glass windows. During World War II the fifteenth-century windows were shattered, and temporary ones took their place until 1966, when enough money was finally raised to commission an artist: the French painter Jean Bazaine, a fine colorist in abstract art who also did the mosaic at the UNESCO building in Paris. Bazaine drew his inspiration from the Bible, using quotations about fire, earth, and water. The bold primary colors of the windows set in solid shapes, one next to the other, create a striking contrast to the quiet strength of the stone.

When you leave the church, glance at the notices on the wall: classes in the French alphabet for North Africans, information on the history of the church, announcements of concerts (excellent and always full) to be held in the church, marriage banns, retreat dates, and so on. This is a marrying church. Come any Saturday morning and you can be sure to see a wedding.

Outside and across Rue St Séverin at **no. 22** is one of the narrowest houses in Paris; it is eight feet (two windows) wide. This was the house of the abbé Prévost, an eighteenth-century minister who wrote voluminously, though only one original manuscript remains, *Manon Lescaut*. We are convinced that the inspiration for his book came from his promimity to St Séverin and a shocking practice the church then indulged in: each year an award was given to the five most virtuous maidens in the parish. It was not enough, however, to praise the good. To warn against immorality, the church placed the most scandalous and unvirtuous women of the parish in cages and displayed them outdoors to the scorn and not-so-tender mercies of the passersby. It was the Last Judgment—the blessed and the damned—translated from life to art.

In 1763 the abbé Prévost, then living in a suburb of

Paris, succumbed to a stroke of apoplexy. An autopsy seemed in order, but when the good doctor used his scalpel on the corpse, it rose up and called out. The abbé was not dead after all! A few minutes later, the abbé obligingly passed away, not of apoplexy, but of the doctor's deep cut.

The corner house, **no. 24,** is a lovely rounded building, and on the corner above the blue street sign you can still see the street name cut into the stone, as you saw earlier. It says RUE on one line and on the next line SEVERIN. The SAINT was scraped out here as elsewhere during the Revolution, when the passionately anticlerical populace ravaged all things religious. Look for evidence of this on other streets named after saints. (The number 18 cut into the stone refers to the old divisions of Paris before the Revolution.)

Above the door at **no. 13** there is a fourteenth-century *enseigne*, a standard, for what was once an inn, depicting a swan whose neck is wrapped around a cross. This is another rebus, like the Y on the Rue de la Huchette. A swan in French is *cygne*, a homonym for *signe*, meaning "sign." Combining the *cygne* with the cross yields the "sign of the cross," the standard for lodgings.

Look down the long narrow hall of **no. 30** at the plaster and wooden construction of the walls. In the seventeenth century, walls were built of timber framing with a gravelly mixture filling the spaces between. This mixture was held together by pieces of wood and rags, just as clay bricks are held together by straw. This filler was usually covered over with white plaster, with timbers exposed, but the heavy incidence of fire in these oil-lit interiors led King Henri IV to decree that any wall with exposed timbers had to be completely plastered over. A white clay, which was found just below ground not far from here, in Paris, was quarried and used widely in the area—at Notre Dame, St Julien le Pauvre, and St Séverin. "Plaster of Paris" has become the generic term for any white plaster. Many walls were so weighted down with their coat of plaster, however, that they buckled and even collapsed.

**No. 34** is the most elegant building of this street. It was a stylish private home in the seventeenth century; one sure sign is the presence of a large coach entrance for the carriages of the proprietor, now filled with assorted vendors. (The other residents of the quarter obviously were not expected to own coaches or, if they did, were expected to keep them elsewhere.) The Ministry of Cultural Affairs has classified as monuments the entrance doors, the courtyard, and the iron stair rail. The wide and graceful courtyard is decorated with eighteenth-century *mascarons* just above the first floor. One is missing, however, as a result of fire.

## Rue de la Harpe

Turn left into the Rue de la Harpe. This was one of the great streets of Paris from Roman days until the middle of the last century. It ran parallel to the Rue St Jacques and wound its serpentine way from the river down toward the South of France. This long street, which was the principal north–south thoroughfare of its day, was amputated by two-thirds when Haussmann laid out a new, wide, straight north–south route across the Left Bank, the Boulevard St Michel, which took over much of the old right-of-way.

From the earliest times at least fourteen different names for the Rue de la Harpe have been recorded, several of them used concurrently. To some the street was known by a standard or an inn or a school, to others by the people who lived there. It was the street of Reginald the Guitarist or Reginald the Harper, the street of Old Jewry, the street of the Old Buckler, street of new St Michel, and so on.

A standard of King David playing a harp finally won out and gave the street its present name. The standard is said to have identified the house of Reginald the Harper but may bear some relation to the fact that in the eleventh and twelfth centuries there were Jewish schools on the Rue de la Harpe between Huchette and St Séverin.

The first recorded synagogue in Paris, tenth-century, stood on the corner of the Rue de la Harpe and Rue Monsieur le Prince, approximately four blocks south. Nothing at all is known about it, except that it stood at the wall of King Philippe Auguste, which encircled and protected Paris. When the Jews were expelled from Paris and their synagogue confiscated in 1182, Philippe Auguste gave their houses to twenty-four drapers and eighteen furriers.

The Rue de la Harpe has been the heart of the Latin Quarter for centuries. Roger de Beauvoir in *Paris Chez Soi*, published in 1855, describes it as it was in the early sixteenth century when Latin, though losing ground to French, was still spoken.

> There was a time when a mass of strange costumes could be seen milling around the greasy dirty street. There was first of all the *mire*, the first doctor of early times, who sold his drugs and unguents in the street, escorted by a child with a monkey which was bled by the "practitioner" *on request* [what for we can't imagine]; then the hanging sleeves and furs of a professor as grave as Erasmus; the flowing cloaks of the students mixed in with the jackets of the men at arms, the pointed hats of the Jews, and later on the wig of Dr. Diafoirus. . . . How many little working girls, the girl-friends of the students, did these black, filthy houses not shelter? Girls singing like canaries in their cages, the frightful cages of the seventh floor of the Rue de la Harpe. The whole anthill of the schools . . . begins every morning to move its thousand legs from the bottom of the Rue de la Harpe—the medical student who goes off, nose to

the wind, hand in pocket, looking at his coloured anatomical plates, the High School student buying a cake, the law student ogling a shop girl, the tutor taking the rich man's son to his exam for the baccalaureate. The point is that rents were reasonable; even so, no chance that a Chinese, a Turk, an Arab, or even an Englishman would lodge there. It is a special people that enlivens this quarter; a people with ink on its fingers and in its lips, an undisciplined, haughty, noisy people, the people of the schools, the drinking joints, the furnished rooms, the Rue de la Harpe with its thousand side streets is the "heart of the students."

Today it is not the "heart of the students" but the heart of the tourists. As you have noticed, the Arabs and the Vietnamese, if not the Chinese, the Greeks, and the Turks, have found their way to this quarter and have changed the business of the street from student housing and small food shops and workshops to one of restaurants, cafés, boutiques, jazz clubs, and hotels. The street must be seen at night, and Saturday night is the best night of all.

People in brightly colored costumes, very strange and unpredictable, swarm on all sides. They do not tell us the business of the wearer—doctor, soldier, student, girl-friend—for most of the milling passersby simply look like travelers on the tourist beat playing games with one another. Overheard conversations reveal, however, that many of these exotic birds are settled and serious and probably change their plumage during working hours. The "frightful cages of the seventh floor" are now restored studios (one room and a cubby of a kitchen and bath) renting for large sums, and are snapped up before the rental sign is put up.

On the corner of Rue de la Harpe and St Séverin is a simple French restaurant called the **Prégrille.** In the sum-

*Tunisian bakery on Rue de la Harpe*

mer, take a table outside, enjoy a *steak-frites*, and watch the crowds roll by.

**No. 33** is a narrow, one-window house called La Petite Bouclerie. Remember the street was once called the street of the Old Buckler. The name is written inside a sculpted stone frame inside the door.

Look up at **nos. 35** and **45**. You will see elegant eighteenth-century houses with impressive doorways, rounded stone window-frames, and sculpted façades. The

old coach entrances are now filled in, the courtyards occupied by restaurants; but up above, the ceilings are
twelve feet high and the rooms are large and bright. The
cellars, once filled with mud from Seine floods or used
as wine cellars, are fast giving way to restaurants and
movie houses.

Look in the courtyard of **no. 35,** past the entry on
the right. You'll see a staircase with a classified iron railing and a wall of beige building stones.

ar*iswalks*

This wide street, closed to traffic, is a pleasant place to walk despite some poor-quality clothing stores. In pleasant enough weather musicians and singers vie for the corner of Rue de la Harpe and Rue de la Huchette (one block north). Enormous crowds gather and often richly fill the empty hat in appreciation of good music or just the pleasure of the spectacle. We once heard a violinist who really was first class, probably on holiday from a symphony orchestra, we decided after listening to him.

## Rue de la Parcheminerie

Turn left into the Rue de la Parcheminerie. In the Middle Ages this street was the "bookshop" of the Rue de la Harpe. Before 1530 it was called the street of writers (Rue des Escrivains), then renamed for the parchment the writers wrote upon. The first parchment paper was thick and rough and lent itself poorly to handwriting. It was only in 1380 that the experts developed a grain so tight they were able to write the whole Bible in one small volume. The scribes who worked here were privileged souls, exempt from taxes and held in high esteem, though their morals were infamous. This street has just been cleaned up and widened, transforming it from its former dark-alley appearance to a quiet and pleasant residential street.

The odd luxury of the street is **no. 29.** It was built for a gentleman named Claude Dubuisson in 1750. One of its beautiful doors was removed when the building served as a wine depot. Each pair of the tall, curved, graceful windows, all three stories of them, opened on to a large room. Today these rooms have been divided into apartments and the previous occupant, who was there during the restoration of the splendid façade, explained to us that the architects had made the space to squeeze in the necessary bathrooms in the thickness of the wall.

The second door of no. 29 now opens to **The Abbey Bookshop**, competition for Shakespeare and Company. The Abbey Bookshop offers a large and carefully chosen selection of secondhand scholarly and literary English-language books. The proprietor, Brian Spence, claims that in this busy and crowded part of the Latin Quarter, his bookstore is a quiet refuge for the poet, the scholar, or the pilgrim. Sheri Aldis tells stories to children three to ten years old every Wednesday at 3:30 P.M.

The newly built **Hôtel Parc St Séverin** at **no. 22** benefits from a sunny, open disposition in this neighborhood of crowded, twisted streets. No. 70 is the penthouse suite, with a circular terrace that spans views from Notre Dame to Montmartre.

In 1935, plans were drawn up that called for a complete modernization of the area, a transformation of these winding, narrow streets into neat, airy thoroughfares flanked by modern apartment buildings. But then the campaign to save old Paris took over; the Ministry of Cultural Affairs classified every possible treasure and forbade the destruction of most of the buildings, though they could be restored. Alterations were usually permitted in the interior, hence the opportunity for profitable conversion to new commercial uses and to luxury apartments. And so, the restoration goes on at a galloping pace, but always far behind the rise in demand.

The medieval name of the Rue Boutebrie (on your right) connects it to the Rue de la Parcheminerie. It was the street of illuminators (Rue des Enlumineurs) when the other was the street of writers. This was the book center of Paris, and Paris was the intellectual center of the world. Follow the continuation of Parcheminerie to the Rue St Jacques and turn left.

## Rue St Jacques

Immediately cross the Rue St Jacques to the store side—the better to see the back of St Séverin, which was smothered by shops until the street was widened a hundred years ago. The stores on this street change with time and style, but many of their names—the Cloister, the Pilgrim—still tell the history of past centuries.

To the left of 31 Rue St Jacques and to the right of no. 27, on the wall that juts out, there is a plaque that tells of the death of a soldier, a policeman who was killed at the barricade in 1944. Above the plaque, high on the wall, are the remains of a sundial.

Look into the hole-in-the-wall café, **Polly Magoo.** Most of the patrons here seem to be permanently settled behind their chessboards, surrounded by timers, kibitzers, smoke, and drinks. Chess players come from everywhere to play as they did in certain cafés in the early 1900s. The owners of the Polly Magoo also own the **Caveau de la Bollée** at 24 Rue de l'Hirondelle, where even more serious chess players go at it all night.

**Métamorphoses** is true to its name, so it changes its wares. It was originally an eccentric 1900s store. Today it is strictly jewelry with a collection of mainly Deco reproductions done by the same companies who made the jewelry in the 1920s. Her pieces are more expensive than others in Paris but the quality and selection are superior.

**Baby Train,** a strange name for this highly technical store, has an enormous selection of electric train equipment and models that should prove irresistible to the hobbyist. Although the current is different (you'll need a converter if you buy anything), the pieces of scenery are fascinating.

## Quai St Michel

Cross the street to the corner of Place du Petit-Pont and the Quai de Montebello, and walk right, toward the Pont au Double. You will pass in front of the famous bookstalls of Paris and be across the street from the beginning of Walk 1. The booksellers (*bouquinistes*) represent one of the oldest trades in Paris, and one that has changed very little. The men and women who are lucky enough to get a spot on the parapet to hang their metal boxes consider themselves a special breed. They love the outdoors and the freedom to open and close at will. When the *quai* is quiet, they sit and read, or sleep, or knit, or smoke, or play chess with their neighbors. Story has it that they are never sick and live to very old age. Most of them have a specialty, but many buy whatever looks saleable.

The real fear of the *bouquinistes* is the automobile. The noise is deafening, the air polluted, and the traffic so dense and steady that they see themselves under siege. And rightly so. Although plans to transform the *quai* into an expressway have been abandoned, the fear is always there. It was former President Giscard d'Estaing who stepped in to protect traditional Paris. He forced the Paris Council to abandon its planned motorway by withdrawing the government's 40 percent financial contribution.

We found the stalls between the Petit-Pont and the Pont au Double more interesting than those near the Pont St Michel. Some stalls down, opposite La Bûcherie, M. Lanoizelée has a serious stand. He collects first editions, many of which have inscriptions from the author on the flyleaf.

Opposite Shakespeare and Company is the stall of M. Korb, **Box 109,** a postcard dealer who is president of the Bouquiniste Union. He took on the task because he felt these independent individualists would have more *esprit de corps* than normal businessmen. He has since learned that they hate to pay even $10 a year in dues, and he

*Produce stand at the Buci Market*

often spends his own money on stationery and postage. Korb's postcards are wonderful. Often the messages on the back are as fascinating as the photography and style of the card itself.

The rest of the bookstalls offer the usual fare of pages torn from old books, reproductions of Daumier prints, and modern paintings of children with large liquid eyes. But it's worth browsing.

One of the best of the stalls is **no. 103** (at the corner of the Pont au Double), where M. Leleu sells old and beautiful leather-bound books, mostly from the eighteenth century. He has a private collection of more than fifty thousand volumes. If you are especially interested he might invite you to his home to do some serious buying. Leleu also restores old manuscripts. One day he showed us a medieval Arab manuscript bound in crumbling leather and clasped in bronze fittings that he hoped to revive in about a month. We must warn you that he is not always pleasant; he says so himself. His books mean too much to him, and he is exasperated by the careless handling—as well as the occasional rip-off—from pass-ersby. Back to the corner of the Petit Pont and the Quai de Montebello: diagonally across you will see the usual souvenir and poster shops that fill the Quai St Michel, but tucked in between are serious galleries and entrances to choice apartments that look out on the Seine and the bustle of the *quai*.

A gallery of fine engravings has moved out to make way for a *métro* elevator for the physically handicapped. We wonder how a handicapped person could ever get through this street. We agree with the residents; it is not a good location.

**Sartoni-Cerveau** at **no. 15** begins a row of serious collectors' stores. Sartoni-Cerveau's shelves are packed with antique books and etchings. The major topics of his collection are travel, maps, landscapes, and decoration. His motto is, "The love of books unites us."

The cupboards on the walls of the **Galeries Michel, no. 17,** are filled with original seventeenth-, eighteenth-, and nineteenth-century prints. M. Michel, whose father ran the gallery before him, is both informative and friendly. The labels on his cases cover any subject you might think of—circus, interiors, romantic, mountains—as well as individual artists. Michel will be glad to give you a chair and a standing wooden frame to rest a folder in and leave you on your own. Prices range from numbers with one zero to numbers with many. Most of his business is done with collectors by mail, despite his location on this very busy street of tourists. Ask to see the back room, which is a small museum of fine etchings.

**Musique** has walls lined from top to bottom with folders of new and secondhand sheet music. The shop is always crowded with serious musicians. Classical and jazz guitars are displayed in the window.

**Gibert Jeune:** there are three of these, two on the

*quai* and one around the corner on the Place St Michel. They are offshoots, though now separate, of the older firm of Gibert, chief bookseller to generations of students at the Sorbonne and the Lycée Louis le Grand farther up the Boul Mich.

Gibert Jeune, like every other Paris enterprise that can get away with it, sets up displays of merchandise on the pavement outside to catch the fancy of the passersby. These take up a good half of the pavement, and although they create a minor pedestrian traffic jam, it's fun. Take your time walking through the crush during morning and evening rush hours. At those hours parking is not tolerated on that side of the *quai*, and cars tear along in the outside lane a foot or two from the pavement.

These pavement displays are usually filled with loss leaders and sale books. If you want to buy one, give it to the salesperson outside, usually perched on a high stool and sheltered (in winter) by a glass box. He or she will then give you a ticket, which you take inside to the cashier. She (invariably it's a she) will take the money and stamp the ticket. You can then go back out and collect the book. This is another example of the tight control French storekeepers hold over the cash box. They have more faith in their customers, however, than we do in this day of shoplifting. Gibert Jeune and Galeries Michel leave merchandise out unattended, something of a surprise for Americans.

The first Gibert Jeune offers art books, guidebooks, books for collectors (about dolls, playing cards, trains, buttons, pipes, anything) at remainder prices. An example of their offerings was a large book, illustrated in color: *Delacroix* by René Huyghe, reduced 50 percent.

The second Gibert Jeune has perhaps the largest selection of schoolbooks in Paris; they range from beginning readers in the back of the store to Keynes on economics in the front. When secondary school starts in the fall, lines stretch around the corner, and students wait for hours with their lists of books in hand. The shop closes at five, the line at three.

The third, and the largest, is on the Place St Michel. Turn the corner and you will see a book and stationery shop literally in the street. Every morning and evening the stands are carried in and out. The ground floor has all kinds of stationery and office equipment. Enjoy yourself buying new kinds of pads and pencils and paper clips.

It is certainly time to sit down at the corner café, **Le Départ,** for espresso, fresh lemonade, hot chocolate, or beer. (If you like lemonade with bubbles, ask for a *siphon*, or seltzer bottle, with your *citron pressé*.) Le Départ is a choice spot for people-watching.

You are now back where you started, but there are a few more remarks we would like to make. The *métro*, with its easy map of instructions, will take you anywhere faster than the taxis on the riverside of the *quai*. This particular entrance is one of the seventeen remaining in Paris that were built around 1900 by Hector Guimard, the architect of the period. Go to see the façade and interior of one of his prize-winning houses at **no. 14 Rue La Fontaine** in the sixteenth *arrondissement*. Sometimes the art of the period, Art Nouveau, is called Style Métro because these subway entrances typify the imaginative floral spiralling that marked the style so clearly. Note the side railings of the *métro*. An Art Nouveau show at the Museum of Modern Art in Paris in 1960 appropriately used a *métro* entrance as the passageway into the exhibit. The appreciation of 1900s métro entrances soared, but the Museum of Modern Art in New York managed to buy one before Paris realized their future worth. The entrance in the Place St Michel is missing its curved arch; this has been replaced by a straight pole, typical of the Art Deco of the 1930s, which holds up the rectangular nameplate.

If you look down the boulevard, you will see how jammed it is with people and pavement vendors. The Cluny Museum is three blocks south, away from the *quai*, and the Sorbonne, five.

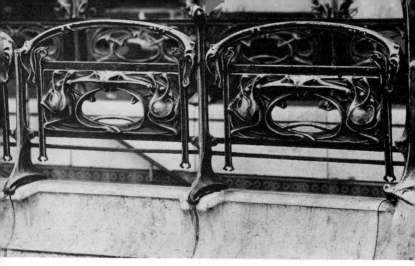

Art Nouveau métro *railings designed by Hector Guimard*

### Rue St André des Arts

If you wish to begin Walk 3 now, cross the boulevard to the Rue St André des Arts. You will pass by a large and impressive fountain, which is a meeting place and haunt. St André des Arts is a fascinating street with interesting shops, elegant doorways, and better buildings than Huchette. **Allard,** the once-famous one-star bistro, had fallen on hard times with the death of Mme Allard, but it's on track again.

Continue up this street of little shops to the arcade, the **Cour de Commerce.** Look at the shops here: a decorator's shop with copyable ideas, a modest bookbindery that does elegant work. Leather, unfortunately, is not cheap, and the day when you could get a fine morocco binding for a few dollars or so is long gone. Cloth binding is much cheaper. The shop is always busy, partly because large French books come out in paper rather than cloth and have to be bound if they are to see any use.

Now go out into the little street beyond, which is closed to traffic, and turn immediately off it to the left into an enchanting island of old private homes and rich, privileged tranquillity. Whenever we had an errand in the area, we used to wander in there just to see the entrances, to walk on old-fashioned giant cobbles, and to get away from the noise and crowds and dirt right outside on the Rue St André des Arts.

Go on back to St André, where there is hardly enough room to walk, through the **Buci marché**, one of the best, busiest, and liveliest markets in Paris, down the Rue de Buci, and out onto the Boulevard St Germain.

# Walk · 3

---

## St Germain des Prés

*In my last letter, I told you that the guillotine is taking care of some dozens of rebels every day, and that about the same number are shot. Now I want to inform you that several hundreds are to be shot every day so that we will soon be rid of those scoundrels who seem to defy the Republic even at the moment of their execution. . . .*

*—From a loyal republican to his section*

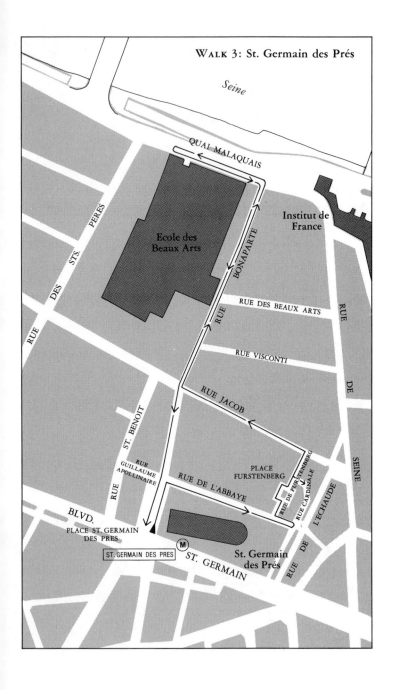

WALK 3: St. Germain des Prés

*Seine*

QUAI MALAQUAIS

Ecole des
Beaux Arts

Institut de
France

RUE BONAPARTE

RUE DES BEAUX ARTS

RUE VISCONTI

RUE JACOB

RUE DES STS. PERES

ST. BENOIT

RUE GUILLAUME APOLLINAIRE

RUE DE L'ABBAYE

PLACE FURSTENBERG

RUE DE FURSTENBERG

RUE CARDINALE

RUE DE L'ECHAUDE

RUE DE SEINE

BLVD.

PLACE ST. GERMAIN
DES PRES

ST. GERMAIN DES PRES

ST. GERMAIN

St. Germain
des Prés

RUE DE

**Starting Point:** Place St Germain des Prés
**Métro:** St Germain des Prés
**Buses:** 48, 63, 70, 86, 87, 96

As you take in the busy and curious scene of St Germain des Prés, wander over to the garden on the side of the church at the corner of Rue de l'Abbaye and the Place St Germain. We suggest you begin this walk by taking a seat in the garden and reading a bit about its illustrious abbey and the bloody events of the French Revolution that took place on and around this spot.

In Roman and Merovingian times this area consisted of open fields (*prés*) stretching westward away from Paris, and there was a temple to the Egyptian goddess Isis on the site where the Eglise St Germain now stands. The modern suburb of Issy les Moulineaux took its name from this ancient temple.

In 542 Childebert, son of the first Christian king, Clovis, went on a crusade in Spain to punish the Visigoths, who, though Christian, were guilty of heresy. The inhabitants did not defend themselves in any way, and Childebert laid siege to their key city, Saragossa. The Visigoths, despairing of their fate, paraded around the walls of the city in hair shirts, carrying sacred gold relics and the alleged tunic of Saint Vincent. The men chanted psalms; the women, with hair unkempt, sobbed hysterically, as if in mourning. Childebert was fascinated by this procession, and, when he saw the relics they carried, offered to lift his siege in exchange for these treasures. He returned triumphantly to Paris with the sacred tunic and the objects of gold. There is evidence, however, that the Bishop Germain (later Saint Germain) of Paris, as well as the chronicler of this tale, Gregory of Tours, considered Childebert a fool to have settled for so little. They felt his father, Clovis, would have done better.

In any event, the bishop took the opportunity to get Childebert to build a church to house the sainted relics on the location of the former temple of Isis. There a magnificent basilica with marble columns and gilded rafters was built in two years. The outside was covered with gilded copper and gold mosaic radiant in the sunshine, and it was called St Germain le Doré, "St. Germain the Golden."

Three hundred years later, Norsemen, drawn by the glitter of what looked like pure gold, descended on Paris and ransacked the church four times in forty years, between 845 and 885. They were disappointed each time; the true gold relics that Childebert had brought back from Spain, along with the tunic of Saint Vincent, lay safely somewhere in the country. In the meantime the devastated church was left a ruin for more than a century. Then, in the beginning of the eleventh century, it was rebuilt. The central bell tower dates from this reconstruction and today is the oldest church structure in Paris.

What decided the fate of this area for many centuries was the establishment there of an abbey, with rights to the land and its revenue over an enormous area stretching from the Seine all the way to what are now the suburbs of Paris. The abbey also received exclusive jurisdiction in all religious and legal matters within its territory. The fortified walls that enclosed the abbey proper formed a square between the present Boulevard

*The bell tower of the church of St Germain des Prés*

St Germain and rues Jacob, St Benoît, and de l'Echaudé. The size and riches of the abbey of St Germain rivaled those of the city of Paris.

The bishop's abbey was his palace; his clerics were his court; and the peasants who lived outside the walls (bakers, butchers, prison guards) were his servitors. This imitation of courtly life did not go unnoticed by the king, who kept a close watch on the rival power just outside the city walls.

The most interesting tales come to us from the thirteenth century and concern the perennial conflict between the monks and the students of the Latin Quarter nearby. The students used to come to talk and sport on the fields that stretched along the Seine north of the abbey. They made noise, trespassed on areas the clerics would have closed to them, and troubled the peace of the local residents—as students are usually accused of doing. In return the residents of the abbey harassed the students at every opportunity. From time to time this hostility broke into violent conflict.

The worst of these confrontations took place in 1278, when the abbé Gerard built some houses along a path that the students customarily used in going from the Latin Quarter to the playing fields. The students saw this as a provocative impediment to their passage and proceeded to dismantle these structures. The abbé rang the tocsin, summoning monks, vassals, and serfs to defend the rights of the abbey. Chroniclers tell us that an armed company fell on the students with swords, pikes, and clubs, shouting, "Kill! Kill!" The students took a terrific beating. Two were killed, one blinded, several badly wounded. Prisoners were paraded bareheaded through the marketplace and thrust into the abbey's dungeons, on the site of the present Hôtel Madison (no. 143 Boulevard St Germain).

However great the provocation offered by students, the abbé was felt to have overreacted. The students appealed to the papal legate and the king, and, surprisingly, got a quick and sympathetic response: perhaps this was because both the Church and the Crown had come to feel that the abbey was too rich, powerful, and arrogant for anyone's good. The leader of the abbey forces was exiled; the chapter was compelled to build and endow two new churches in memory of the slain students; the parents of the victims were granted substantial indemnities. And the students were confirmed in their legal use of their sporting meadow, the Pré aux Clercs, so called because the term "clerc" denoted all men of instruction, whether or not they were members of the clergy. The students were overjoyed at this victory, and in the following years continued to exercise whatever rights of destruction they felt appropriate.

Three centuries later, Henri II, plagued by student uprisings, decided to dampen their ardor and sent Parliament orders to pursue persons guilty of acts of violence. Its action culminated on October 6, 1557, with the burning at the stake of a student named Croquoison, who received the bleak mercy of being strangled before being burned on the Pré aux Clercs. This seems to have been the last major incident in the student–monk war, although their mutual animosity produced incidents well into the eighteenth century.

In the spring of that same year, the people of the *quartier*, as well as those who came streaming from all over Paris, had been treated to a more dramatic execution at the stake. Two Huguenots, who had been captured at a secret religious meeting two weeks earlier and had refused under torture to abjure their faith, were brought into the square that is now Place St Germain, in front of the church, and asked one last time to renounce their heresy in order that they might be strangled before being burned. If not, their lying venomous tongues were to be ripped from their mouths. They refused. After the executioner had done the terrible deed (to the roaring approval of the crowd), the heretics were bound and hoisted onto the stakes, which were placed high above the wood in such a manner that the lower halves of the bodies would be reduced to ashes while the top halves were still intact.

Less gruesome stories are told about the fairgrounds that were a central feature of the abbey's power. Every year for a month after Easter a great fair was held in the place where the *marché* St Germain is today, although in those days it spread all the way to the Luxembourg Gardens. This was one of the great medieval fairs, drawing people from all over France as well as Spain, England, Burgundy, Flanders, and the Holy Roman Empire. Here were hundreds of stalls selling every kind of product and service available then; troupes of performers, dancing bears, and minstrels; the most impressive swirl of colors, smells, and noises a commoner would ever see. This fair served as a gathering point for students as well as courtesans and men of state. The rest of the year the area was far from deserted. There was always some activity, and it seems to have been the place to find whomever it was you sought in Paris. In addition to attracting courtiers, merchants, and students, the fairgrounds were frequented by a group of Italian ruffians, ironically called *braves*, because they hung out in groups of five or six. They were available, at the right price, for carrying out whatever vengeance one might seek, as the following story illustrates.

In the court of Henri III there was a nobleman whose mistress dumped him rather rudely. Having given her large sums of money in happier days, he wished to collect his "loans." His former lady, believing that in love, money loaned is money given, refused to comply. Had she stopped there, no one would have blamed her, but she continued her vengeance by finding a new lover. One night, the nobleman was returning home after a walk through the St Germain fairgrounds. On the *champ crotté* (the dunged field of the cattle market), which was understandably solitary, a band of *braves* jumped him and held him by the nose, which the leader began to cut off with a knife. The victim's screams aborted the full oper-

ation, and the nobleman was left watching his assailants
flee as his nose dangled by a thread. The nose was sewn
back on, but, in the testimony of a contemporary, slightly
off-center. The story had unpleasant results for some of
the actors; one does not lightly cut off a nobleman's nose.
One *brave* was hanged, and the lady and her friends had
to buy their way out of trouble, no doubt with the hap-
less victim's money.

Henri III also appreciated the promenade, where he
would stroll in the company of his *mignons* (literally
"cuties," the name given to his favorite young men) with
their curly hair, powdered faces, and makeup. They rapidly became the butt of student jokes. Returning one day
from Chartres, the king had several students imprisoned
for following his suite with long pieces of curled paper
and shouting out loud in the middle of the fair, *"A la
fraise on connaît le veau"* ("You can tell the calf by its
birthmark"—a French proverb that meant in this context,
"You can tell the faggot by his curls").

The monastery reached the end of its 1,200-year history when the French Revolutionaries moved in and took
over. They replaced intermittent violence with the organized violence of the Terror. They filled the abbey's jail
until it was overflowing with prisoners (aristocrats, clergy,
and common people), and then set up tribunals to thin
out the crowd. These tribunals made use of "guest
houses," which stood on the corner of the Rue de l'Abbaye and Rue Bonaparte, just outside the entrance to this
garden. These houses had extra rooms called *chambres à
donner*, which meant rooms that could be given to guests
of the abbey. These rooms, which once provided shelter
and comfort, were turned into tribunals of condemna-
tion—swift and deadly. The stories about the trials held
there are hard to believe.

One concerns Mlle de Sombreuil, a carefully brought-
up young lady who rarely left her house unaccompanied.
One day, however, she left, alone, on a terrible mission.
Her father, a prisoner, was scheduled for one of the in-

famous swift trials in which no one was found innocent. When she appeared at the tribunal, she begged for her father's life. The guards found the situation amusing and offered to make a deal. If she would drink the still-steaming blood of the latest victim, they would spare her father. She did, and her father lived, for a few days.

During September 2 and 3, 1792, these tribunals carried out the ostensibly judicial massacre of more than two hundred victims. Each defendant was dressed in his best clothes, because he had been told when arrested that he was being sent away. The questioning that followed demanded simply a yes or no; either answer proved the defendant guilty. After this mock trial, the prisoners were led out of the tribunal into the courtyard of the abbey and were there hacked and stabbed to death by two rows of hired citizens, in many cases local inhabitants.

One hundred and sixty-eight men and women, including several of Louis XVI's ministers, his father confessor, and surely many "irrelevant" people were executed in this fashion on September 3 alone, because Judge Maillard (nicknamed "the Slugger") insisted on having them killed at once. The executioners, however, were soon to rue their zealous slaughter when they learned that as a prize for the day's work they could claim the clothes of the victims. These were so badly cut up that they were worth little. The massacre continued with the slaughter of the king's personal Swiss guard. Late in the afternoon, another judge came onto the scene, and, drinking to the nation, shouted to the executioners (whose arms still dripped with blood): "People, you slaughter your enemies, you do your duty!" On September 4 the slaughter was followed by a long auction of personal effects while the pile of corpses lay in this garden, alongside the church.

In all, the number of citizens killed in Paris during the month of September 1792 is estimated at 1,614. Many victims were burned at the door of the prison, and even at the door of the church, but the largest number was massacred in front of the tribunal, at the corner of the Rue Bonaparte and Boulevard St Germain.

After the Revolution, Paris was very different from what it had been. The church of St Germain was reconsecrated but simply as the parish church it is today, and the abbey served, as it still does, the social needs of its parishioners. The neighborhood today is an intellectual center of Paris in which the church of St Germain des Prés simply happens to be found.

Now it is time to look at the garden itself, the **Square Laurent-Prache**. This quiet spot, in the midst of a confusion of cars and people, is a lacy and shady retreat in summer and a startlingly bare sculpture garden in winter. The first piece of sculpture you see is most unexpected; it is the strange and powerful bronze head of a woman, dedicated to Guillaume Apollinaire, sculpted by his loyal friend, Picasso. The bust sits on a four-foot-high white stone pedestal; it is dated 1959, although Apollinaire died years before in 1918 at the age of thirty-eight. Picasso and Apollinaire, the artist and the poet, were favorites of the arty café world and were courted by all the would-be artists and hangers-on who spent their days drinking and talking together.

One of these admirers, an employee of the Louvre Museum, wishing to show his appreciation and respect for the two, presented each of them with a statuette. Picasso and Apollinaire thanked him, put the objects away, and thought no more about it. Several months later the guards at the museum, shocked out of their negligence by an important theft, realized that other objects were missing as well. It wasn't long before they found the culprit, and he led them directly to his friends, pleading that he had simply given Picasso and Apollinaire the statues as gifts. Because he was not a French citizen, Picasso was let off with a few sharp words and warnings; but the case was different for Apollinaire. The officials not only

*Pablo Picasso's* Head of a Woman,
*dedicated to Guillaume Apollinaire*

entangled him in the ever-present web of French papers and procedures but also questioned him so harshly that the poet was driven to ask why in the world they didn't accuse him of stealing the Mona Lisa. That did it. The Mona Lisa *had* just been stolen, and Guillaume Apollinaire was put in prison. The situation could have been merely ludicrous, but for very special reasons this experience became tragic.

Apollinaire was born in Rome of Polish parents named Kostrowitsky, but he turned from this background to a love of France that led him to change his name and his allegiance and to fight valiantly in the First World War for his new country. To be accused of stealing the nation's treasures and imprisoned was too great a blow. He died soon after, a disappointed and unhappy man. It is, therefore, particularly suitable that tribute was finally paid him by placing this statue here, among medieval remnants (the dog head of the gargoyle on the grass is now gone, broken off and carried away by "lovers" of Gothic architecture) and archways, the treasures of France.

These treasures are fragments from the thirteenth-century Chapel of the Virgin, which stood within the walls of the abbey, diagonally down the street at the present no. 6 bis Rue de l'Abbaye. The chapel, begun in 1245, took ten years to build and was the work of Pierre de Montreuil. (Montreuil was the builder of the perfect small chapel for Saint Louis on the Ile de la Cité, La Sainte-Chapelle.) The remains that you see on the two walls of the garden, pieced together stone by stone, make clear how delicate this masterpiece of thirteenth-century flamboyant Gothic must have been.

The chapel was partly destroyed in 1794, when the refectory and library next to it exploded and burned. It was completely dismantled in 1800, when the street was cut through. Additional remains of the chapel decorate the garden of the Cluny Museum.

If you have not been in the church yet, you may

wish to go now, or you may enter later, when the walk ends back here. This is one of the few churches that is still painted inside with blue vaulting decorated with stars and gilt capitals. Today we are accustomed to plain stone, but originally churches were very colorful. The entire façade of Notre Dame and the interior were brightly painted and gilded in the Middle Ages. The modern clear glass doors keep concert music in and street noise out.

The entrance to the garden Laurent-Prache was the site of the Revolutionary tribunal. It was here that the incredibly bloody hacking to death of 168 persons took place. This street was cut through in 1800, and shortly after was given the whitewashing name of Rue de la Paix (the "street of peace") but finally took the name of its earlier history, Rue de l'Abbaye. The Place de la Concorde on the Right Bank, the site of most of the guillotine murders and crowd madness of the French Revolution, has somehow managed to keep its name, despite its violent past.

## Rue de l'Abbaye

**No. 18** Rue de l'Abbaye is **Librairie Le Divan**. This is one of many publishing houses and bookshops in this neighborhood.

At **no. 16** is a chic beauty shop, **Claude Maxim**. Check the prices in the window, no appointment necessary. In typical French fashion, chic women are treated graciously; others, less so.

Next door is the spot where the refectory of the abbey stood. It was built by Pierre de Montreuil in 1239. Nearly five hundred years later, in 1714, a library was built over the refectory. During the Revolution the refectory served as a magazine for powder, which exploded on the night of 19 August 1794. The refectory collapsed; then fire broke out and completely destroyed it and the library above. Fortunately, most of the manuscripts were saved, including the original *Pensées* by Pascal, written on little bits of paper.

It was thought that no trace of the refectory remained. But a few years ago the government was in the midst of putting up moderately priced housing on this spot when the workers uncovered a marvelous windowed wall that had been the outside wall of the refectory. Its two and a half flamboyant windows, tall and graceful and intact, had been covered by plaster and totally forgotten for almost two hundred years.

The wall is preserved on the right-hand side of the entrance hall to the apartments. Some of the stones below are part of the old wall as well. The monks' cells in the *cave* are now filled in with brick walls and serve as storage rooms for the tenants. Niches for holy statues and prayer dot the walls. The door to this building, like most doors, is locked after 1:30 P.M.

**No. 14, La Hune** ("Crow's nest"), is a contemporary art gallery. Notice the bronze door handle in the shape of a man's face. When you leave the gallery, look at the back of the man's head on the handle.

Enter no. 14 and walk to the back of the courtyard. To the right you will find a neat, small white stucco house. Until 1983 the place was in ruins and overgrown with bushes. Now it has been completely redone.

The door of **no. 12** can be opened by pushing the button at the bottom of the code pad. To leave, push the button on the wall to your left.

It was a small rectangular cloister, thirteenth-century, plainer than the larger one across the street. The bays have been filled in and rebuilt, but the shape remains the same. If you look all around, you will see the perfect symmetry of the four sides.

In **no. 13** are the remains of the abbey's larger cloister (built in the thirteenth century, restored in the seventeenth), and in which the priests could walk. Remember that the Rue de l'Abbaye did not exist at that time and these cloisters were in fields surrounding the church. Note the three floors built above the arches of the cloister.

**No. 10** Rue de l'Abbaye houses an interesting shop, the Technical and Commercial Services of the National Museums. Here you can buy books, catalogues, and posters that are printed for the Louvre. They also have a gift catalogue (free) of all the museum reproductions and exhibit a number of the jewelry and sculpture items that are for sale in the Louvre gift shop.

To enter the shop go in the *porte cochère* and down the hall that leads to the courtyard. The shop entrance is on the right. In the courtyard itself there is a stone copy of a carving from Notre Dame de Paris of a man with a scythe, representing autumn. The round metal disc in the pavement is a turntable for delivery trucks.

**Nos. 11, 9, 7,** and **5** have recently been restored. They belong to the parish of St Germain des Prés. Nos. 11 and 9 block a fine view of the church that is not likely to be uncovered for a long time to come, if ever. No. 7 has a hook for a pulley on its gabled top window.

Look into the glass door of **no. 8,** a *grand standing* apartment house (built in 1963), at a variously marbled, tiled and flowered entry. Notice the spectacular wood sculpture shaped like a series of abstract totem poles. In the courtyard is a carefully tended (unusual) walled garden with pool. Look next door between the curtains of the glass-fronted modern office here in order to see how it has been constructed around the remains of the second pillar of the Chapel of the Virgin. This pile of thirteenth-century stones seems quite at home with the computers and other accoutrements of the twentieth century, and lends a touch of class to its surroundings.

**Nos. 1–5** are the remains of the palace built in 1586 for Cardinal Charles I of Bourbon, the abbot at St Germain. The unusual style is marked by a sharply slanted slate roof and open pediment and particularly by the use of both brick and stone for the façade. The few remaining examples of this style are the houses on the Place des

Vosges (see Walk 5) built under Henri IV, and the apartment houses that form the prow of the Ile de la Cité, facing the famous statue of Henri IV. Brick is, in general, rarely used in Paris. When you spot some turn-of-the-century brick apartment houses here and there, you will probably agree that stone suits Paris better.

Until recently these buildings were hidden by a temporary wall that also hid a gallery, a garage, and a social services center. Now two thirds are owned by the Institut Catholique and one third is still the social services office for this parish. Go in the door of no. 5 to see the restored stone staircase and the lovely garden. The main staircase at no. 3 originally served as the grand entrance to the abbey from the Rue de Furstenberg, behind you.

**No. 6 bis** is another of the many decorating shops in this area. These shops often work with their neighbor **Manuel Canovas** at no. 6. Manuel Canovas's wallpaper and fabric designs are the rage of Paris. He also has showrooms at 7 and 5 Place Furstenberg. Note the Art Nouveau floral motif of the building.

Stand on the steps of no. 3 to look at **no. 4.** The building, once a dilapidated part of the Sorbonne, has been restored and rebuilt (preserving the two Medusa-like heads) into a house for one family. Notice the sculpture in the garden, hidden in summer by the trees.

For a light bite, pack a vegetarian lunch at the **Guenmai.**

**No. 2** is an old building with odd triangular windows on the right side of the house that follow the line of its staircase. A Greek restaurant, Au Vieux Paris, was opened by M. Nico on December 6, 1941 during the German occupation. When M. Nico could get meat he would call his best customers and serve it to them concealed beneath puréed potatoes. By the time you walk here either a new decorating shop or a restaurant will have moved in.

Retrace your steps to the Rue de Furstenberg.

## *R u e   d e   F u r s t e n b e r g*

When Egon de Furstenberg was abbot of St Germain des Prés in the last decades of the seventeenth century, he opened a new entrance to the palace, one that led into the Rue Colombier ("street of doves"), now the Rue Jacob. This entrance descended from the grand staircase of the abbey into the Rue de Furstenberg.

The square in the middle of this short street, with its four pawlonia empress trees, benches, and old-fashioned light globes, is a picturesque spot. Although the trees are named after Anna Pavlova, daughter of Czar Paul I of Russia, they are Chinese (some sources say Japanese) in origin. They are admired in the spring for their perfumed mauve blossoms and large leaves. Symmetrical houses were built on either side of the street; **nos. 6** and **8,** still standing, and recognizable by their low doorways and brick-and-stone painted façades, were stables of the abbey.

Walk through the stable archway of no. 6, across the courtyard to the center door, to the **Delacroix studio,** home of the painter for the last six years of his life, 1857 to 1863. This small museum shows fine drawings and small sketches of his completed masterpieces. Go through the museum to a small orange building with a pebbled garden. This was the infirmary of the abbey, where the invalids were kept, more as protection for the healthy than care for the sick.

Outside once more, walking left toward the Rue Jacob, you will notice at the point where the street narrows a sculpted stone torch on the pillar of no. 4. It is the remains of the decoration of the Court of Honor, a place where ceremonies were performed when the palace on the Rue de l'Abbaye was Furstenberg's private domicile. The house was sold to the government in 1797 and taken down. Only this pillar, an entry, remains.

Directly across the street is an ultra-chic Canovas retail store of items made with gorgeous fabrics and prices to match. Pillars from the Abbaye are carefully enclosed in glass, preserving traces of polychrome decorations.

As you head out to the Rue Jacob look to your right, down the small, picturesque **Rue Cardinale**. The street once lay within the boundaries of the Abbaye St Germain and was named for the abbot, Guillaume de Furstenberg. It was originally the abbey's open-air tennis court but became a street in 1701. The house at the elbow of the street, **no. 3,** has an attractive terrace with wrought-iron grillwork, a sagging roof, and flowers that evoke a lost picture of this city's past. A few steps to the right of this house at **no. 5** is **Cipango**, selling creative costume jewelry made from natural materials.

There are interesting shops on your way to the Rue Jacob: choice seventeenth- and eighteenth-century antiques at **Yveline,** and at **no. 1, Aux Armes de Furstenberg**, a fine antique shop, specializes in scientific instruments and military objects. One more decorating shop at no. 1 has replaced a serious bookshop.

## Rue Jacob

Streets in Paris are often named after famous people, important places, or interesting signs, but rarely do they get the name of a Biblical patriarch like Jacob. The name was given in memory of a vow taken by Marguerite de Valois, whose colorful life has left its mark on the history of this area and is worth recalling in some detail. Marguerite, known as "*chère* Margot," was the daughter of Henri II and Catherine de Médicis, the sister of two kings, and the wife of Henri de Navarre, later Henri IV. In addition to this noble background, she was beautiful and learned. Her memoirs are among the best written by nobility, but when the French say "*chère* Margot" with a knowing smile, they are thinking less of what she wrote than what she left out.

As one historian put it, "She knew love at eleven,"

and thanks to this early start was able to collect a long list of lovers in the course of her career. She had, of course, good teachers: her brother Henri III and his flamboyant *mignons*, as well as her cousin and husband, Henri, who is recorded as having had fifty-six mistresses. But history can't know everything.

Margot was married at the age of nineteen in 1572 to her Protestant husband, Henri de Navarre (who was second in line for the throne), very much against her Catholic convictions and the will of the Pope. This mattered little compared to the determination of her brother Charles IX.

It took more than marriage to slow Margot down. She had her establishment; her husband his. All went well until one day in 1583 when Margot's brother Henri, now Henri III, denounced his sister's debauchery before the entire court. The actual cause of his anger was that Margot openly parodied her brother and his court of homosexuals.

This denunciation made it harder for Henri de Navarre to put up with her scandalous behavior, and finally, in 1587, under social pressure, her husband put her away in the Château d'Usson in Auvergne, where she managed to seduce her jailer. She made the best of her exile—eighteen years of a small court—writing memoirs and adding to her list of conquests. Nevertheless, she missed Paris and swore to raise an altar to Jacob if ever she was allowed to return. Jacob had also suffered exile, had worked and waited fourteen years for Rachel, and had finally been able to go back home, where he had given thanks to God for his safe return by building an altar.

The happy day came in 1605. (By this time Henri de Navarre, now Henri IV, had long since divorced Margot and married Marie de Médicis.) The king installed her in the château of the Archbishops (an ironic touch) of Sens, located on the Right Bank of the Seine at the entrance to the Marais quarter. (This château is now open to the public.)

Margot was then fifty-two, fat, bald, but as insatiable as ever. Her weight was so great she ordered the doorways widened. Her hair was so thin she snipped the locks of her blond valets for her wigs. Jean Duché, in his *Histoire de France racontée à Juliette*, claims she wore around her ample waist amulets containing pieces of the hearts of her dead lovers.

Her lover of the moment was the twenty-year-old Count of Vermond, but finding him perhaps too old Margot brought in the eighteen-year-old son of a carpenter from Usson. The Hôtel de Sens became a place of revelry. Vermond couldn't stand it. He lay in wait for his rival and shot him in the head right in front of Margot, who was returning from her religious devotion in a nearby church. Margot was enraged. She had Vermond pursued and arrested, and when he was brought before her, she cried out, "Kill the wretch. Here, here are my garters. Strangle him!" They cut off his head instead, while Margot looked on.

But all this blood and gore depressed her, and two days later she decided to leave the Hôtel de Sens and inhabit a house she was then building on the Pré aux Clercs, at what is now nos. 2–10 Rue de Seine. She remembered her vow and built the convent of Petits Augustins (now no. 14 Rue Bonaparte) in the back of the garden of her château. There she installed fourteen Augustinian friars, who took turns every two hours singing praises to Jacob with words and music written by Margot. Five years later she chased them out, claiming they sang badly. The name of the street is all that remains of Margot's celebrated gesture of thanksgiving.

This street is what we call one of the hidden streets of Paris. The unknowing eye sees shop after shop below five-story apartment buildings that show little decoration and little difference from one to the other. Not so. There are gardens, courtyards, staircases, even ceilings to uncover on the piece of the Rue Jacob that runs from the corner with the Rue de Furstenberg left to Rue Bonaparte.

The street to the right is just as interesting and leads to a lovely square, old houses, and modern shops, but today we are turning left and will keep crossing back and forth until we reach the corner of the Rue Bonaparte.

The building at **no. 5** is the spot where one of the towers of the surrounding walls of the abbey stood. It was twenty feet in diameter and stood next to the dove-cote (hence the old name of the street, Rue Colombier) of the abbey.

Enter the courtyard of **no. 12** and go through the archway. You'll find a small garden at the back and to your right an Indian dress shop called Mohanjeet, which seems to attract a trendy clientèle.

Contrast the renovated house at the back of the court-yard with the untouched building at the left. Note the stone steps of the staircase, the old railing, and the rafters.

**No. 12** is an antique shop that has replaced an old bookshop which was once the meeting place for lovers of Paris. The Huysmans Society met here every Saturday from three to six. Joris Huysmans is the famous nineteenth-century writer who described Paris in a manner so poetic, so unbelievably full of love, that his books today are collectors' treasures and are sold at auction for very high prices. Huysmans could write about the garbage smells of Paris in a way that would make you mourn the passing of the garbage truck.

**No. 7** dates from 1640 and was called the Hôtel St Paul. Racine lived here with his uncle in 1656, when he was seventeen years old. The gallery housed here, Antoinette, specializes in naive paintings.

Richard Wagner lived at **no. 14** for six months in 1841–42.

In a new building for this street, built in 1928 (note the Art Deco style), **Languereau** at **no. 18** is one of the oldest and most important children's publishing houses in Paris. Inside on the left-hand wall at the base of the staircase is a poster of dancing children, taken from the nineteenth-century cover of Boutet de Monvel's famous songbook, *Chansons*. They also publish *Bécassine*, the humorous tales of this naive but sensible Breton nanny.

In the seventeenth century **nos. 9, 11,** and **13,** built next to the old abbey wall, were all one house, belonging to a member of Parliament, M. Chabenat de la Malmaison. Later, the building was the Hôtel de la Gabelle, the main office for the collection of the salt tax.

**No. 11** is **Le Petit Atelier,** a studio where children seven to sixteen years old learn English. It is open only on Mondays, Wednesdays, and Thursdays. The Atelier teaches through play-acting, mime, and music "in the language of Shakespeare." Since English is their business, go in and ask if you can go upstairs to see their ceiling. You will see hundreds of rafters in Paris but none like these remarkably well-preserved and painted ones. They date from the end of the fifteenth century; the painting, however, was done later. Various trades of the City of Paris are pictured in the medallions in the center. Part of this building was owned by an antique dealer, who had never uncovered what was certainly the most valuable treasure his store had ever seen. The entire ceiling had been hidden (and preserved) by plaster. Very skillful restoration has saved most of it. Imagine the beauty of this room when it was two floors high and the fireplace on the side wall was huge enough to reach this height.

When you reach the entry to **nos. 11** and **13,** stand back and look. The tall, rounded doorways are topped by the typical eighteenth-century mask decorations called *mascarons*. These two must have been done either at different times or by different people. One of the nicest pieces of iron sculpture, a flamboyant S projecting tridents, is attached to the wall above the two doorways.

Go into no. 11 (push the release button and the door will unlatch), turn left through the entrance before the courtyard, go up a few steps, and you will find an imposing, wide stone staircase. What is truly impressive is that the banisters and railing were cut in stone by hand—a tremendous task, in comparison to the already difficult

Mascarons *at nos. 11 and 13 Rue Jacob*

one of turning a banister in wood. The Louis XIII style is often used for wooden staircases, as is the case on the upper floors of this building. In summer this wide stair-well is a cool, quiet spot; in winter, when it gets dark early, turn the *minuterie* light on until you have seen it all. Please be discreet and polite if you meet residents.

On the other side of no. 13 is an antique store that specializes in period furniture and particularly in games: chess, backgammon, games tables, ivory counters, and so on.

Much has been said and written about **no. 20**, but today little can be seen. A little Temple of Friendship, such as were built during the Revolution to replace churches, stands in a presently neglected garden behind

locked iron gates at the back right-hand side of the courtyard. We did once gain access to the temple, which is
low and rectangular with Doric columns. The words *"A
l'Amitié"* ("To friendship") are inscribed on it. This
neighborhood was rich in such Revolutionary clubs, but
few remain. The garden and the temple are owned by
Michel Debré, former right-hand man to de Gaulle and
then to Pompidou.

Natalie Clifford Barney, a very French American
woman, lived here until her death a few years ago. She
was called in her youth the Amazon or the Sappho 1900.
She was beautiful, intelligent, and at the forefront of a
literary movement that championed women's independ-
ence. In her second-floor apartment she received a pro-

cession of the greatest writers and artists of the twentieth century: Hemingway, Joyce, T. S. Eliot, Colette, Rilke, Apollinaire, Anatole France, Max Jacob, Anne de Noailles, and many others. She was a legend to the people, a lesbian in her personal life, and catholic in her hospitality. Her generosity was legendary; she once hosted a boat trip around Greece for fifty friends. She did as much for the artistic life of the quarter as did the better-known cafés on the Boulevard St Germain.

As you leave the courtyard notice the classified wrought-iron banisters and gate and the consoles of phoenixes in the entry hall. The policemen are on duty here day and night—they guard the Debrés.

**Nos. 17** and **26** are two bookshops that indicate the range of specialized bookshops in Paris. One is agricultural and horticultural; the other, specializing in maritime books and overseas editions, shows maps and prints in the window as well. Look also at the old houses above the shops.

Within the interstices of **no. 19,** down hallways, through doors, past offices of the publishing house Editions du Seuil, there is a private house and garden with a view of the back of the Delacroix Museum. Prud'homme, an active pamphleteer against the *ancien régime,* lived back here. He was an editor of the *Revue de Paris,* a revolutionary journal, and it was in the quiet of this garden that he wrote the incendiary articles that led to numerous arrests.

**No. 21,** the **Hôtel des Maronniers,** with its courtyard of chestnut trees, is one of the many attractive medium-priced hotels on this street. At no. 25 the **Hotel des Deux Continents** is a similar establishment.

**Anaïs,** at **no. 23,** is a fine and old-fashioned needlepoint and knitting shop. The ladies are skilled, capable of drawing your design for you or supplying their own. They send you on your way either with marked canvas, needles, wool, and samples of each stitch already begun on your canvas, or with their lush wool and a knitting pattern. The store was named after their aunt, Anaïs, not Anaïs Nin.

**No. 28** is a shop selling rare stones and minerals—some of the petrified wood looks like slices of caramel. The lady in the shop explained that the precious stones came from thousands of miles away, from a place called "Ah-ree-zo-na." M. Boullé specializes in agate and septaria.

There are no old houses or antique staircases in the back of the courtyard of **no. 30,** but you will find a collection of young artisans who restore paintings as well as and probably better than their predecessors hundreds of years before them at **Restoration-Depretz.**

The first time we visited these young artisans they were barefoot and hirsute, seemingly antiestablishment. The following year they wore jackets and shoes, but the ambience remained the same. They move within one another's work areas, talking and joking all the while. This easy atmosphere, this seeming lack of concentration, is the setting for the highest degree of delicate, technical, and artistic work.

We were shown how a Poliakoff painting was being transferred from its original decaying canvas to a new one, how one and a half years' work on a Dürer was finally removing slash marks and deterioration. We witnessed the uncovering of mushrooms, grapes, and a butterfly that had been blacked out by the Victorians—no doubt for being too earthy, too sexy, and too frivolous. A young painter named Lagrue had set up his easel near the entrance to the shop and amused himself and his audience by reinterpreting famous paintings, turning a Crusade into a Chaucerian pilgrimage, a Renoir garden party into a Bacchanalia.

Twenty years ago the Editions du Seuil, an important French publishing house, took over the lovely private home and front garden of **no. 27.** Ingres, the champion of classical painting, lived here more than 150 years ago.

**No. 29** replaces a traditional hotel with a whole new

look for this St Germain neighborhood. **La Villa** is a high-fashion, Memphis-decorated hotel. It is rated as a four-star hotel (more luxurious than most in this area) and the furniture and colors have all been carefully chosen to make a "statement." Try their bar and jazz club at night.

Mme Castaing's (she is still dressed and made up in the style of the 1930s) antique shop at **no. 32** is an odd one. Room after room filled with strange furniture from the colonies or from England stretch from here to the corner of the Rue Jacob. Elephants' feet serve as ashtrays, goats' legs hold up tables, and palms and rubber plants flourish everywhere.

## Rue Bonaparte

Despite too many cars in the road and too many people on the street, the Rue Bonaparte is still a favorite of visitors and Parisians. The shops are rich with the art of today and yesterday; the colorful history of the street is less obvious but nevertheless there to see and imagine.

Seven hundred years ago there was no street here at all, simply open fields that belonged to the abbey. You will recall the stories of the university students battling violently with the priests of the abbey over the use of these lands. These conflicts were settled only in 1368, when the monks built a wall and moat around themselves for privacy and safekeeping. At that time they also dug a canal, sixty-five feet wide and twenty-five feet deep, which ran from the Seine down the present Rue Bonaparte to the corner where you are now standing, Rue Jacob and Rue Bonaparte.

Here is where this arm of the river, La Petite Seine, emptied its waters into the moat of the abbey. Boats sailed up and down, bringing and taking away goods. But the canal's most important function was to provide a natural division between the field frequented by the students, which was a small piece of land that covered the area between what are now the rues Jacob and Visconti up to the Rue Bonaparte (called the Petit Pré aux Clercs), and the larger field on the other side of the canal favored by the priests (called the Grand Pré aux Clercs).

For almost two hundred years the little Seine characterized the *quartier*, and when it was eventually filled in in 1540, it gave its name to the paved road that took its place, Rue de la Petite Seine.

In 1606, when the famous Margot received a gift from her ex-husband, Henri IV, of a piece of land on the Rue de Seine, she built the beautiful château whose walled gardens and walks cut through the Rue de la Petite Seine, closing it off from the river itself. But Margot was generous with her new domain and allowed her meadows and gardens and shaded walks to go on giving pleasure to the simple folk of the neighborhood.

Marie de Médicis, Margot's successor as wife to Henri IV and whose money no doubt paid for Margot's château, was jealous of the latter's reputation for generosity and her popularity with the people. And so Marie tried to outdo her by building the Cours de la Reine (the "queen's way"), a wide and beautiful road on the right bank of the Seine, parallel to the Champs-Elysées. These two ladies, Marie and Margot, spent more time outfoxing each other than Henri spent thinking about either of them; his constant love was Gabrielle d'Estrées.

Margot's gardens and the convent of Petits Augustins, which she had built farther up the street, lasted until 1628, thirteen years after her death. At that time her property was divided among many, and the street was once again opened up, this time named for the convent, the Rue des Petits Augustins. Look across the street to see this old name cut in stone above the tapestry shop on the corner.

The name Bonaparte was not given until the year 1852. Why is there no Rue Napoléon in Paris? Was he too formidable a hero? Perhaps the idea of the republican Bonaparte is more acceptable.

And now for the street, to find what is new and what remains of the old. Your route will turn right at the corner of Bonaparte and Jacob, continue up the right side to the top, and then cross to the other side and back down the street to return to the Place St Germain.

Very few establishments in the ample old-fashioned style of **Bulloz**, at **no. 21,** still exist in Paris or anywhere. The moment you enter the large, uncluttered, quiet premises and are greeted by the gentle ladies who serve you, you realize that although their type of photographic service is greatly in demand today, they remain unaffected by the passing of time. Here you can have a picture of yourself, or a landscape, or a document, or a painting, or anything blown up to any size you specify. Their work is excellent as well as dependable. Pictures come in black and white or in color, and there are thousands to choose from if you like the idea but don't have the picture.

The door to the courtyard of **no. 21** is on the left. It gives you an idea of the grand houses that surrounded the abbey in the sixteenth century. The garden of Queen Margot's palace on the Rue de Seine extended all the way to the other side of this street just a few yards up from here. The grand house before you now was built in 1760, around the courtyard of an earlier one, for Prévost de St Cyr, and was lived in during the Consulate (1799–1804) by the Princesse de Rohan-Rochefort, who was secretly married to the Duke of Enghien. After the Revolution these houses changed their tenants and their appearance, as the neighborhood turned popular. Today it is once again a street of high rents, coveted apartments, and very special shops and galleries. It is also one of the most heavily trafficked streets in Paris.

This large courtyard is picturesque, with its thick ivy, ornamental ironwork on the balcony windows, and large iron hook for a pulley on the dormer or mansard above to the left.

The dress shop **Vicky Tiel** is worth a visit. This is the place to find designer clothes. Vicky Tiel puts together two collections a year from her nearby workrooms on Boulevard St Germain and sells her samples here in this small, elegant shop.

Elizabeth Taylor is an old friend and customer (she buys dresses in the sample size, swearing she will get into them). It was through Vicky's husband, who was Richard Burton's makeup artist, that the initial contact was made. Some other customers here include Farrah Fawcett, Shirley Fonda, and Ivana Trump. Vicky's gowns start at $1,000 and go up from there. Like other fashion entrepreneurs, she is also bringing out a perfume and a book on how famous women seduce men.

We were told that d'Artagnan's stables were here, but then again we were also told that about the Rue St Gilles on the other side of town. Continue up the street to the corner of Rue Visconti.

The **Librairie du Cygne** at **no. 17** specializes in books on the history of art. Their window display usually consists of books relating to a scholarly theme.

You are now at the intersection of the Rue Bonaparte and the Rue des Beaux Arts. If you wish to take the time to see a beautifully appointed hotel, called simply **L'Hôtel**, walk a few steps down to the right. Wander in under the atrium and walk to the back of the reception rooms, where there are bowers of plants and a parrot flying free. Oscar Wilde had a room here.

On the corner of Bonaparte and Beaux Arts is the **Restaurant des Beaux Arts.** This is a local hangout with good classic food like herring filets or *boudin* sausage or steak-frites and crème caramel for dessert. The service is quick and pleasant. Come early for a table.

Art galleries abound here and the twentieth century seems to be king. **No. 7** sells Deco furniture and **no. 5** sells Deco and Nouveau *objets* of high quality. Most of these galleries don't open until 11 or 11:30 and then close at lunch for an hour at one. **No. 5**, like no. 21 (Vicky Tiel), is typical of the eighteenth century, presenting an impressive wall and entry on the street and

*Ecole des Beaux Arts: a local café*

apartments that look down on the beautiful courtyard.
Check and see if the gleaming Bentley is still parked
there. Note the plaque on the outside wall: "Here, formerly 5, Rue des Petits Augustins, was born Edouard
Manet, 1832–85."

The **Galerie Damien** sells exquisite sculptures and
figurines of the Art Deco period.

You've reached the Quai Malaquais; to the right is
the Institut de France, home of the French Academy,
where the renowned dictionary writers and protectors of
the purity of the French language work. Election to the
Académie Française is open to only forty "immortals,"
who choose their own colleagues. The ceremony of ad-
mission calls for an ornate dress uniform with sword.
These swords are much too expensive for most acade-
micians to buy themselves, so friends usually contribute
to the cause. Across the *quai* there is a romantic foot-
bridge over the Seine to the Louvre.

The little low house across the street, **no. 4,** with
dormer windows (and with hook and wheel for loading
above one of them), was built in 1620. This site was
originally a Brothers of Charity hospital until Queen Mar-

got forced them out in order to build her neighborhood estate. The **Paris American Art** is a huge art supply store serving the Ecole des Beaux Arts, the school of fine arts down the street.

There are two modern art galleries at **no. 6.** Look up at the roof garden on top of the building and the small corner room that leads into it.

At **no. 8, Félix M.** has collected some beautiful pieces of Art Deco and Art Nouveau. They are few but extremely fine. **Librairie E. Rossignol,** also at no. 8, is an antique bookshop passed from father to son since 1906. They moved here in 1940 when they were dispossessed by the Germans. They publish a yearly catalogue and maintain special-interest files in order to notify customers of relevant acquisitions.

At **no. 10, La Porte Etroite** is exactly that, a narrow door. (This is also the title of a book by Gide.) This bookshop was probably a hallway. Also at no. 10, **Jacques de Vos** buys, sells and appraises art of the period 1910–50.

At **no. 12, M. Roux-Devillas** spends his days surrounded by memories of the past. He specializes in old books, old documents (autographs), and old scientific instruments. The collection ranges from sundials and eighteenth-century dental tools to treaties signed by kings. One home inventory of the wife of a French lieutenant general in Martinique in 1791 divided her possessions into three sections: furnishings, silver, and slaves. All the slaves were identified and described in the same way: name, job, age, and price. There was Jurançon who took care of the boats, thirty-two years old, and worth 3,300 francs; Caroline, no duties, five years old, worth 500 francs; and Lucille, who was too old and incapacitated to do or be worth anything at all, but was listed simply to note her existence, *"laissée pour mémoiré."* Documents of this kind form the basis of historical research on slavery today. This is one of the few shops that offers valuable historical items at reasonable rates.

The **Ecole des Beaux Arts** is at **no. 14.** This site is

a mini-stage for the history of Paris. The first record of inhabitants dates from 1603 when Marie de Médicis, Henri IV's Italian wife, brought five priests from Florence and built for them, here, a charity hospital. These priests were not only Italian but also surgeons and pharmacists. Clearly Marie de Médicis felt she needed more than serving ladies to accompany her to her new country and established, in effect, for her use as well as that of others, an Italian hospital and an Italian pharmacy. The Brothers of Charity Hospital moved three years later to the corner of the Rue des Sts Pères and the Rue Jacob, where it became a large and important hospital, lasting until 1937, when it was taken down.

After the removal of the original hospital, the eccentric Margot, Henri IV's first wife, built her promised altar to Jacob here. Although the continual singing of litanies by the monks was stopped after five years, the convent remained until the Revolution, at which time it was forced to close down. It was left abandoned, but not for long.

During the French Revolution it was the sworn duty of each citizen to remove every symbol of religion and royalty he could find (see page 90 for the altering of street signs). A young painter and critic, Alexandre Lenoir, was quick to see the threat to all the art treasures and manuscripts in Paris. After eloquent and anguished pleading, he received permission to take or buy all the treasures he could find, to store the books and manuscripts in two other convents, and to store the art treasures in this one. There followed frenzied years of snatching books from fire, saving statues of precious metal from the mint, and rescuing kings from their coffins at St Denis. A bayonet pierced Lenoir when he threw himself upon Richelieu's tomb in the church of the Sorbonne to save it from the mob in 1839. He was unable to save the row of statues under the first balcony of Notre Dame (the one in *The Hunchback of Notre Dame* that the beggars climbed to save Esmeralda from the hands of the Hunchback). These statues, meant to represent the kings of the Bible but done in the anachronistic style of Merovingian kings, were taken to be kings of France and were pulled down. They were presumed lost—until a few years ago, when they were found buried in the basement of an apartment house in the seventeenth *arrondissement*. They are now in the Cluny Museum. But Lenoir got whatever he could, however he could, and gathered it in, until this old convent became an amazing storehouse.

When the Terror was over, Lenoir could stand back and look at the most eloquent creations of eighteen centuries of French art. He was inspired to make this cave of Ali Baba into a museum of French monuments. In 1795 that became a reality. Chroniclers describe the display of treasures as the most beautiful and impressive ever gathered in one place. It lasted through the Directory (1795–99), through the Consulate (1799–1804), and through the Empire (1804–14). Napoleon, in his zeal to preserve the glory of France, showered gifts and privileges on it. Perhaps that is the real reason for the present name of the street. But Louis XVIII made the irresponsible decision (one of many) to close the museum and disperse its contents. He allowed each locality to reclaim its old art treasures.

Although the collection was dispersed, it has reappeared in the sixteenth *arrondissement* at the Place du Trocadéro as the Museum of French Monuments, with copies (magnificently done) of religious art from throughout France. The monastery here was then turned into a school of fine arts, the Ecole des Beaux Arts, familiarly called just "Beaux Arts."

Pass the jumble of motorcycles as you enter the courtyard, and on the right, high in a niche, should be a statue of Alexandre Lenoir. He was missing on our last visit, but we hope he was gone only for a cleaning and restoration (he needed it desperately). The odd remains of the château doors and pieces of sculpture that decorate the courtyard are all classified historic monuments. The classical building at the back, just cleaned, was put up in

*Ecole des Beaux Arts: sculpture studio*

1858 and was the original building of the school. Go
through the main door to see the neoclassical frescoes,
lecture rooms, and students' work in progress.

When you are back in the courtyard facing the street,
enter the middle of the wing to your left and go into the
delightful Cour du Mûrier (the "court of the mulberry
tree"), which was a cloister of the convent. If the weather
permits, sit on the grass (a good spot for lunch), look
around, and listen. The empty pedestals in each cloister
bay once were capped by pieces of sculpture that had

142

won the Grand Prix de Rome. This coveted prize allowed the winner to go to Rome to study the antique and Renaissance masters in the Villa Médicis. Critics claimed, however, that as long as the best talent got such training, French art was likely to remain "classical." The absence of sculpture in this courtyard shows not only that the decline of the Italian influence still persists today, but that there is a general lack of *esprit* at the Beaux Arts.

It is impossible to get information about the school or the buildings, a legacy of the events of 1968. It turns out

that the students at Beaux Arts were among the most dis-
ruptive in the revolt of 1968, and they destroyed and damaged a good deal of the school. At that time the school
granted all sorts of student demands, including one to separate the faculties for painting, architecture, sculpture, and
so on, in order to improve the level of teaching, which the
students felt was too general. The administration, cleverly,
has continued this idea of division to such a degree that it
has weakened the communal role of the students. Classes
are held all over Paris, painters never see sculptors, and even
the famous costume ball of the Beaux Arts has not been
held since the uprising. Political interest has waned although there was a poster inviting everyone to a Saturday
evening demonstration denouncing imperialism.

We were sitting on a stone ledge in the big courtyard
on the Quai Malaquais, wondering where the spirit of art
students had gone, when we were suddenly doused with
cold water from a balcony above. Amid gales of laughter, we
were told how lucky we were it hadn't been ink or paint.

Return to the Rue Bonaparte, where, at **no. 20, Boulakia** exhibits twentieth-century art. On the other side of
the door, **Sala** has a magnificent collection of antique
furniture from the Spanish Renaissance and the Haute
Epoque. They showed us a marvelous twelfth-century
Gothic door and several important Spanish chests.

This building is one that marks this area as Henri
IV's. Of all his women, Gabrielle d'Estrées was the one
he loved most, and in the back of this courtyard is a
house in which their son, César de Vendôme, once abbé
of St Germain, lived. He was born illegitimate in 1594,
recognized the following year, and would have been king
had Louis XII not been born.

At **no. 22, Simone de Monbrison** sells antiques and
primitive art from Africa, Oceania, Greece, Rome, Meso-
potamia, and Byzantium. They carry mainly statues,
masks, and some jewelry.

Go into the courtyard of **no. 28** to look at the elegant
open staircase with its fountain and thick, flowering vines.
Look at the modern art in the **Galerie Jacob.**

**Le Mur du Nomade** has its entrance on the Rue Jacob. The nomad's wall is, of course, tapestry-hung. These hangings are completely French, from Renaissance reproductions to Lurçat (the reviver of tapestry art today), and contemporary artists like Arp and Picart-le-Doux. Whether or not tapestries interest you, go into this shop to watch the young man or woman who is weaving a tapestry on a loom exactly as it was done hundreds of years ago at the Aubusson factory. Today, Aubusson is still France's national school and factory for tapestry weaving and rug making, the only place one can be trained for this work. School is followed by three years of apprenticeship and then five years more before the weaver is permitted to work alone. Tapestries that are woven at Aubusson sell here, the price depending on size and the fame of the artist. Eight copies of a design are made, six for sale, one or two for the artist. Less expensive "walls of wool," as Le Corbusier called them, can be purchased here also—for example, an artisanal tapestry of woven wool on which a picture is printed. The shop has rooms in the back and upstairs; the people here are most helpful and instructive.

This next section of Rue Bonaparte (between Rue Jacob and Rue de l'Abbaye) seems to belong to **Nobilis**, an important interior decorating firm. They occupy **nos. 29, 31, 32, 34, 38,** and **40.** At no. 29 they sell finished goods made from their own fabrics, including very nice traveling bags and lap rugs. Very chic and expensive.

The **Hôtel St Germain des Prés** at **no. 36** has one of the most charming lobbies in Paris. The back wall is a sheet of glass sandwiching a beautiful display of flowers growing in a hothouse against the stone wall of the building. The building is eighteenth century and although the decor reflects this, every room provides all the modern amenities at reasonable prices.

**Fabrice** at **no. 33** specializes in jewelry and accessories that are always unique and avant garde.

Following the Rue Bonaparte on the opposite side of the street from the church of St Germain you come to a wide pavement used in the summer months for late-night plays, pantomimes, and acts by sword swallowers, fire-eaters, and chain breakers. A stage is set up here and the crowds gather to watch, as in medieval times. A hat is passed for contributions.

Also on this side is the very proper and dignified **Arthus Bertrand.** This 150-year-old firm specializes in museum reproductions of jewelry and honorary medals. They reproduce in gilded bronze the Louvre's artifacts, which are sold only at the museum shop. At this shop they sell the same pieces but in sterling or 18-carat gold. This is a serious shop; the merchandise is exhibited in cases and you must sit at the table and have trays brought to you for inspection as the saleswoman consults a separate price list. Arthus Bertrand is especially famous for military medals and decorations. They supply 80 percent of the medals for the African nations and the individually designed academician's swords for the Institut de France. These range in price from $7,000 to $20,000.

We are now back to our starting point, St Germain des Prés. If you have already visited the church, move directly ahead to the boulevard for a table at the famous café **Les Deux Magots,** or its rival, the **Flore.**

You are now in the heart of what was, and to some extent still is, the artistic and literary center of Paris. Before the First World War, Picasso and Apollinaire were already installed at the Flore, in the back, although they were also habitués of the even more popular cafés of Montparnasse: the Dôme, the Rotonde, and the Closerie des Lilas. How many cafés can one frequent? When did they work, and where did they work? The "lost generation" of expatriates after the First World War, some of whom drank themselves into oblivion, frequented both St Germain and Montparnasse. One distinction, however, between the two areas seems to have been that writers favored St Germain des Prés, artists, Montparnasse. Re-read Hemingway's *A Moveable Feast* and *The Sun Also Rises* for the feel of these days gone by.

Les Deux Magots was the birthplace of surrealism, the Café de Flore the home of the existentialists. Simone de Beauvoir and Sartre had their regular table at the latter, drawing young intellectuals like a magnet. Camus came, but not often, because Sartre was supposedly jealous of Camus; at any rate the two did not get on.

Today café life is still fascinating. The talk is at once stereotyped and unbelievable. It is about ex-husbands and weekend houses or business deals concerning art, films, and books. Most of the publishing houses have offices in this *quartier*, so a constant stream of intellectuals will be around for lunch or a drink. Tourists come to look at everyone else; the French come to be looked at. It is still true that many of these people know one another, and the neighborhood keeps the character of a small town.

These cafés got their odd names the same way so many other places and streets in Paris did. A small statue of Flora (goddess of flowers and mother of spring) used to stand at the door of the Café de Flore. There is an interesting room on the second floor of the Flore decorated, as the French say, "in the English style." Les Deux Magots was the name of a novelty shop that planned to move to this spot from the Rue de Buci in 1873, but before that actually happened, a bar opened, used their name, and has been here ever since. The *deux magots* are the two wooden statues, inside the café on the central pillar, of Chinese dignitaries (most often portrayed in porcelain) that were to be the standard of the novelty shop.

In 1984 the Deux Magots was sold at auction. M. Mathivat, who has operated the café for the last twenty years, bought it. "I bought it for sentimental reasons. Don't worry. It will always remain what it has been. I don't want to start a fast-food joint." The auction was carried out in the Chambre des Notaires tradition. After the bidding was finished, the auctioneer lit two candles. As they burned, those with a possible change of heart had the opportunity to come in with a higher bid. Under

147

*Café de Flore*

the law M. Mathivat was not the true owner until ten
days later. A bid of 10 percent more than his could still
be accepted.

Before his death, our late friend, Georges Perec (author of *La Vie: mode d'emploi*), had—as have others like
him—ceased to come to St Germain any more. But the
small cafés off the beaten path are still frequented. Cafés
are not only an important part of people's lives, about
which they write, but are also the places where literature
is made. Even if you don't make films or write books, a
regular table at a café of your choice is a great idea. You

will find the same people coming back, and the owners of these little cafés in your neighborhood (if you are lucky enough to be here long enough to claim one) are fascinating people. Besides, these are the traditional spots for letter writing. In the old days you would have been supplied with writing paper, ink, and a quill pen.

Two restaurants owned by a father-and-son team are on the Rue Guillaume Apollinaire one block behind and parallel to the Boulevard St Germain. **L'Assiette au Beurre** is the more elegant, in an authentic Art Nouveau setting. The decorations were brought here from other buildings, but the tiles, wrought-iron railings, bar, and furniture seem to have been made for the room. They serve a moderately expensive *prix fixe* dinner with changing entrées.

Next door, **L'Assiette au Boeuf** is a bustling but acoustically quiet restaurant that seems to appeal to businessmen. They serve a terrific steak-frites and their signature dish is a huge bowl of chocolate mousse—serve yourself.

Behind the Flore on Rue St Benoit are several restaurants with outside tables in the warm weather. In particular **La Grosse Horloge,** with a huge clock as its standard, is worth trying. They serve classic French food, very tasty, the kind you wish you could make at home.

**Le Drugstore** across the street from the Flore and the Deux Magots on Boulevard St Germain will sell you a hamburger or ice cream, but somehow these seem more French than American. It is a modern complex of restaurant, cinema, bookshop, *charcuterie* (providing a fabulous picnic at fabulous prices—$75 a pound for smoked salmon), pharmacy, gift shop, and newsstand. Le Drugstore is open until two in the morning every day.

There are two more good restaurants nearby. **Brasserie Lipp, No. 151** Boulevard St Germain, is a restaurant that has done what we would have considered the impossible. The French, as you know, consider themselves the arbiters of fine taste, and the country they might least copy would be Germany. The namesake of the restaurant, Lippmann, was an Alsatian who was desperately unhappy about the separation of his home from France. The food and drink he served, however, was totally German: frankfurters and sauerkraut, light and dark beer. The amazing fact is that this dish caught on; it appears today on almost every Parisian menu. *Choucroute alsacienne* is sold fresh in every charcuterie, in cans in every grocery, and is now the raison d'être of countless restaurants in Paris.

In the early 1900s Lipp was *the* after-theater place to

dine, as the Plaza Athenée was fifty years later. The lovely ladies shown in engravings, picking up their long dresses as they step from horse-driven hacks, were no doubt going to dine at Lipp. By 1924 the area had become so much the *quartier* of editors (two steps to Grasset, four to Gallimard, and six to Hachette) and their prize-winning writers, that Lipp was forced to enlarge—not like the Deux Magots, which could extend its stomach onto the pavement—but by turning and twisting into the recesses behind the restaurant. In the 1960s Lipp was the eating place for politicians as well as writers. François Mitterrand, president of France, used to dine here, perhaps still does. Ben Barka, a Moroccan militant, was arrested here.

**Vagenende, no. 142,** is a joy to behold. Here is 1900 in all its fantasy and variety. You will see many a floral door on the Boulevard St Germain, but they are a product of the 1970s. This restaurant and the even more fantastic restaurant of the Gare de Lyon (which was shown in the films *Travels with My Aunt* and *Murder on the Orient Express*) are the real thing, built when the creation of Art Nouveau was at its height.

Although you have walked and talked and looked for a good two hours, these few streets are only a sample of what the neighborhood has to offer. It is no doubt time, however, to sit down at a café or restaurant and restore yourself. *Bon appétit!*

# Walk · 4

## Mouffetard

De par le roi, défense à Dieu
De faire miracle en ce lieu.

By order of the king, God is
  forbidden
To perform miracles in
  this place.

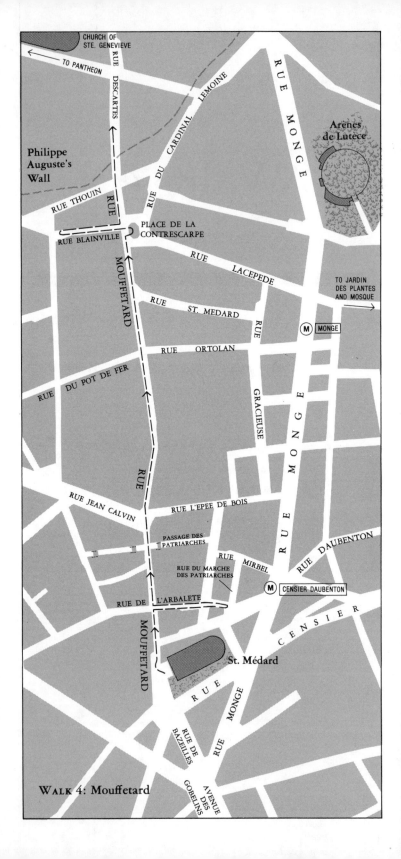

CHURCH OF
STE. GENEVIEVE

TO PANTHEON

RUE DESCARTES

RUE DU CARDINAL LEMOINE

RUE MONGE

Arènes
de Lutèce

Philippe
Auguste's
Wall

RUE THOUIN

RUE

RUE BLAINVILLE

PLACE DE LA
CONTRESCARPE

RUE LACEPEDE

RUE ST. MEDARD

RUE ORTOLAN

MOUFFETARD

RUE

RUE

TO JARDIN
DES PLANTES
AND MOSQUE

(M) MONGE

RUE DU POT DE FER

GRACIEUSE

RUE MONGE

RUE

RUE JEAN CALVIN

RUE L'EPEE DE BOIS

PASSAGE DES
PATRIARCHES

RUE
MIRBEL

RUE DAUBENTON

RUE DU MARCHE
DES PATRIARCHES

(M) CENSIER DAUBENTON

RUE DE L'ARBALETE

MOUFFETARD

St. Médard

C E N S I E R

RUE MONGE

RUE DE BAZEILLES

AVENUE DES GOBELINS

WALK 4: Mouffetard

Starting Point: Eglise St Médard
Métro: Censier Daubenton
Bus: 47

## Rue Mouffetard

The Rue Mouffetard is different from our other walks because, although it is one of the liveliest streets in Paris and has a fascinating history, many of the events that happened here have left no traces. We recommend that you read this walk beforehand so that you won't be try-ing to read while you're being jostled by the crowds of shoppers. This will also allow you to spend your time discovering the pleasures of the *marché* for yourself. You can do your advance reading in the garden of the church of St Médard before you venture into the market. After you have left this garden, you will be unable to find a place to sit other than cafés, curbs, and the public library (when open) at no. 74.

There are three good times of the day to come and visit this neighborhood: the best is between nine and noon, particularly on a Saturday or Sunday (closed Monday), when you can see the most colorful outdoor food market in Paris; the second is in the afternoon,

155

when the crowds have gone home and the buildings become visible once more: and the third is at night, when all the restaurants and cafés are open and the youth of Paris (and the tourists) are out to eat and people-watch.

In ancient times the Rue Mouffetard was important as the main Roman road to the southeast, Lyons, and Italy, but it owes its real development to the Bièvre River. This river flowed across the base of the hill where the street ends today (originally the road continued to the Porte d'Italie). Its banks offered excellent land for settlement, and in the twelfth century the area, called the Bourg St Marcel, was a village where wealthy Parisians had farms and country houses. The list of residents of the mid-fourteenth century reads like the social register. In a huge area (currently delineated by three streets—Mouffetard, Lacépède, and Geoffroy St Hilaire—and the Bièvre River) there were only two roads, Mouffetard and Daubenton and, apart from the church, only seven estates. These were owned by bishops, lords, the president of the courts, and Charles V's architect.

Nevertheless, the dominance of the upper class was not long lasting, again because of the Bièvre. The river ran with sweet water, which encouraged cultivation, and was famous for its freshwater shrimp, described by Madame de Maintenon as "the best that could be imagined." However, the river was soon discovered to contain properties efficacious in skinning and tanning hides. Rabelais offers his own bawdy explanation for this phenomenon in *Pantagruel*, book 2, chapter 22. In this story Panurge takes revenge on the finest lady in town, who had scorned his love. He kills a bitch in heat and carefully prepares "that part [about which] the Greek necromancers knew." The following day was a feast day, and, finding the woman in her best clothes in the church,

> Panurge deftly sprinkled the drug that he was carrying on to various parts of her, chiefly on the

pleats of her sleeves and her dress. . . . All the dogs in the church ran up to the lady, attracted by the smell of the drug he had sprinkled on her. Small and great, big and little, all came, lifting their legs, smelling her and pissing all over her. It was the most dreadful thing in the world.

. . . She ran to hide, with the dogs after her and all the chambermaids laughing. But once she was inside and the door closed behind her, all the dogs ran up from two miles around and pissed so hard against the gate of the house, that they made a stream with their urine big enough to swim in. And it is this stream which now passes by St Victor, in which Mme Gobelin dyes her scarlet, thanks to the specific virtue of those piss-hounds, as our master Dungpowder once proclaimed in a public sermon.

In the sixteenth and seventeenth centuries the population of the Bourg St Marcel became working class—tanners, slaughterers, skinners, dyers, and similar craftsmen. They named their bridge the Pont aux Tripes ("tripe bridge"). The famous Gobelins' wool factory is the only survivor from this period. It was because of the Flemish tapestry weavers at the Gobelins' that the second characteristic of the neighborhood developed. The Flemish were great beer drinkers, a tradition they would not leave behind, and soon cafés and cabarets proliferated to serve them. The successors to these establishments are still here.

Industry, together with the rotting animal wastes, rapidly polluted the purity of the Bièvre. By the nineteenth century this neighborhood was the commercial and shopping center of the Left Bank, but the fumes from the Bièvre were more noxious than ever. There is a theory that the name of the Rue Mouffetard comes from these sewerlike qualities of the river: the French for "skunk" or "bad smell" is *mouffette*. There is also a less amusing

*Shellfish at the market on the Rue Mouffetard*

explanation that claims that the hill was called in Roman times *mons cetardus*, perhaps named after a now forgotten Roman, which became *mont cetard*, then *montfetard*, and finally *Mouffetard*. In 1828 a portion of the river was covered; in 1840–48 studies were done to try to save the Bièvre; in 1910 the only possible solution finally came to pass: the river became part of the underground sewer system. Even now, in the summer, in certain corners, the foul odor of garbage still seems to emanate from the pavement under your feet.

The door to the church of **St Médard** faces the market on the Rue Mouffetard. Architecturally, this church is not particularly notable, though some of the events connected with it are. The first church on this spot is thought to have been built in the seventh or eighth century, in dedication to Saint Médard, but there is no evidence to support this theory. The first positive proof of the existence of this church is in a papal bull of Pope Alexander III. It dates from 1163, when the pope came to Paris to consecrate the choir of St Germain des Prés and to lay the first stone for Notre Dame. This bull mentions, under the rights and lands of the Abbey Ste Geneviève, the Bourg St Marcel and a church, St Médard, on the left bank of the Bièvre. There are no physical traces of this church except for the bell tower, since renovated, which was originally separate from the body of the then much smaller church. The actual building is from several periods. The nave and the façade, in flamboyant Gothic, are from the middle fifteenth century. The money for their construction probably came from a donation from the sister of Reilhac, the lawyer of Charles VII. She wanted the priests to say 261 low masses a year for her brother, who was buried there. In 1736, three hundred years later, the priests had cut this down to sixteen; today there is no one to remember him.

During the years 1560–86 the choir was enlarged and chapels rebuilt in the style of the Renaissance. The windows of the nave are also from this period. This time the money came from fines imposed on Protestants after a religious battle. The money ran out when it came to the vaulted ceiling, however, and it had to be completed in wood. It remains wood to this day, a refreshing change from stone vaulting. In 1665 the side aisles were added, although the vaulting, which had served as buttressing for the church, is earlier (sixteenth century). At this point the church was considered complete and St Médard became a parish. In 1784 the church was again redone to fit the existing fashions. The columns are fluted in the neoclassical style, and the apsidal Chapel of the Virgin, behind the choir, was built. The walls are completely covered with votive tablets that give thanks for miraculous recoveries, exams passed, and life in general. During the Revolution the church was made into a Temple of Labor—a citizens' meeting place—and the standard still hangs over the choir. In 1901 the *petit charnier*, a small roomlike enclosure for common graves located behind the church, was condemned and transformed into the catechism chapel. In this and other chapels there are some interesting paintings: note *The Merchants Being Chased from the Temple* by Matoire and the *Multiplication of the Bread* by Restout. In the last left-hand chapel (as you stand with your back to the entrance) is a painting of Sainte Geneviève that was at one time thought to be by Watteau.

Outside the church there was once the cemetery of St Médard. Originally, it included the area in front of the church, where the square now is, and the entire south side back to what is now the Rue Censier. At the beginning of each winter, before the ground froze, a large ditch was dug to serve as a common grave for all who died during the winter. It was closed in the spring, and several smaller ones were dug to take the few summer dead. (In primitive conditions on the margin of subsistence, the winter months were always far more deadly than the summer, if only because the poor could not get enough food to keep warm and sustain resistance to disease. The combination of the Bièvre and the rotting corpses must have been overwhelming.) The church buried about three hundred people a year in this fashion. After nine years they would reuse a large ditch and after three or four, the smaller ones. When the Rue Censier was opened in 1913, a layer of bones twenty-four inches thick was uncovered ten feet down. A coin found among the bones dates from the 1590s.

In 1765 a law was passed forbidding any burials within the limits of the city. The people of the neighborhood had no desire to be buried at Ste Catherine, which was far away, so with the complicity of the old beadles, who had the cemetery keys in their safekeeping, they continued to be buried at St Médard in secrecy. This went on through the Revolution, until the police, in 1795, became indignant about this *"manie de perpétuer l'ancien régime"* ("nonsense of perpetuating the old regime").

The most famous corpse of St Médard was a young

Jansenist, François Pâris. (Jansenists were so called after Cornelius Jansen [1585–1638], bishop of Ypres, who held doctrines the main body of the Catholic church found heretical.) Pâris was a novice with a great reputation for humility. He preferred to spend his life performing menial tasks, such as knitting socks for the poor, and he died at the age of thirty-six on May 1, 1727, at the height of the Jansenist persecution, exhausted from a life of extreme abstinence and self-punishment. Pâris was buried with the poor in the *charnier*, having insisted before he died that he was not worthy of the cemetery. The Jansenists declared him a saint, and a black marble stone was laid over his tomb. The grave became a gathering place for his admirers, and before long the word spread that the site was holy and capable of miraculous cures. This was the beginning of an unbelievable history of hysteria that lasted thirty-five years. Young girls, fanatics, began coming to the *charnier* to eat the dirt of the novice priest's grave. There they would fall into religious ecstasies or convulsions and have to be restrained. At first there were eight to ten girls, but after two years the number had risen to eight hundred. The girls' activities escalated from day to day, changing from mere convulsions to atrocities. They would ask to be beaten while crying out, "Oh! How good that is. Oh! How good that makes me feel, brother. I beg of you, continue if you can!" They wanted to have their tongues pierced, twenty-five-pound weights placed upon their chests, their bodies raked with iron combs, or their breasts, thighs, and stomachs trampled on until they fainted. Pain was voluptuous, and it had no bounds. They had their breasts crushed or were hung head down. Some girls had themselves tortured in this way more than twenty times.

On 27 January 1732, the government, in desperation, had the cemetery walled, locked, and guarded. The next day at St Médard, on the locked gate, the following rhyme appeared:

*De par le roi, défense à Dieu*
*De faire miracle en ce lieu.**

The girls had to move their activities to private houses; the tomb of the novice priest became no longer necessary. In fact, in March 1733 another law was vainly passed, forbidding all those seized by convulsions to turn their affliction into a public spectacle or to arrange meetings for this purpose in private houses. Some girls were imprisoned, but this only made the others more impassioned and caused some of the most unusual scenes to occur. The girls borrowed an idea from ancient Miletus and began strangling themselves; they also swallowed live coals and leather-bound editions of the New Testament. Sister Rosalie, we are told, lived for forty days on air sipped from a spoon, and one girl had herself nailed to a board and was thus crucified.

In direct association with the ecstatics were the *mélangistes*, who pretended to distinguish between useless, indecent acts and true religious ecstasy. The *secouristes* were those who gave aid to the convulsive girls. They gave "small aid" and "big aid." Small aid consisted of helping to prevent falls and other accidents and helping to defend the girls' modesty by rearranging their often disordered clothing. Big or "murderous" aid entailed inflicting all the forms of martyrdom that the girls begged for.

Not everyone was so helpful. In a convent near St Médard the nuns would meow ecstatically in unison for several hours every day at the same time. It was a disturbance, and the neighbors were up in arms. The nuns were told if one more noise was heard from their convent, the Garde Française, which was posted at their gate, would come in and whip them. There was complete silence.

The activities of this Jansenist cult continued for

---

*By order of the king, God is forbidden to perform miracles in this place.

thirty-five years, until August 1762, when the Jesuit society that had, with the help of the government, persecuted them for so long was disbanded and expelled from the country. As for the girls, French historian J. Dulaure points out, if a girl is brought up by people who believe in possession of the soul by the devil, and the girl herself believes this, she is bound to become very anxious at a certain age about new and unavowable emotions that seem to be tormenting her. She finds it easy to believe she has become possessed. Dulaure also offers another explanation: if a girl has been reared by very devout people and is herself religious, her own devotions and abstinences may continue increasing until she reaches a point of religious ecstasy. In her case it is love that has taken a wrong turn. Dulaure alludes only in passing to the explanation that we today might find most plausible, namely, that this was a search for a form of sexual release that would be acceptable to the religious and social milieu of the day.

In 1807 Pâris's tomb was opened in order to give certain eminent Jansenist families relics of this saint; the rest of his bones lie under what are now the unmarked stones of the Chapel of the Virgin.

St Médard has also played a small role in literature. Fans of Victor Hugo's *Les Misérables* will remember, perhaps, that it was here that Jean Valjean accidentally encountered Javert. There was always a beggar by St Médard, posted under the street lamp, to whom Jean gave a few sous. One evening the beggar lifted his head briefly to look at Jean under the light. Jean shivered with fear, for he was certain that he had seen the face of his enemy, Javert, and not the old beggar.

Today, the **marché** stretches out from the Carrefour des Gobelins, which is not on our walk, to the Rue de l'Epée de Bois and spreads right and left almost a block on each side street. The scholars tell us there has been a street market in this area since 1350, and it is this that shapes the character of the street. The origins of the market, however, are a bit disquieting. We are told that, in the fourteenth century, on the Ile de la Cité under the shadow of Notre Dame, there was a butcher who sold the finest pâté in Paris. One day, however, his unusual sources of material were discovered; the meat used in his excellent pâté was human flesh. The butcher and his friend the barber had been abducting students who lived under the auspices of the church (away from their families) and were killing them behind the barber shop. Some readers will remember the play *Sweeney Todd*, which tells a similar story. These poor youths, living anonymously among the crowds of students, were not missed until the day the barber picked out a young man who owned a dog. When his master did not return from the barber's, the dog put up such a howl that the youth's friends came to investigate and caught the barber and the butcher in their bloody work. Judgment was swift: the two men were suspended in cages in front of Notre Dame and publicly burned.

The clerics of the cathedral, however, were in a more ambiguous position. The well-fed priests had long enjoyed this pâté, but to eat human flesh, even unknowingly, is the sin of anthropophagy, and is punishable by excommunication. Several of the priests of Notre Dame, therefore, had to be exiled from their cathedral. They banded together in their exclusion and decided to make a pilgrimage to the Pope in Avignon to plead their cause and beg forgiveness. They set out barefoot one morning on the road to the southeast. They arrived twenty minutes later at what is now the Carrefour des Gobelins (then just outside the city limits). There they decided that their feet hurt enough and that they should stop at that very spot and become mendicants. They lived from their begging until later in that same year when Jean de Meulan, the new Bishop of Paris, came to visit his property and farms on the hill of Mouffetard. During his visit he was attacked by thieves and would have been killed if not for the aid of the mendicant priests. In appreciation, Jean de Meulan gave the priests absolution and, taking account of their record, allowed them to open a market on his property to sell *"toutes marchandises et objets dont on n'aurait pas à rechercher l'origine"* ("all goods and objects of unquestionable origin").

There are official records of 1654 of a vegetable market held every Wednesday and Friday in the courtyard of the Maison du Patriarche, then owned by the family of the Maréchal Biron. An ordinance of 20 September 1828 authorized the clearing of this site, and the architect Châtillon was given a commission to build a covered market in place of the house. It was inaugurated on June 1, 1831. At that time the market sold primarily old clothes and ironwork, with only a small section for food.

The actual building was later used as a garage, for a long time as a public bathhouse (there was one on the Rue de Lacépéde), and today it is a gymnasium with a paved square in front, suitable for roller skating.

The street market we see today is devoted almost exclusively to food. It's an interesting and especially nice *marché*, because unlike the peripatetic markets assembled from temporary stalls that are set up in a given street one or two mornings a week, Mouffetard consists almost entirely of permanent shops that lay out their goods daily, covering the pavement. The street is reserved for pedestrians. This is much closer to the medieval system, in which each shop had a large, horizontally-split shutter that was opened for selling. The top half was a shade to protect against the sun and the rain, and the bottom was used as a table on which to display the goods. Hanging out past the shutters was the shopkeeper's standard with a symbol representing the shop's name, which in itself was symbolic of the business. The room behind was used for storage, or, if the shop was owned by a craftsman, for a workshop. Although the shutters are gone, and the displays are richer than in the Middle Ages, the room behind is still used to store the crates of vegetables and fruits; in some cases (butchers and fishmongers) it has become part of the shop.

The array at the *marché*, particularly on Sunday morning, is dazzling. The fresh vegetables and fruits are neatly piled in bright and tempting displays, looking somehow fresher and more delicious than at home. The tomatoes are redder, the white peaches more fragrant, and even the carrots seem more robust and flavorful. There are even two stands of exotic produce from Africa on the Rue des Patriarches. The stall in the square in front of the church has been run by the same family since 1910. They also own the produce store at no. 132. They start work daily at 4 A.M., when they first buy their goods from the central market, Les Halles in Rungis, and then come to Paris to set up and begin selling from nine until seven in the evening with only Monday off. When we asked them some time ago if it was a profitable business, they confessed it was. Today their stand is much smaller and they bemoan the rise in popularity of prepared foods sold in supermarkets.

Take the time to walk around, comparing quality and prices; one man will sell the cheapest carrots and onions, another, the best apples and bananas. If you are staying in Paris for a long time and can shop, there is almost no better way to feel French and a part of the city than to buy each type of food from your own favorite merchant. Patronizing your own carefully chosen bakery can be a most pleasant, as well as fattening, experience. Be adventurous. Try all kinds of *charcuterie* salads and meats, including the ones you have been brought up to think are unswallowable. Also try the cheese. Contrary to popular belief, the smell of a cheese does not necessarily indicate how strong it is. Chaume, a mild, creamy, sinful cheese, reeks. Avoid the supermarket versions of cheese; the cheese store sells the unpasteurized, purer version at lower prices.

The Mouffetard market fulfils every food need possi-

*Poultry shop at the Mouffetard market*

ble, a reputation this street has had for a long time. August Vitu wrote about Mouffetard in the late nineteenth
century:

> There is an average of two shops in each building,
> and all of them are dedicated to the daily subsis-
> tence of a very large, very crowded population
> with little time to spare and a large appetite to
> satisfy. On the ground floor of the 142 houses on
> the Rue Mouffetard there are 52 wine merchants,
> plus 9 wine merchants who also cater food and
> roast meat—yours or their own—16 grocers, 8
> butchers, 6 bakers, 6 dairies, 5 delicatessens, 5

pastry shops, 4 lemonade stands, 3 tripe butchers, 2 café-bars, 1 horse-meat butcher, 3 coal sellers, 1 coffee shop. This, which could feed an entire city, was complemented by fish, fresh vegetables, fruits, and flowers sold from outdoor rolling carts. The housekeeping of the Rue Mouffetard is kept up by three stove and pottery shops, one bottle shop, two glaziers, two brushmen and shoe repair and tool shops, one lighting shop, one wallpaper and business supply shop. Between the butchers and delicatessens with their reddish tinge and the pastrymen and bakers with their crusty tidbits are six linen and sewing shops; eight shoemakers for men, women, and children; four umbrella shops; three hatmakers for men, three for the women; and four gift shops spilling their wares out into the street, closely followed by a launderer-stain remover. While five barbers are caring for the heads hatted by the hatters, two watch and jewellery shops represent luxury, two wash-it-yourself-by-hand laundries represent cleanliness, teamed with a bathtub and bathroom fixtures salesman. The health of the body is watched by a doctor, two pharmacists, two *herboristeries*, two dentists to whom are attached three midwives in case of need. There is an office for job placement, one post office, one barracks of the Garde Républicaine (once the Garde Française), to guarantee security. For intellectual culture one finds on the street one kindergarten and one reading room. Even art has its representative in the person of a photographer.

There is a greater variety of shops now, though certain trades, such as wine shops, lemonade stands, hatters, and coal merchants have all but vanished. Today they have been replaced with a supermarket, a natural foods store, a computer store, and even a Baskin-Robbins. What hasn't changed is the animation and dedication to good eating—a line of thirty people at the bakery attests to that.

An aspect of the street Vitu didn't see in his day is the construction and renovation that is so common now. Whole blocks of eighteenth-century buildings have been condemned; one has already been torn down for senior citizen housing. Asked about the destruction, any old-timer will shake his head and mourn the changes in the neighborhood, "It's just not the same, the atmosphere has changed." Although we were frustrated several times searching for vanished historical sites, for us, having come from the New World, the atmosphere and age are still palpable and exciting.

As you walk up the Rue Mouffetard, take your time to look at the buildings and courtyards. The houses are almost all from the seventeenth century and are generally very plain with simple mansard windows and undecorated façades. They were built for ordinary people of modest means. **No. 134** (to the left of no. 132; the number is not clearly marked), however, is very different. Its façade was extravagantly decorated by an Italian artist, Aldeari, a friend of the family, in the 1930s. On the second floor are panels of painted wood depicting country people at their tasks. (There are other panels similar to this on the bakery on the corner of the Passage des Patriarches and the Rue Mouffetard.) Above on the stucco is an unusual scene showing wild game and birds intertwined with a floral pattern. Even the seventeenth-century mansard windows have been decorated. The shop below, **Fachetti**, is, appropriately, that of a butcher and *charcuterie*. Seven to eight people work full-time in the basement kitchen to produce the pâtés, sausages, cured meats, and savories enveloped in golden crusts. Even if you don't need any food, go in and sniff the perfumed air—you'll soon change your mind.

Next door is **Produits de la Nature/Les Comptoirs**

**de Provence**. Here is the store to find wonderful, hard-milled soaps from natural ingredients such as seaweed, honey, almond, and floral extracts. They are artisan made and are inexpensive. This is one of the few good buys in Paris and is the perfect gift for everyone you left at home. The store also sells natural perfumes and cosmetics and makes up gift baskets to order.

**No. 122** is decorated with the oldest original standard on the street, **A la Bonne Source** ("At the good spring"). Look above the doorway and notice the bas-relief of two boys, dressed in the style of Henri IV's reign, drawing water from a well. In 1592 this shop was owned by M. du Puy (the name means "of the well"), who sold wine and used the name of the shop as an implicit seal of approval. This type of pun as well as the link to the shop owner's name was typical of the play on words of medieval standards and necessary in a time without street numbers or the Yellow Pages.

Standards go back to the thirteenth century and beyond, when noblemen marked their houses with their coats of arms. If you were not a nobleman, you might distinguish your residence by placing a statuette of your favorite saint in a niche above the door. That way you got a little holy protection besides. Nos. 44 and 45 of the Rue Mouffetard still have niches in their façades, although the statues are long gone. The first commercial standards were put up by taverns and hotels so that a foreigner could find a place to eat and sleep in a strange city. These standards generally represented a bundle of straw, which gives a good idea of the character of the sleeping accommodation. Even today there is hardly a city in France without a hotel called the Lion d'Or, the "golden lion," or, in rebus form, *le lit [où] on dort*, "the bed where one sleeps."

The commercial standard was soon understood to be a smart way to advertise, and a problem almost nonexistent in the thirteenth century became serious by the fifteenth. The standards were made from sheets of iron, cut and painted, and hung on long poles to extend into the street past the large shop shutters. Like signs today, they were hung out as far as possible and made as large as possible to attract the most attention. Although Mouffetard had always been the same width that it is today, the combination of the shutters and an open sewer running down the center of the unpaved street—the whole overhung with huge groaning and clanking signs that blocked the sun—must have made for a dark and cluttered street. A *parfumerie* had a standard of a glove, each finger of which could have held a three-year-old child. A dentist hung a molar that was the size of an armchair. These standards were constantly threatening to fall; one man was reputedly killed when the dentist's tooth fell on his head. For reasons of safety rather than aesthetics, the government tried to pass legislation to limit the size of signs. In 1667 they said the signs could be no more than thirty-two inches wide and had to be hung at least fifteen feet above the ground, so that horsemen might ride safely in the streets. It was not until 1761 that standards were banned altogether, to be replaced by wall decorations like those at A la Bonne Source. A few of these decorations and old names still remain.

Not all signs designated the trade of the shop below so clearly as A la Bonne Source did. Since literacy was rare, the names were more often simply visual recognition or mnemonic devices. Actually this decorated house had previously been called The Bat, which tells us absolutely nothing. There are several old names that leave the business inside unexplained: The Bottle Tennis Court, or The Small Hole, or The Cage. Other names were clearer: The Tree of Life was a surgeon's house; The Red Shop, a butcher shop (the surgeon might have used that one too); The Reaper, a bakery (another possibility for the surgeon). One common name whose symbolism was clear in the Middle Ages was the Salamander. Salamanders were at that time believed to be impervious to fire, and therefore salamander was the old name for asbestos, the "wood that wouldn't burn." Bakers often took this name to symbolize their clay baking ovens, and the word is still in use today for the ceramic room heaters commonly found in Europe.

Many of the names were religious, some specifically so: The Golden Cross, The White Cross, The Red Cross, The Name of Jesus, The Fat Mother of God (which was not vulgar but, rather, complimentary in the hungry Middle Ages). Some names were only vaguely religious in that they used the number three and thus invoked the Trinity. The number three was extremely popular: The Three Catfish, The Three Goddesses, The Three Pruning Knives, The Three Torches, The Three Panes (this was a bakery and not a glazier's), The Three Nuns' Coifs, The Three Doves, The Three Fish, The Three Pigeons. These were only a few of the names used on the Rue Mouffetard, for each shop had as many as its changing ownership required. Today, with the return of the small boutique, interesting names are again common.

On your right, a little farther up the hill, is the Rue de l'Arbalète, which leads to the Rue du Marché des Patriarches. It was here that the **Maison du Patriarche** once stood. This estate occupied the land between the rues Daubenton, Mouffetard, L'Epée de Bois, and Gracieuse. The house was set back from the street and was approached from an alley located where you are now. The first owner was Jean de Meulan, the Bishop of Paris who pardoned the mendicant priests. The property passed through several hands before Simon de Cramault, Archbishop of Rheims and Patriarch of Alexandria, bought it. It was then that the estate received the name Maison du Patriarche. This was changed gradually to Maison des Patriarches, when Simon de Cramault was mistakenly associated with the Patriarch of Jerusalem, Guillaume de Chanac, and it was assumed that they had lived on the same property.

The fate of Simon de Cramault is disputed by historians. Some say that he was evicted from his house for

*No. 80 Rue Mouffetard*

not paying a tax to the Abbey Ste Geneviève. Others say, more logically, that he was forced to abandon the house when Jean Sans Peur, Duke of Burgundy, pillaged the entire village on his way to Paris, followed by the Armagnacs who occupied it, and finally the English who devastated it. Whatever the reasons, Cramault did not have enough money to run the estate and in 1443 abandoned it to Thibault Canaye, a hotel owner on Rue de la Harpe and husband of the wealthy Gobelins' wool factory heiress, Mathurine Gobelin.

The house remained in this family until, in the sixteenth century, Jean Canaye, a great-great-grandson and militant Calvinist, rented it to a friend who opened the house to the Huguenots. The Huguenots turned the house into a Protestant temple, one of the two that had been allowed in the villages outside Paris. The Catholics of the Bourg St Marcel were not at all pleased to see the Huguenots installed right beside their church, and on Saturday, December 27, 1561, religious violence broke out here. It was the holiday of St John the Evangelist, and two thousand Protestants had gathered to hear Jean Malo, the former priest of St André des Arts, give a special sermon. The congregation was unable to hear the sermon, however, because the sexton of St Médard (only two hundred feet away) insisted on repeatedly ringing the bells for vespers. Malo sent four men to the church to ask the priest for quiet, but that was a serious mistake, for they fell into an ambush. When they arrived at the church doors, one man was snatched inside and beaten by parishioners. He was never seen again. The other three helplessly faced a locked-up church front, while stones and slates rained on them from above.

The three men returned to the Maison des Patriarches ready for blood. The Huguenots quickly armed themselves and stormed the church of St Médard. They killed and wounded parishioners, broke all the religious statues and windows, profaned the altar and sacked the sacristy, throwing holy wafers to the wind. The Catholics, in retaliation, set fire to the temple and then called for government support. Constable Anne de Montmorency, head of the royal army, authorized the Catholics to raze one section of the house and to execute four of the Protestant offenders. The Catholics turned the execution into a public spectacle. Near the portals of St Médard the prisoners had both hands cut off and their tongues pierced. Then they were gently strangled so as not to expire entirely and finally burned to death. As a final measure the Catholics confiscated all their goods to pay for the repairs to the church. There were only six buildings, a garden, and some dependencies left to the Maison des Patriarches when it passed into the hands of Maréchal Biron, who authorized the construction of the *marché* on the site of the house.

Today the *place* is clean and open and children roller skate and ride skateboards in the piazza. A new gymnasium stands on the site of the Maison des Patriarches, replacing a public baths. On the street facing the gym (Rue Daubenton) new shops keep opening. The most interesting is charming **Evelyne Gray**, at **no. 35**. This is the kind of store the French do so well—tea sets and porcelain, tin boxes, and adorable knickknacks you suddenly discover you don't want to live without.

Return to the Rue Mouffetard. The **Brasserie, no. 116,** is decorated with designs of grapes and masquerons and the windows are hung with lace. Stop for a quick lunch.

To the right is the Rue de l'Arbalète with its impressive stand of produce from Africa, Asia, and South America. The spices and fruits are fascinating but even better was the codfish *accras*, a hot (temperature and spiciness), fresh fritter of fish and spices that warmed us as it went down. Every cuisine has its fine points. The owner explained what to do with the different bananas he sold. The black are for fritters, the yellow are for boiling and sautéing, and the green are for boiling and mashing.

Back again on the Rue Mouffetard on the corner to

your right are two superb bakeries. The first is **Les Pane-tons** (a *paneton* is a cloth-lined basket in which bread can rise) selling much more than the standard baguette. Here you find a varied array of breads of different shapes and different grains. Some say that French bread is not as good as it used to be. White bread is no longer de rigueur and new breads are on the rise (pun intended). The second bakery, **Le Moule à Gâteau, no. 113**, is also not a traditional bakery. Here you won't find eclairs and napoleons. Instead, pastry cream has given way to fruit-based mousses, flourless chocolate cakes, fruit tarts on almond crusts, and even brownies. Don't wait to stop in here. By noon they are almost all sold out.

Across the street there used to be a coal and wood merchant's. This was home base for some of the last of the *bougnats*, coal deliverers. A highly respected, old yellow-toothed woman, Mme Courtine, owned this business. She sat wrapped in layers of black, dunking her croissant in her coffee, and told us that the business was started in 1903 by her husband's father. When she married in 1923, she came to work here and stayed until her recent death at the age of ninety. She told us that, when she had first come here, the street was very *charbonnier* (coalish); there were thirteen coal dealers. People bought their coal in the summer when there was time to sort it and wash it and the price was lower. Everyone stored it in the basement. Now no one buys in the summer be-cause, Mme Courtine said, they can't leave it anywhere— it will be stolen. She planned to retire to the country, but never did.

According to her, the street had changed. It used to be a street of workers. It was "proper." Now it is a "cab-aret." Once a street of food, ranging from the best quality to medium quality, it is now a "bazaar"; everyone is a foreigner or a student. Work went on once from 6 A.M. to 10 P.M. every day; today shops close at noon on Sun-day and stay closed until Tuesday. Her final comments to us were to the effect that her heart bleeds for her old *quartier* and that the *"fameux mazout"* ("famous"—or "in-famous"—"oil") not only ruins her but the whole world as well.

As you walk up the street, look at the buildings on the left. They are mostly new, **nos. 100** and **98**, for example. The old ones that were replaced were certainly decrepit, but these are well on the way to fitting in.

**No. 85** hides a treasure deep within. Press the main button and go down the long dark hallway until you come back outside, and look to your right. There is a garden and a charming stone house that has been restored. Notice the wooden lintels and the old glass in the windows. Here the country atmosphere that is all but lost from Rue Mouffetard still exists. The new library is nearby at **no. 74.**

The doorway of **no. 81** is unusual for this street. It is all that is left of a former chapel built in the beginning of the early seventeenth century.

The **Théâtre de la Mouff (no. 73)** finally has a new home. It spent many years struggling to exist in a run-down building across the street. Today it is in an interior courtyard in the midst of a new apartment complex.

Above the entrance to **no. 69** is a curious decoration in the form of a tree. The sign is carved from an old masthead taken from a sunken ship. There were two identical standards carved from the wood, and both advertised a restaurant named **Au Vieux Chêne** ("At the old oak tree"). The second once stood on the Right Bank, but the building there has been demolished. Wood from sunken ships is said to have a strange power, and mastheads that have been refashioned are supposedly even more potent. Legend has it that the two restaurants bearing these trees were cursed, particularly this one. Every seven years there was supposedly an unexpected argument at Au Vieux Chêne, and someone would die a violent death, right in front of the other diners. The first restaurant owner was forced to sell the property, because he could not cope with its macabre reputation. A second

owner also fell victim to the curse and eventually sold out to a discothèque owner, who sold out to the present owner. M. Francis Tartar has been here in his restaurant for seven years—nothing has happened yet.

**No. 64** is a true working-class shoe shop. Here you can find real peasant *sabots*, wooden shoes that farmers and laborers wear to this day. They also sell woollen slipper *sabot* linings, rubber boots, and plain espadrilles. This shop has no pretensions. It was started in 1890 and the wooden boxes with brass handles which you see on the wall were made for shoes. They are still in use.

**No. 62** is a beautifully restored seventeenth-century building. Go in the apartment entrance and down the stone hallway with the beamed ceiling. On your right is an excellent example of a Louis XIII staircase with its solid, rounded oak balustrades. The first diagonal section is a reproduction; the sections above are original. At the end of the hall is a small stone courtyard; to the left is a stone balcony with plants. It is just this sort of restoration that is changing the character of the Rue Mouffetard and many other streets of old Paris. And no change is so expensive as the kind of controlled renovation-plus-preservation that is required in Paris.

Aesthetically this is progress, but socially it means dislocation of residents. These fine houses, on their medieval foundations, must be repaired and restored, and the high rents that follow limit occupancy to the well-to-do. The municipal government has tried to help by renovating some buildings for the tenants, who are placed in temporary housing while the work proceeds and are then allowed to return at subsidized rents. But there are limits to the city purse, and most of this work is being done by private investors. The result for now is a widening of the social range: many of the poorer residents are still there, but they have rich company. And in a strange way, this is a return to the social arrangements of long ago, when Paris buildings were microcosms of the larger society and these old neighborhoods in the center housed the rich as well as the poor.

**No. 61** was once a convent devoted to poor and sick women. The nuns of the Convent of Notre Dame de la Miséricorde bought this property, which stretched back to Rue Gracieuse, in 1653. By the beginning of the eighteenth century, however, the buildings were falling into ruins. In 1717 help came from an unexpected source. Madame de Maintenon, between her marriage to the poet Paul Scarron and her secret marriage to Louis XIV, had lived in a similar convent on the Rue des Minimes. She was always grateful for the hospitality she had received, and so now, as an all-powerful marquise, she arranged for all the convent's expenses to be paid by the royal treasury. She ordered the lieutenant general of the police, Marc-René d'Argenson, to supervise the reconstruction. The convent's problems were not, however, at an end. D'Argenson did not have the morals a man in his position was expected to have, and when he came to supervise the work he had just separated from his latest mistress. During his brief inspection d'Argenson fell madly in love with a young and innocent novice; he tried to seduce her with promises of money. When the mother superior heard of the scheme, she took steps to make it impossible for the novice to leave. D'Argenson was furious and in retaliation informed her that he was suspending all construction until she gave in to his demands. The mother superior was thus forced to choose between the soul of her novice and the stones of her convent. The restoration took precedence, and the novice was yielded up to d'Argenson. (Whether the novice ever got her promised fortune is not known.)

Next door on the corner at **no. 60** is an unusual wall that masks a fountain built in 1624 (redone in 1671). The fountain exists because of Marie de Médicis. When Henri IV built the palace at the Luxembourg Gardens for her, she demanded a plumbing system that would be able to handle enough water for the palace and for the gardens. The only way to do this was to reopen and repair the ancient Gallo-Roman aqueduct. This brought so much water into the Left Bank, however, that fourteen new fountains had to be built along the aqueduct's route to pump off the excess. This remaining fountain on the Rue Mouffetard is now a classified historical monument, which has finally been restored. Formerly it was black and smothered in posters; today it is clean and at the top a frieze of *coquilles* and flowers has miraculously appeared.

A buried treasure was found inside the walls of the building that once stood at **no. 53**. In 1938 it was condemned by the city for reasons of safety, and a crew of men was assigned to tear it down. On the first day of the job, a wrecker, Flammo Maures, ripped open a wall and was astounded to see "medals" pour forth. In no time at all the workers gathered around and divided up the booty. When Maures went home that night, he showed his discovery to his wife, who immediately recognized the medals as gold. A law-abiding citizen, Maures took his "medals" to the police, where they were identified as louis d'or gold pieces. The treasure was reassembled, and the walls carefully searched, finally yielding a collection of 3,351 22-carat gold coins, in the form of double louis weighing 16.3 grams each, single louis weighing 8.7 grams, and half-louis of 4.7. With the gold, an identifying piece of paper was also found: *"moi, sieur Louis Nivelle, écuyer et secrétaire du Roy, lègue ma fortune à ma fille, Anne-Louis Nivelle"* ("I, Sir Louis Nivelle, assistant and secretary of the King, bequeath my fortune to my daughter, Anne-Louise Nivelle"). The paper was not dated, but it was not difficult to determine that Nivelle had been the secretary of Louis XV and had played a main role in a still unclarified mystery: he vanished in 1757 without a trace.

The police, searching for the descendants of Anne-Louise, finally found General Robert de St Vincent, who, although surprised, said that he had been brought up with a family tradition of a lost inheritance. It was not until 1952 that a legal division of the gold was arranged. Two hundred and fifty-four pieces had to be sold to pay the genealogists for their research, 538 were given to the city officials, and the original wrecking crew and the eighty-four descendants of Anne-Louise Nivelle split the remaining 2,559 coins. The gold was valued at sixteen million old francs (about $32,000) at that time, simply as metal. Its historical value is untold. (100 old francs = 1 new franc; in 1960, the franc was revalued, and new francs introduced.)

**Nos. 52, 42,** and **34** all have small gardens hiding behind their entry doors. Why is it that one struggling tree in a slightly shabby courtyard can still lift the spirits in a big city? Another spirit-lifter for you might be a stop at **Baskin-Robbins** at **no. 26.**

**No. 23** is a very old house with bulging timbers. Above, to the left of the door, plaster has been removed to show the original structure. Note the old wooden door.

Above the door at **no. 12** is a recent wall decoration that is quite surprising. The name of the building is Le Nègre Joyeux, "the happy Negro," and the painting depicts a young black servant waiting on his mistress. Most people in America have long since rejected and condemned the image of the "happy black servant," but up till now in France few objections to the stereotype seem to have been raised.

## Place de la Contrescarpe

To your right the street widens to form the **Place de la Contrescarpe.** Take a seat in the center and look around. These cafés can be expensive and the service rude. This square has been described as the most picturesque in Paris, and although we would not go as far as that, the *place* is certainly one of the most interesting ones, especially on a summer night. Contrescarpe is a meeting place and has been one for hundreds of years. The name goes back to the Middle Ages, when the Porte Bourdelles, one of the gates in Philippe Auguste's wall around Paris, stood just beyond this point on what is now the Rue Descartes. Outside the gate and its guard towers was the moat, rising to another earthen wall or counterescarpment (*contrescarpe*). At this time the Bourg St Marcel was not really populated above what is now the Rue l'Epée de Bois, and so the land outside the gates became a no-man's-land. It gradually developed into a spot where people naturally congregated, although no one lived there. During this early period in the fourteenth century, there were only three streetlights in Paris, none of them here, making the Place de la Contrescarpe a dark and dangerous area at night. Throughout the sixteenth century hopeless ordinances were passed (in 1504, 1526, and 1551), ordering each house in Paris to burn a candle in the first-floor window from 9 to 12 o'clock every night. Either this was ignored or the candles were ineffectual, for the police estimated an average of fifteen bodies every morning from the killings of the night before—a fantastic murder rate for what was by today's standards a small town.

In 1662 a priest, l'abbé Caraffe, invented mobile lighting. Place de la Contrescarpe soon picked up this innovation, and lamp carriers, or *lampadophores*, would wait here for customers. The lamp bearer would offer to accompany you right to your door, whether it was on the first or seventh floor, for five sous per slice of wax on his torch, or three sous for one-quarter hour with an oil lantern. In the eighteenth century this practice spread to umbrella carriers, who would protect you from showers on a time basis, and chair carriers to keep you out of the mud. At the turn of the eighteenth century lanterns attached to housefronts with a rope pulley were tried, but the candles blew out and the glass darkened. Besides, the city chose to save money by not using the lighting on moonlit nights or in the summers. It was not until the 1770s that any kind of effective street lighting was instituted, and the *lampadophores* were put out of business.

The actual *place* as it stands today was not created

until 1852. By this time the area had the taverns and action that made it a logical site for a barracks of the Garde Républicaine. Today the Garde Républicaine is mostly decorative; the ruffians who used to inhabit the area have been replaced by "winos" or *clochards*, who have long staked their claim here. For them this area offers every convenience: the Rue Mouffetard has the wine shops, the *marché* throws out spoiled food twice daily, the students and tourists are good for begging (a cigarette, if not money), and the Place de la Contrescarpe and the Rue Lacépède offer *métro* heating vents to sleep on. On almost any night you will see the *clochards* huddled on the vents in groups of three or four. They are bundled in rags and coated with a layer of protective dirt. When a rehabilitation center tried to help by taking the *clochards* in off the winter streets and giving them food and showers, before returning them to the city, the center discovered to its shock that some of the *clochards* could no longer survive without their layer of dirt and died of the cold. The misery of their condition seems in a strange way to keep them going. They show little interest in a good meal and a bed; they have the opportunity to go to a hospice in Nanterre by free bus every night and be returned to the city the next day, but as one wino explained to us, no self-respecting *clochard* would consider this, except in time of dire need. In fact, they carefully cultivate their deterioration for the sake of their begging. A café-owner friend of ours says that one day a *clochard* came in begging for a free drink. Rather than oblige him, she asked the wino how someone so young could get into such a position. The *clochard* was visibly upset that she could tell he was still a young man. He had grown his beard and hair and not washed for days in order to look older and more pitiful, but his eyes had given him away as a still unseasoned bum. (The *clochards* are harmless and you need not fear them. They will call out for change or a cigarette as you pass, but you can refuse them or comply, whichever you prefer, without being afraid.)

The French are generally disapproving of these out-casts and have little understanding or patience for them. Compared to some of the contemptuous comments in guidebooks of the Victorian era, however, progress in social attitude has been made. Here is a prize comment, made by an Englishman, F. Berkley Smith, in a book called *The Real Latin Quarter*, written about 1901: "That women should become outcasts through the hopelessness of their position or the breaking down of their brains can be understood, but that men of ability should sink into the dregs and stay there seems incredible. But it is often so."

In the 1950s the *clochards* of the Place de la Contrescarpe began having to share their territory with the students. Now the takeover is almost complete, and French and foreign youth dominate the night scene. The restaurants and cafés put their tables out on the pavements, the food is cheap, and conversation is easy. Sometimes on the weekends a fire- and sword-swallower will come to entertain. First, these performers talk interminably, passing the hat all the while; then when the crowd is about to leave in disgust, they quickly prepare to begin their act. At that point the police invariably appear to break up the crowd and chase away or arrest the performers.

The building at **no. 1** Place de la Contrescarpe has *La Pomme de Pin* ("the Pine Cone") carved into its wall, referring to an old café that once stood on the square. The café was not in that building, however, which is modern, but in what is now a *charcuterie* on the corner of the Rue Blainville, behind you as you face La Pomme de Pin. It was here that the Pléiade Society came into being. This was a literary group begun in 1549 by Pierre Ronsard, Joachim du Bellay, and Jean Baïf. These young men had all come to Paris for their education and were engaged in studying the classics, which they did avidly, straight through the night. From their interest in classical poetry they felt a great need "to defend the French language and render it illustrious." The society had a strong influence on the French language, and their stylistic theories are still in use today.

## Rue Blainville

Turn left into the rue Blainville to find a group of very old houses, **nos. 1, 3, 4,** and **5.** At **no. 4** look at the cleaned rough beige stones and the long beam across the front. **La Truffière** is one of the very few French restaurants in the area with a serious menu. The inside has been restored as carefully as the outside, including a corkscrew staircase to the *caves* below.

At **no. 6** enjoy Korean food at the **Maison de Corée.** Try their fried chicken with scallions and garlic and the caramelized noodles. Prices are very reasonable.

Return to the Place de la Contrescarpe and continue up the Rue Mouffetard. The **Crêperie de la Mouffe** at **no. 9** is a good way to manage a light meal in Paris. This restaurant is beautifully decorated with Breton yokes, *sabots*, Quimper dishes, photographs of Breton life, a closet of colorful traditional Breton costumes. They offer almost eighty kinds of crêpes here, approximately forty of buckwheat (*sarrasin*) with main-course-type fillings and an equal number of dessert crêpes made with white flour. Prices are comparatively low.

## Rue Descartes

At the intersection with the Rue Thouin, the Rue Mouffetard becomes the Rue Descartes. Where you are standing was the emplacement of the Porte Bourdelles and its guard towers; they were demolished in 1685. There are still remains of Philippe Auguste's wall, however, at **no. 47** Rue Descartes. If the door is open, go into this historically classified building and notice the half-timbered walls.

Look closely at the stone slabs you are walking on. Two on the left have numbers carved into their faces. These are stones that were taken from the cemetery of Ste Geneviève when it was destroyed in the eighteenth century. (Again, a little saving in construction costs.) The numbers probably refer to lists of the people buried in communal graves dating from the sixteenth and seventeenth centuries.

Continue back to the second hall with its huge stone building slabs. The third staircase on the left is unfortunately now locked. It winds up to a door that leads outside. Suddenly it was as though you were on a secret street, above ground. You were actually standing on the top of the medieval wall. The buildings along the old wall all made thrifty use of it as their fourth side. A curved building ahead of you on the right was that way simply because, when the original house was built, that was the contour of the wall at that point. This was one of the most charming secret spots of Paris and, although we understand, we are unhappy that more and more building owners close off their houses.

At **no. 39** there is a plaque stating that the poet Verlaine died here in 1896.

From here you are within walking distance of the Arènes de Lutèce, the remains of a Roman arena on the Rue Monge; the Jardin des Plantes, the botanical gardens with a small zoo; and on the same street, Rue Geoffroy St Hilaire, the Mosquée, the only mosque in Paris. It also includes a charming Turkish café. In the other direction in the Place du Panthéon there is the Panthéon, a burial place of famous Frenchmen, and the church of Ste Geneviève, with its unusual architecture and famous rood screen.

# Walk · 5

## Place des Vosges

*C'est le coup de lance de Mont-gomery qui a créé la Place des Vosges.*

It's the blow of Montgomery's lance that created the Place des Vosges.

—Victor Hugo

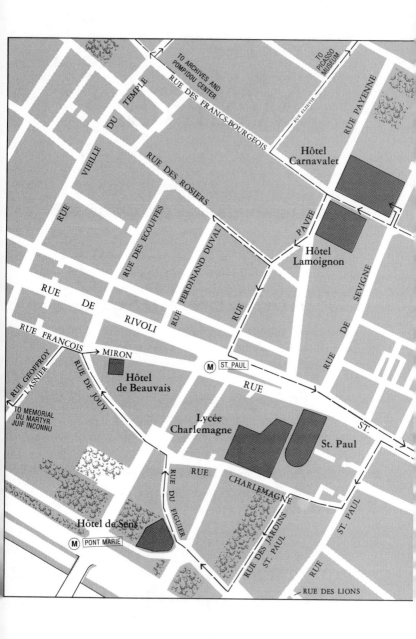

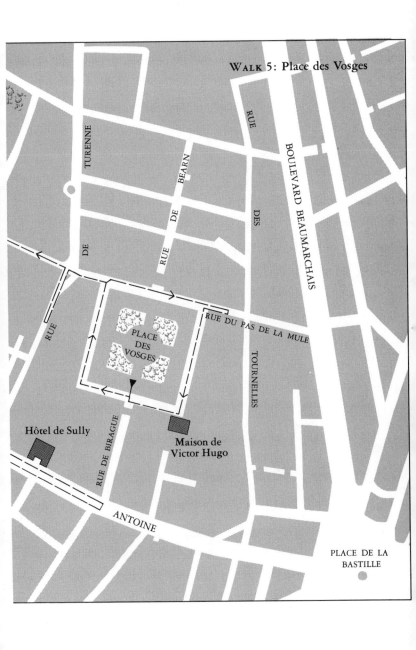

WALK 5: Place des Vosges

RUE TURENNE

RUE DE BEARN

RUE DES

BOULEVARD BEAUMARCHAIS

RUE DE

RUE

PLACE DES VOSGES

RUE DU PAS DE LA MULE

TOURNELLES

Hôtel de Sully

RUE DE BIRAGUE

Maison de Victor Hugo

ANTOINE

PLACE DE LA BASTILLE

**Starting Point:** Rue de Birague, the south entrance of the Place des Vosges
**Métro:** Bastille or St Paul
**Buses:** 20, 29, 69, 86, 87, 91, 96

The Place des Vosges is a square on the right bank of the Seine with a large park in the middle and symmetrical townhouses all around. Take a seat on a bench in the park to read the history of this *place* and some of its surroundings. Sit near the sandbox, so that you can watch the children play *à la française* despite the diminishing mix of Hebrew, Yiddish, and Arabic you'll hear. If it is cold, try the café, Ma Bourgogne.

This walk is our only walk on this side of the Seine. While the Left Bank was inhabited as far back as the sixth century, the Right Bank, or Marais ("marsh"), was not settled for another five hundred years or more because the area was too wet to be habitable. Even at the height of the Middle Ages, in about the thirteenth century, this land was still largely field and meadow, much of it Church lands. The major buildings were churches, chapels, and monasteries, with smaller dependent structures nearby. The one built-up street was the Rue St Antoine, which was the major road out of Paris to the east.

One hundred years later, the Marais was to become the center of fashionable Paris. The Rue St Antoine, because of its width from what is now the Rue de Sévigné to the Place de la Bastille, offered the best site in the city for the jousts and games that were the delight of the court and for the solemn processions, arrivals, and *cortèges* that were the public pageants of the day. When the center of Paris—that is, the Ile de la Cité—became dangerous for Charles V in the fourteenth century (a very troubled time, complicated by war with England, civil conflict, and urban uprisings), he moved to the Palais Saint-Pol (Saint-Paul) near the Bastille, where he could take care of business and pleasure and yet get out of town in a hurry. The king's presence drew to the neighborhood wealthy courtiers, who built large residences that, with their fields and gardens, towers, and walls, seemed like so many *châteaux* in an urban setting. One of these, called the Hôtel des Tournelles because of the small towers that marked its walls, came under the Crown in 1407 and replaced the Palais Saint-Pol as the royal residence. Tournelles was on the north side of the Rue St Antoine and included the area that is the Place des Vosges today.

Charles VI, who reigned from 1380 to 1422, was the first king to reside in the Hôtel des Tournelles. Six of his successors followed suit, although in 1527 François I moved the principal residence to the Louvre, reserving Tournelles for less serious activities. Among other things, there was a menagerie that featured camels, ostriches, and lions (recalled today by the Rue des Lions nearby). The custom of games, processions, and spectacles in the Rue St Antoine continued throughout the sixteenth century with the addition of *autos-da-fé* at which heretics (that is, Protestants) were burned for the salvation of their souls and the edification of the populace. It was here that Henri II, in June 1559, engaged in the joust that cost him his life and ended the role of Tournelles as royal residence.

The king had fought and won two jousts already that day, but he insisted on a third against the captain of his

Scottish Guards, Gabriel de Lorges, sire de Montgomery. At the first pass, both knights splintered their lances. The king wanted another run; Montgomery was reluctant. Of course, the king, savoring his success, had his way. Once again Montgomery's lance broke, but this time, by a freak accident, the point pushed up the visor of the king's helmet and entered his head above his eye. For ten days Henri suffered. The greatest doctors were called in; Ambroise Paré and Andreas Vesalius came all the way from Brussels. Four criminals under sentence of death were decapitated so that the doctors could study their cranial anatomy, but to no avail. Henri died, of infection if nothing else, and his widow, Catherine de Médicis, persuaded her son Charles IX to demolish the palace with its unhappy memories.

The ground on which the palace had stood was given over to a succession of improved roles. The militia used it for its exercises. The city installed stables and used some of the buildings to store powder. For many years the interior courtyard housed an active horse market that attracted many rogues, posing a growing problem for the authorities. The answer was found by Henri IV: the horse market would be replaced by a development project, Paris's first, a spacious, symmetrical public square to be known as the Place Royale, a place of respectable residence and assembly. The parceling of terrain began in 1605, and the first building finished was the large pavilion at the south end of the square. It marked an epoch in domestic architecture and set the example for the remaining construction.

The Place Royale was only one of Henri IV's three urbanization projects. Another, a set of large avenues that would radiate out from the *place*, was never built, and the third, the Place Dauphine on the tip of the Ile de la Cité, was only partially completed. (Today at the Place Dauphine you will find the splendid statue of the gallant Henri IV on horseback looking over the Seine.) The Place Royale, however, was the king's pet project, and he visited the construction daily to speed the workers along. In his plan for the large square, he reserved the south side for himself and the north for a silk factory *à la façon de Milan*. The east and west sides were to be sold in parcels to private owners.

The façades were to be all the same, built of brick with cut-stone (*pierre taillé*) trim. The ground floor was planned as a covered walkway with four arcades per lot; there were to be two floors above that, the whole capped with a steep slate roof encompassing another two floors decorated with mansard windows. At the center of the south end would be a raised pavilion for the king. Within a year or two, when the silk project failed, the north end was given its own pavilion for the queen and private residences matching those opposite. The open space in the center would be promenade, tournament ground, and stage for public events, functions that no street, however wide, could perform. There was no other public square in Paris at this time, and it was Henri's intention that all visiting foreign dignitaries arriving in Paris would enter by the gate just to the east of here at the Bastille, travel down the Rue St Antoine, and then turn into the Place Royale from what is now the Rue de Birague.

If, in principle, the buildings around the square were to be made of brick with stone trim, in fact only the first structures, including the Pavillon du Roi, lived up to the plan. It took a long time to lay brick, and Henri was in a hurry. Bricks and mortar were also expensive, especially in a city that had never before (and has never since) considered brick to be fashionable (and no doubt lacked skilled workers). In any event, the owners of the later buildings were only too happy to construct them of plaster on wood framing and then paint them to resemble brick in colors ranging from dusty pink to dark red. Some of this *trompe l'oeil* is still visible. It is surprising that these masterpieces of French architecture, praised for concept, size, proportions and colors, should in fact be mostly façade, but they are.

The artifice does not seem to have dimmed the square's glory, however. Although no king ever lived here (the Pavillon de Roi was far too small to accommodate the king and his retinue), the square was inhabited in the seventeenth century by the best society. Before the Faubourg St Germain des Prés became the chic neighborhood, the Marais, and especially the Place Royale, was the place where anyone who was anyone lived.

Unfortunately, Henri IV was assassinated shortly before the square's completion, and it was therefore inaugurated by the young Louis XIII. This is why the equestrian statue in the center of the square is one of Louis XIII, and not Henri IV. On April 5, 6, and 7, 1612, a fabulous tournament was held at the resplendent Place Royale. Jousting was, of course, forbidden; but five equestrian ballets were organized for the cavaliers, each with different exotic costumes, including one group dressed as American Indians. A description of one of the *quadrilles* will give you some idea of how elaborate these festivities were: the Duke of Longueville and his retainers were dressed in gray violet satin with silver embroidery; the pages and the horses were dressed in red velvet; four winged horses pulled a chariot with two rhinoceroses harnessed to the back; and two giants in blue satin preceded the duke himself, who rode a horse draped with repoussé plaques of silver and gold. There were 150 musicians in the *place*, continuous parades, fireworks at night, games, and this time, no untimely deaths. The square was packed with ten thousand people, some crowded onto viewing stands, some at the windows. (Members of the royal entourage had been assigned different houses and balconies from which to observe the tournament. In fact, the residents had been required to make their balconies available to the noblemen assigned to them. It was the first time that houses had been built with real balconies; until then Parisians had had only small stone ledges to lean on. Of course once the Place Royale had shown the way, balconies quickly became *de rigueur.*) The common people had to hang from the chimneys or squeeze into the recesses of the arcades.

The Place Royale was used frequently in the seventeenth century for tournaments and spectacles. Visiting ambassadors staged elaborate processions to show off the riches and costumes of their home countries. For many Parisians this was their only contact with a foreign culture, and dress and appearance were carefully scrutinized and discussed. Of one delegation Madame de Motteville wrote, after describing their rich clothes studded with jewels, "In general they are so fat that they give you heartburn, and concerning their bodies, they are dirty."

The Place Royale was also the favorite dueling ground for the hotbloods of the French aristocracy. The fashionable ladies of the *place* enjoyed the spectacle, and the swordsmen were encouraged by these ardent admirers. The fights were more than show, however. In 1614, three out of four antagonists were killed in one encounter, and over the years France lost some of its most valiant cavaliers in this square. In 1626, then, Richelieu, first minister of Louis XIII, forbade dueling on pain of death. The very prohibition was a challenge to French manhood. Only one year later there occurred a six-man duel (two principals and four seconds, who were expected to do more than hold the antagonists' coats) right in front of the Pavillon du Roi. Results: two dead, two fled to England, and two off to Lorraine. The latter two were caught *en route*, brought back to Paris, and decapitated, over the protests and appeals of the nobility of France. Richelieu was not a man to take insolence lightly. The incident cooled the ardor of the young blades, but only for a time. In 1643, after Richelieu's death, the last scion of the Protestant Colignys dueled with Henri, duc de Guise, grandson of the man who had killed Coligny's grandfather, Admiral Coligny, in the aftermath of the Saint Bartholomew's Day Massacre (1572). The duel was supposedly fought to champion two quarreling women, but who is to say that old, unavenged grievances did not enter into it? Anyway, the ladies watched and cheered their men on. Guise was wounded first, but managed to grab Coligny's épée, hold it, and simply finish him off. This time the king chose not to punish the victor.

Not all the action in the *place* was outside. The Place Royale was the center of Parisian social life, and such highborn ladies of the neighborhood as Ninon de Lenclos and Marion Delorme invented a new and durable institution, intimate gatherings (*ruelles*), at which the elegant guests rivaled one another in wit, fine speech, and social finesse. Molière parodied their excesses in his play *Les Précieuses Ridicules*. The predecessors of the fashionable salons of the eighteenth century, these encounters took place in the hostesses' bedrooms, perhaps because an amazing number of the hostesses were as renowned for their sexual as for their social prowess. Several of the great ladies of the Place Royale could hardly keep track of their lovers. We shall meet them later as we visit each house individually.

The fashionable lifestyle of the Place Royale spread to the rest of the Marais, and large *hôtels* (private residences) sprang up everywhere throughout this sparsely settled part of the city. Houses here were larger and more elegant than anything Paris had ever seen. With the streets filled with traffic, all it took was one noblewoman and her carriage to block everything and cause a great commotion. (Women wealthy enough to do so in the seventeenth century always traveled in carriages; the streets were too dirty to walk in and too dangerous, particularly at night.) The moneyed inhabitants of the Marais, and its location right at the edge of town, made the area ripe for thieves.

During the day the streets were thronged with soldiers, people in religious orders, and especially the poor, who stayed in the streets as much as possible to avoid their miserable and dingy huts. When night fell, however, anyone with honest intentions went home. There was no protection from those who roamed the dark streets. Lanterns were lit on moonless nights only, and one toss of a stone could throw an entire area into total darkness. What guards there were, were generally not interested in losing their lives to some brigand, so they chose to appear only after the battle was done and the bodies lay dead. Tallement des Réaux, chronicler of the Marais, reports that one night the Duchess of Rohan was returning from a ball when she was stopped by thieves. "Immediately," he recounts, "she put her hands on her pearls. One of these gallant men, to make her let go, grabbed her where women ordinarily defend themselves best; but he was dealing with a tough lady: 'That,' she said, 'you can't carry off, but you can take away my pearls.' " Fortunately, someone happened along, and the duchess was saved.

Beginning in the eighteenth century, the Marais went into a decline. The center of Paris fashion and social activity moved steadily westward. The aristocracy moved to the Faubourg St Honoré (where the Elysée Palace and the British and American embassies are now located), and the superb palaces of the Marais were abandoned to manufacturing and trade. Heavy machinery was bolted to elegant parquet floors; paneled walls were stripped or covered over; large reception rooms were divided into two-floored apartments; the spacious courtyards were filled with homely utilitarian sheds and shops. The whole area grew into an industrial center of small enterprise and craft shops, running from the old market (Les Halles) in central Paris to the Faubourg St Antoine east of the Bastille. With each updating of this walk, we find, with some regret, the steady disappearance of the small factories and craft shops. If not for these small enterprises it would have been the Place des Vosges that disappeared. They kept the buildings heated, roofed, occupied, and accessible.

This tendency continued into the nineteenth and twentieth centuries. The fashionable neighborhoods grew toward the west, in part because the prevailing winds came from that direction and carried the unpleasant odors of central and eastern Paris away from the residents of fine *quartiers*. And then, in the years after World War II, the trend reversed. The newly elegant districts of Passy and Auteuil filled up, and well-to-do Parisians, unwilling to settle in distant suburbs, began to look again at the long-abandoned buildings of the older neighborhoods. Antique residences came to have a new cachet—like old furniture and *objets d'art*.

The first areas to benefit from the new mode were on the Left Bank; we have talked about some of them in previous walks. Renewal of the Marais came later, with a special push from the Malraux law of 1972 requiring that the façades of all buildings be cleaned at least once every fourteen years. The law created an industry of this *ravalement*. It also transformed the appearance of Paris. Suddenly black and gray structures took on the colors of their youth. Paris became once again a city of light.

The Marais was one of the *quartiers* that benefited most from the new cleanliness; the *hôtels* were spectacular once one could see their lines and details. Some of them were now restored by the state; others were taken in hand by developers. There was no lack of customers waiting to pay small fortunes for apartments in renovated buildings. But there was also no lack of residents who were very happy to stay in their old quarters at low rents. The result was a small, quiet civil war. French tenancy laws made removal hard enough; politics made it far harder. There were abuses on both sides. Tenants organized themselves into defense committees and solicited support. Some of them were eventually scared or bullied into leaving; later, tenants held up badly needed improvements even when generous provision had been made either for their subsequent return or their relocation into what were often better accommodations. Militant denunciations and calls to resistance covered neighborhood walls. We found one slogan in a courtyard and started to copy it down. The concierge came out and asked us what we were doing. She was furious at the "troublemakers" and tried to scratch out the poster right in front of us. She was on the side of the "improvers" because they would bring in better and richer tenants and that would mean a substantial gain in status and income for her.

Now the tumult has quieted down. The new procedures are fairer; the worst abuses are behind. The Marais has become the neighborhood of choice for intellectuals, professionals, and those who want the feel of old Paris. Jack Lang, the Minister of Culture, lives in the Place des Vosges.

Before you begin a close look at the different houses in the *place*, take a look at the garden and the façades. The gate that you see today, in the railings surrounding the garden, is merely a poor imitation of the wrought-iron version with elaborate gold trim that originally stood here. The gate was locked at night, and each resident had his own key. During the Revolution the railing was almost torn down to be made into spears but was saved because a depot for military equipment already existed in the *place*. The gate inexplicably was torn down, however, during the reign of Louis Philippe, despite the eloquence of Victor Hugo on its behalf; it was replaced in 1839 by the uninteresting grill that you see before you today.

During the Revolution the Place Royale was renamed the Place de l'Indivisibilité, after the new Republic, one and indivisible. Then in 1800 the name was changed again: it became the Place des Vosges to honor the region that paid its taxes first.

At first glance you might think that all of the houses in the square are identical. But although the architectural plans for the square were strict, the individual owners still managed to put their marks on the buildings in discreet yet effective ways. The original plan for each dwelling or *pavillon* called for four arcades, and each *pavillon* was to have mansard windows, two round *oeil-de-boeuf*

*Northwest corner of the Place des Vosges*

("bull's-eye") windows and two square windows, all framed by the roofline. Yet every set of windows is slightly different. Look to see how, with time, ownership has changed the original four-pavilion plan into any number of variations.

Today, however, the most noticeable difference between buildings is between those that have been restored and those that have not. When you get inside the courtyards you will see that some with glowing façades are in terrible shape on the inside, and that some with marvelous courtyards are in disrepair outside.

The garden before you is the subject of great controversy: to keep or not to keep the trees, this is a recurrent question. To preservationists and purists, the large leafy trees are an intrusion. They weren't there in the first place, for a good reason: they block the view of the *place*. The French have always been devoted to vistas, which is one reason why Paris is such a beautiful city. Here in the Place des Vosges the original garden was minimal—lawns with paths cut on the diagonals—in order to leave an unobstructed view of the whole square.

The trees that are here today are the second set of trees to be planted in the garden. The circle of trees that originally surrounded the statue were stricken with Dutch elm disease and had to be replaced. The new trees obstruct more of the view of the entire *place*. When you visit the Musée Victor Hugo, look out of the windows from the second story on to the *place*. You will be astounded to see how magnificent the whole square looks when it is uninterrupted by the trees. You too may be tempted to side with the historical preservationists.

The children move about freely in a relaxed atmosphere that is unusual in Paris parks. The older people can sit on the benches in the leafy shade and converse, knit, and play checkers and chess while their children and grandchildren play happily. The park really fills with children between noon and 2 P.M. when the three schools tucked away in these imposing houses plus two more schools backing onto the *place* come out to play. This park, once the social center of the seventeenth-century upper class, has now become a playground for the highly diverse neighborhood population.

Begin walking at the Pavillon du Roi at no. 1 Place des Vosges, the center of the south wing. (As you face the Pavillon, odd numbers are on your right, even numbers are on your left.) The pavilion was never occupied by the king but by his concierge, or gatekeeper, who was the first resident of the building. Since 1666 it has been rented to different tenants and today is divided into apartments that are served by the unattractive stairs and lift built into the right-hand side of the entrance arcade. This blocking of the arcade is a very touchy subject to Parisians. The building is a classified historical monument and therefore should be returned to its original condition. But how, then, would the residents enter their building? Even more important, the stairwell blocks part of the vista from the Rue de Birague into the *place*, and as we have already noted, vistas are serious matters. As early as 1752, the writer Germain Brice said that these three arcades themselves should be torn down to leave the view of Louis XIII's statue unobstructed from the Rue St Antoine. That is perhaps too much to ask, but he also wrote:

> It has to hurt to see one of the three arcades under the pavilion blocked to make a nasty stairway which defaces entirely the entrance from the side of the Rue Royale [Rue de Birague today]. But we have such little care for public embellishments in Paris that we do not hesitate to spoil a vista or an entire square for the minor interests of some private person who has influence with the officials who are supposed to look after the decorations of the city.

Looking up at the façade of **no. 1** you will see that the balcony here is stone rather than wrought-iron and that the building is adorned with a bust of Henri IV, which was added at some unknown time. Walk through the arcade and look at the other side of the building from the Rue de Birague. On this side the pavilion is decorated with the arms and initials of Henri IV just above the arches; these date from the original construction. In the spring and summer many of the residents place window boxes filled with flowers on their balconies, and the building looks more as if it should be part of a narrow Mediterranean street than a king's pavilion in Paris.

Re-enter the *place* and look to the left at **no. 1 bis.** This residence, the Hôtel de Coulanges, is the last to remain in the hands of a single owner, Mme Cotin. More than twenty years ago she undertook the gigantic task of restoring the entire structure. She changed architects and contractors every few years, working first on the façade, then the interior, and back again. It has been a source of wonder to the neighbors, who watch what goes on with great interest. The present contractor, M. Sachet, of Sachet and Brulet, says with some pride that this is a prestige

job and therefore he decided to face the building with real brick even though false brick was stated in his contract. He is making up the difference in cost himself. Of the six arcades, the last two are in false brick, because each pavilion of four arcades must match and the first proprietor to restore sets the style of brick for the rest. The next two arcades had already been restored in false brick.

The building has one of the oldest wrought-iron balconies in Paris, built in 1655. Its straight, plain support poles are the sign of its authenticity. There are more of these early balconies in the *place*, but most are more modern with elaborately decorated supports. The rooms of this *hôtel* are reputed to have kept their seventeenth-century size as well as the painted walls and beamed ceilings that were so fashionable when the Place Royale was first built. The last windows on the right-hand side of the second floor have seventeenth-century interior shutters (*pan clos*).

The Hôtel de Coulanges is famous as the birthplace in 1626 of the marquise de Sévigné, née Marie de Rabutin-Chantal; note the plaque on the wall. This was the home of her maternal grandfather, Philippe de Coulanges; Marie, orphaned at two, lived here for ten years. At seventeen she was married off to the marquis de Sévigné. She had two children, one of them a daughter to whom she remained very close. After the death of her husband, who was killed in a duel in 1651, when she was still a very young woman, Madame de Sévigné rented different homes, always in the Marais. She was often courted and proposed to, but she chose instead to remain a widow, turning her aspiring lovers into friends. Meanwhile her daughter married the Comte de Grignan, who took his new wife to live in Provence, far from Paris and her mother. The separation was painful for Madame de Sévigné; she often disagreed violently with her daughter when they were together but missed her desperately when she was away. And it prompted one of the most famous series of letters in French literature. In her last years Madame de Sévigné lived in what is now known as the Hôtel Carnavalet. Some of her belongings and portraits can still be seen there.

In 1627 the Count of Montmorency-Bouteville hid here in the Hôtel de Coulanges after the duel, described earlier, that so piqued Cardinal Richelieu. As soon as things quieted down, he took off for Lorraine, but he would have done better to have run immediately. He was caught and put to death. Montmorency was well known in the Place Royale; he had been the lover of many of the women who lived here.

Fashion has been coming to the Marais in the form of the new young designers. Azzedine Alaïa was the first to move in at 17 Rue du Parc Royal. The first major designer has now moved into the Place. At **no. 3, Issey Miyake** has restored a space that was once an art school. The spare stone walls are now the backdrop for a single row of racks, each holding no more than five dresses. Each dress is a sculptural piece of art with a price to match. Other innovations here and beginning to show elsewhere are their incredible fabric imitations. The soft-as-butter "beaver" coat on the mannequin at the front of the store is more furry and more expensive than the genuine article. The color and thickness of the "cashmere sweaters" defy discovery of their composition. The door is locked and you must ring to be admitted—or you can just look in the windows.

The entrance at **no. 3** Place des Vosges is always unlocked. Push the door open and walk into a charming courtyard. This was one of the first buildings in the *place* to have been restored, and the owners are justly proud of their work. The door is open on principle: people should be able to see the interior courtyards as well as the façades. This is also the only building in the *place* with "brick" walls in the courtyard. If you look closely at the front façade of this courtyard you will see that the "brick" is painted, even down to the pipes in the corners.

The pipes are painted pink when they are in front of "brick" and ivory in front of the stone trim. The color is bright, but it has a pleasing effect, especially with the small garden and the elegant glassed-in terrace on the second floor of the back section of the building.

Note the windowed arches on the ground floor below the terrace. They were originally the entrance to a stable; this house was built in 1613 on the remains of the stables of the Hôtel des Tournelles. Two huge bronze urns stand against the back wall.

As you leave this open courtyard note the keystone piece in the center of the archway. The top part of the sculpture has been restored, but the bottom half is original and adds a softening touch to the severity of the stone.

The front staircase, the one on your right as you leave, is due to be restored. It is lovely, with wide stone steps and a wrought-iron railing. During the nineteenth century the banister had been remodeled with wooden inlays, which are handsome but, as a resident informed us, not authentic. They also have plans to return the garden to a classic French pattern but to keep the stanchions that ring it now.

As you go past **no. 5** look at the pavement to see rails installed to facilitate the delivery of heavy loads to the factory inside. If you want to see what the factory-filled Place des Vosages was like, open the door here and look inside.

One of the more exciting results of the bicentennial fever is that the **Hôtel de Sully** has been partially opened up to the public. The main entrance is on the Rue St Antoine but we can now enter through the back door in the corner of the Place at **no. 7**. In the past this was boarded up and children played ball against the wood. Today when you open the doorway, it is like stepping through a magic casement into the courtyard of a seventeenth-century palace. The *Orangerie* (a large, formal greenhouse that all self-respecting noblemen had in order to grow their own supply of fresh fruit in the winter) is on your right. Beyond the formal gardens is the main body of the *hôtel* with another courtyard on the other side of that and the façade with the main entrance on the street. This is what the French call *"entre cour et jardin"*— just what it takes to make a private house complete. Go through to the front to get the proper feeling of entering a magnificent private home.

In typical early seventeenth-century style, the street façade was built to impress, something it does admirably, especially compared to its tasteless neighbors. Two two-story pavilions are divided into three windows each and are crowned by a stately pyramid-shaped roof with an ornate semicircular window. Between the pavilions is the entry for horse and carriage leading into the spacious courtyard. The two wings leading to the main body of the house (the section straight ahead of you) were used for stables, a garage for carriages, the kitchens (noise and smelly cooking odors were kept far from the reception areas, guaranteeing cold meals in drafty rooms) and housing for the vast staff required to maintain a home of this magnitude.

Look up at the sculptured bas-reliefs above the doorways. On the body of the *hôtel* are female figures representing two of the four seasons, Fall and Winter. Spring and Summer are on the other side. The four elements are sculpted on the two wings: water with a rainbow and earth with a wild boar appear on your right; air with a chameleon and fire with a salamander (a mythical animal said to be able to withstand the heat of fire) on the left. The French use the word *salamandre* to designate a small ceramic space heater. The fashion for these symbolic sculptures dates from the end of the sixteenth century, and you will see more of them in the courtyard of the Carnavalet Museum later in the walk. We had always admired these allegorical sculptures in the Carnavalet, but in comparison these are carved with more depth and greater detail.

Pass between the two sphinxes with broken noses and enter the building. A little off-center, to the right, is a staircase that was already dated by the time it was built. It consists of two straight runs of stairs parallel to each other and covered by a vaulted ceiling. An apocryphal story has the Duc de Sully reprimanding his wife for letting her lovers use the main staircase. She may well have had several lovers, for the Duc was already seventy-five years old when he purchased the property. Inventories show, however, that her rooms were, contrary to tradition, on the ground floor and he was on the *étage noble*, or our second floor.

On the left are the portions of the *hôtel* that are always open to the public. The main room with painted beams is used for workshops that are related to the exhibits that are displayed in the suite of rooms behind. When we visited, a huge Lego project was under way with elementary school children. There was a perfect model of the Bastille to study and then the children were asked to build the buildings they would choose to put in its stead. The results were fabulous. This was part of a program initiated by the Ministry of Culture and designed to instill in the children of Paris an appreciation of their architectural heritage. The museums of Paris have become their workshops. This is one more indication of the pride and love the French have for their buildings and monuments. Passing back into the gardens, remember to look up at Spring and Summer over the door as you head back to the Place des Vosges.

Just around the corner there is a tiny shop called **Sifrène**. The owner, Mme Kung, sells fabrics that have been hand-quilted by carefully outlining the pattern in chain stitch. She says that there are two women in Paris who will do this work for her, and that it is very painstaking and slow.

At **no. 9** is the **Hôtel de Chaulnes**. Press the bell for Galerie N.D. Marquadt to enter the courtyard; it is always open because of the art gallery inside. This is one of the larger, more elegant *hôtels*, and it is part of a guided tour given by the Monuments Historiques (once a month only) that will take you inside this building and inside the Hôtel de Sully. The tour, given in French, is announced in *Pariscope* and *L'Officiel des Spectacles*. If you understand even a little French, it is well worth going.

The Hôtel de Chaulnes, built in 1607, was one of the most luxurious houses in the Place Royale. Louis XIII stayed here when the tournament inaugurated the *place*. The Hôtel de Chaulnes was also the site of the royal reviewing stand during all the public events that were held here. In 1644 the building was bought by Honoré d'Albret, maréchal de France, duc de Chaulnes, and peer of France. The Chaulnes were a wealthy family, and much of the decoration was done by them. When the duke died, his widow remodeled the house to include a new dining room and an oratory in the left wing. In 1655 her third son, a man who was accustomed to living well, inherited the residence. (His two older brothers had disappeared.) He hired Mansart, the famous architect, to extend the right wing of the house back to the Rue de Turenne. Mansart designed a façade with a large triangular *fronton* in the roofline. Unfortunately, today this wing is partially obscured by a gallery that cuts into its center. Mansart also built a monumental staircase to serve this newly expanded wing, but the wrought-iron stair rail was sold to someone in England in the nineteenth century. In the expanded courtyard the new duc de Chaulnes had a huge formal garden planted with a fountain and a *trompe l'oeil* perspective painted on the back wall. One of the few touches remaining today from the Chaulnes era is a room with a painted-beam ceiling in the left wing. This was the duchess's oratory, but it was later converted into a kitchen and plastered over, and it was the thick covering of plaster that happily has preserved the wooden beams for us.

In 1695 the building was sold to the Nicolaï family. They restored it in a neoclassical style with stucco ceiling decorations that were recently uncovered when layers of paint were stripped off. Legend has it that during the Revolution, Aimard Charles de Nicolaï hid in his wife's boudoir closet when the *sansculottes* came looking for him. He was discovered, however, and led straight to the guillotine. The *hôtel* itself was seized and not returned until 1795, after the Terror had run its course. By that time only one of the four Nicolaï brothers still had his head.

Elisa Félix (1820–1858), better known as Mlle Rachel and one of France's most famous actresses, lived here in the mid-nineteenth century. She was renowned especially for her performance in the role of Phèdre, which she played for the first time in 1838. Rachel died in Egypt, but her body was returned to Paris, and a great funeral service was held in the synagogue at no. 14, on the other side of the Place des Vosges.

Today the entire second floor of **no. 9** is owned by the Architecture Society, an élite group of one hundred members who use this center for conferences and reflection. It is they who are responsible for the restoration of the building (outside shutters date from the eighteenth century), who cleaned the façade and who did some marvelous work in the interior, which you should try to see.

The courtyard of this *hôtel* is very large. One of the first things you notice is a statue of a satyr. Viewed from the side, it has an amusing symmetry of profile. The right wing of the building still reflects the work of Mansart, despite the gallery at the back. Note the arched doorways with the *mascarons* above them. The large *fronton* gives a pale idea of how grand the newly designed wing must have been in the seventeenth century. A huge warehouse-like gallery, Nikki Diana Marquadt, has moved into the courtyard after the retirement of the owner of a lighting fixtures factory that had been a fixture of the Place since the beginning of the century.

As busy and noisy and full of people as the factory was, and friendly too, this huge empty space contained

*No. 13 Place des Vosges*

only two twelve-foot-high, trophy-shaped sculptures. On the right wall there was a ten-foot-square tile mural, decorated with black-and-white photographs of small people pasted onto it. If this gallery survives you will surely see something equally astounding when you visit.

Look in the doorway of the right wing to get a feeling of the volume of the stairway Mansart designed, even though the railing is now gone. In the left wing, through the last second-floor window—if the lighting is right and the curtains are open—you can see the painted pink-and-green beams of Madame de Chaulnes's oratory. The beams, decorated with a C and a D for Chaulnes and Dailly (the duchess's maiden name), were painted in 1654, among the last in Paris to be thus decorated, for that fashion ended around 1650.

There is a second courtyard behind and to the left of the one we are in now. This is a charming, hidden corner of Paris, one that most visitors to the *place* never see. The houses here are privately owned and may have been the stables or servants' quarters of the original estate. In a tiny garden the statue of a girl holding a bunch of roses is surrounded by real roses.

**L'Ambroisie** at **no. 9** is one of the points of pride in the revitalized Place. One of the newer Michelin three-star restaurants, it is the only world-class restaurant in the Marais. Half of this writing team went there for lunch (dinner reservations were unavailable for at least a month) as an anniversary present from the children. Lunch cost $250 for two of us. The food was extraordinarily fine, in nuance and taste, and yet unambiguous; subtle, and yet the essence of each ingredient remained clear and distinct on the palate. The menu changes, but there are three standard and supplementary offerings that accompany each meal. The *trou normand*, a rinsing of the palate between courses, was a fruit sorbet set in a sabayon sauce. The *trou normand* was originally a shot of alcohol (calvados no doubt) between two courses to clear the palate to make room for more. Maupassant writes (free translation) in his *Contes de la Becasse*: "Between each serving, the norman hole was made with a glass of eau-de-vie that lit a fire in the belly and madness in the head." Custom continues, but in a much weakened form. The other additions to the meal were a feathery light warm chocolate mousse and a mix of citrus fruits in syrup to help cut the sweet but light desserts.

The decor here is in the style of a men's club. The tables are far apart and the seating is luxurious. Service is, as to be expected, outstanding.

**No. 13,** Hôtel d'Antoine de Rochebaron, marquis de Villequier, was originally one of the most elegant houses of the square, and it is now restored to its grand state. According to a description of the house as it once was, it was a gem, with decorations by all the best artists of the time. Stucco ornaments by Van Obstal were painted by Vouet; an alcove was decorated by Buirette, the foremost wood sculptor of the time, who had *"épuisé tout son savoir"* ("exhausted all his skill") in making it. There was a *salon à l'Italienne* with a huge fireplace decorated with silver and gold. The *salon* itself calls for elaboration: it was two stories high, with a ceiling in the shape of a lantern and was lined with mirrors, a rare commodity in the seventeenth century. A chronicler writes:

> When reclining in this salon, if we look to the right, we see, through the two glass doors, opening on to the *place*, carriages, people on foot or on horseback, and all that is happening in the Place Royale; if we turn to the left, the same thing reflected in the mirrors is presented to our sight, so that, without getting out of bed, in summer as in winter, in sickness or health, we can enjoy the diversion.

After the marquis de Villequier, the house was owned by the ambassador to Venice, des Hameaux, who added to its luxurious appointments, installing precious paintings, furniture, and even more mirrors, brought from Italy.

For all the luxury upstairs, some readers may be more impressed by the facilities that existed below, in particular, a garage, which was formerly stables, large enough to hold three carriages and seven horses. Any city dweller who has had trouble parking his car will appreciate what that must have meant.

Today we have new wonders of restoration to see here instead. The property was bought by the Société Française de Promotion et de Gestion Immobilière (SFPGI), which administers apartment houses, and the work was financed by the Banque de Indo-Suez. Elegant as the building looks now, the Société's first set of plans was rejected by the Monuments Historiques as being too pompous for a popular neighborhood.

To see the splendid courtyard of no. 13, look through the windows of the rug shop. The back wings in the courtyard were reextended all the way to the Rue de Turenne, which was how the building stood in the seventeenth and eighteenth centuries, but the wings had been demolished by the twentieth century. The entire back section of the building is therefore new, though built in the style of the eighteenth century, while the front half of the building has been redone in the seventeenth-century brick style. The garden in the center is a copy of a classical French design, but here too, old and new merge; it is automatically watered every evening at eight o'clock by sunken sprinklers. Under the garden is a garage for the residents. This is the first underground garage in the Place des Vosges. (The entrance is just past the back grille and looks like the entrance to an apartment building of grand standing rather than a garage door, and many see it as the beginning of an end to the nuisance of motor traffic and parking in the *place*.)

The apartments are fabulous: parquet floors in the Versailles pattern, restored or rebuilt; huge fireplaces of red marble in the living rooms; ceilings almost sixteen feet high. Many of the rooms have interior lofts accessible by spiral staircases. Elevators have been recessed into the thick walls because the stairs are classified as historical monuments and may not be touched. **Popi Moreni,** an ultra-modern women's shop, was the first clothing shop in the *place*. Their collection is avant-garde with a strong personal style.

At **no. 17** is a new gallery, **Galerie des Indépendants,** replacing a former art gallery. The gallery features ten contemporary figurative painters.

At **Paco Funado, no. 19,** the Japanese designer can often be seen sitting at a small table, designing women's clothes. The store is spare. Each item stands by itself.

Next door, also at no. 19, is the very popular café **Ma Bourgogne.** Stop here for a cup of coffee with milk (café crème), no matter what the time of day, and if it is lunch-time, have one of their *charcuterie* platters from Auvergne. They specialize in these and in wine from Bourgogne and Bordeaux, but they also serve light lunches of all kinds. The waiters here are characters and enjoy teasing; they will offer advice whether asked or not. It also has a good WC. There has been a café here since 1920.

In the seventeenth century this building was owned by the *conseiller d'état*, Robert Aubrey, who lived here with his wife, Claude de Pretevel. Tallement des Réaux, the contemporary chronicler of life in the Marais, wrote astonishingly of this couple: *"Elle le méprisait beaucoup, de sorte qu'elle a pissé plus d'une fois dans les bouillons qu'elle lui faisait prendre."* ("She hated him so much that more than once she pissed into the soup that she gave him.") Hardly an appetizing legacy for a building that houses a café. Fortunately those manners are far be-hind us.

**No. 21** is another one of the larger and more elegant buildings in the *place*, with eight arcades. It was given to Cardinal Richelieu by Henri IV, but no one knows for sure if he ever lived here. Possibly he stayed here briefly while waiting for the Palais Royal to be completed. He bequeathed it to his grand-nephew, who then passed it on to his son. The son never lived here either, but he is rumored to have made good use of his pied-à-terre to know almost every woman in the *place*.

This *hôtel* was restored in the summer of 1978. Res-idents here have put a lot of money and care into the work. The arcades had originally been done in real brick, and the residents wanted to return them to their original condition. The Monuments Historiques was not eager to do it, but the owners insisted. They went to the brick-works in Versailles, which had made the original bricks in the seventeenth century, and they matched the missing parts as closely as possible. Compare this arcade with the fake paint and etched plaster of the others. The beauty of these arcades has now inspired other residents in the *place* to restore with real brick.

From out in the street, look at the façade of **no. 21** above the fifth pillar from the left, at some stones cut in little squiggles like vermicelli, the same kind used to decorate the Seine side of the Louvre. Some of these, the sharply cut ones, are new; the worn ones—the sixth to ninth squiggles on the left column—are the originals. M. Balmès, the owner of the antique shop here, says that the Monuments Historiques helped pay for the restoration of the façade and of the part of the roof that shows from the square and will also pay a small amount for any classified stairways or railings. Other renovations must be paid for by the owners of the building, which is one reason why the work goes so slowly and erratically.

Look closely at the sides of the arcade pillars right above the pediments, and you will find little square stone patches. These patches date from the Revolution, when this section of the arcade was used as a forge for making arms. They cover the points from which metal curtains were hung to close off the forge. As you walk you will notice many more of these patches in the sides of the pillars. Until around 1930 the arcades were filled with shops of all kinds—butchers, shoemakers, and so on— and each shop walled itself in by setting beams into cuts in the stone. There were so many little shops it was supposedly hard to make one's way through the arcade. The last survivor of this era was a shoemaker, who is said to have worked in the arcades as recently as the fifties.

Go into the courtyard (press the button next to the red light). It is large and sunny, well maintained and charming. Face the entry and look up at the windows on the front portion of the building. On the second floor you will see the original *pans clos* that were used in the seventeenth century. The second floor is owned by two brothers (there is a private enclosed staircase on the left as you enter). On the right is a small private garden (you may see a cat stalking the birds) and the entrance to a large staircase. The stair railing here was unfortunately sold to the United States in the last century. M. Balmès explains that Englishmen and Americans would come and ask the building owners to sell stair railings, offering them enough money to restore a whole building. The owners were thrilled then, but the current owners are sorry now.

In the back there is a kind of *orangerie*, dating from the latter half of the eighteenth century. No one knows what it was built for, but now it is a small factory with a small, carefully tended garden. On the left were the stables of the *hôtel*; today they make a sunny apartment with a terrace on top. The buildings in this courtyard all seem to vary slightly, which is partly explained by the fact that they were built at different times. But the layout has been the same since about 1750, as shown by Turgot's famous map of that time.

The **Richelieu** specializes in scientific instruments from earliest times to the twentieth century: clocks, optical devices, navigational aids. M. Balmès has a number of "masterpieces," the graduation projects that guild apprentices have made as a test of their skills and proof of readiness to work on their own. The guilds were all abolished in 1791, so these masterpieces are usually more than two hundred years old. They include small wrought-iron balconies or miniature staircases of exquisite detail. We also learned how lace was made by examining a *carreau*, a box with a square cushion overlaid with a paper pattern stuck with pins to weave the threads around. The threads were drawn from small bobbins, which in this case were still attached to the half-finished piece. M. Balmès is as much a collector as dealer, and his shop often looks empty. But do try the door. He is usually upstairs, but his wife will wait on you. If you are interested in something special, he will come down to help you. He also knows the Place des Vosges very well.

At **no. 21** the owners of **Les Deux Orphelines** collect eighteenth- and nineteenth-century *art populaire*, or country handicrafts, mainly in wood—marvelous ox yokes, wooden shoes, religious statues, and metal objects such as candlesticks, sconces, and planters. The prices are reasonable, and the merchandise is amusing.

Next door is Max Spira, a jumble of old and new twenties-style bric-a-brac. They are open at night.

Every Sunday afternoon and holidays Jacques Doudelle and his jazz orchestra play to more than a hundred admirers in front of **no. 22.** The clarinetist is so good everyone applauds in the middle of the performance. They sell records and cassettes on the spot.

At **no. 23,** notice the heavy wooden door decorated with thick wooden plaques attached with metal bolts. There are several doors of this kind in the *place*, and each one has its own pattern. This was the Hôtel de Marie-Charlotte de Balzac d'Entragues. Not only her name was impressive; her career was as well. She lived here with her mother, who had been the mistress of Charles IX. Her sister, Henriette d'Entragues, had been the mistress of Henri IV. (Decidedly, these ladies did not bring good luck to their lovers.) Marie-Charlotte was the mistress of the maréchal de Bassompierre and gave birth to his son, Louis, in 1610. Their relationship was very stormy, and Marie-Charlotte kept pressing the maréchal to marry her. He refused, reneging on his written promise. So Marie-Charlotte consoled herself with a series of lovers of equal distinction or equal means, among them the archbishop of Paris, Jean-François de Gondi, and the financier, Le Plessis-Guénégaud. We are told that there is a room in the house that still has painted beams dating from her residency, but we have never been inside.

At **no. 23** is the first of two **Galeries Médicis,** the oldest gallery in the Place. Madame Bourgois, the owner, ambitiously organizes thirteen exhibitions a year, with a band of regular artists—Bertière, Ogier, Ten, and others— who exhibit here once or even twice a year. On one visit Mme Ogier was there and autographed a poster of her work for us. This part of the gallery sells watercolors and wonderful inexpensive posters. The other location exhibits oil paintings.

Also at no. 23 is the charming **Guirlande de Julie.** The restaurant's lofty goal is to "make the dining an in-

*An arcade in the Place des Vosges*

termission from the absurd, an instant stolen from daily drudgery." The reality is that the interior is decorated in a soothing bower of green and pink and the food is excellent, beautifully presented and served, bounteous, refined, and with all that, not too expensive. With complimentary smoked salmon hors d'oeuvres, dinner costs about $30 per person. The name is from the history of the Place. The *Guirlande de Julie* was a small book of madrigals, each surrounded by a different flower, that the Duc de Montausier offered to his wife on May 22, 1641. The restaurant, like Coconnas, also in the Place, is owned by the colorful Claude Terrail, impresario of the three-star Tour D'Argent.

The courtyard and house on the right side of **no. 25** are lovely. The ground-floor window just past the doorway is a large hemisphere of glass usually associated with a shop-front window. This, however, is actually occupied as a private house. Formerly there was a trellis with plants rather than curtains, which permitted a glimpse of the living room. Under the frescoed ceiling, a huge stone fireplace on the right wall could hold three men standing upright.

Press the button marked "porte" and enter the courtyard. Pause for a moment to look around. It could almost be part of a farm. If it is warm and you are lucky, you will see rabbits hopping freely about, eating the vegetables that have been left out for them at the back. They have their own doorway cut in the base of the first door on the right. Look at the nicely done modern glass door in the rear to the right; the *mascaron* has been lost, but the stairs and their fine railing are still there. This whole right wing is owned by one family who lives there, we have been told, with untold birds, animals (including chinchillas), and plants!

The left side of the building is much more conventional. The entrance at the back is modern, but the old *mascaron* is still intact above the door.

You have now gone halfway around the square and are standing in front of the Pavillon de la Reine, which is opposite Henri's *pavillon* where we started. This one is exactly the same except for the sun emblem of the Médicis on the façade and the very long iron balcony. The small street here, the Rue de Béarn, was the exit route for all the parades that passed through the Place Royale.

The **Hôtel Pavillon de la Reine** would please a queen more than the Pavillon de la Reine, the central north pavilion of the Place. The *hôtel* is set back from the street behind a classical French garden. It looks as if it has always been there. It has all the comforts and luxuries of new *hôtels*, close to all the new goings-on in the Marais, and yet quiet and private. Double rooms cost $150, a duplex double $200, and an apartment for four $350. Clientele is largely European.

**No. 26** was the *hôtel* of the first *précieuse* of the Place des Vosges, Charlotte de Vieux-Pont. Today the building itself is not very interesting, but the shops that occupy the ground floor are.

The oil painting branch of the Galerie Médicis is here, replacing the Librairie Sylvie, a wonderful browsing bookstore specializing in old books on Paris. In the fifties, M. and Mme. Paillocher presented puppet plays in the square every Friday night. The whole neighborhood would turn out with their own chairs to see the productions. The square needs a bookstore like this and we were sorry when Mme Paillocher took her well-earned retirement.

Above this is an elegant and important gallery called **Jeannette Ostier.** Mme Ostier has been specializing in Japanese art for many years, trying to fulfill her goal of bringing it into historical perspective by emphasizing its artistic purity. She exhibits only traditional art, mainly drawings, engravings, and paintings. Most of her clients are serious collectors who order from catalogues. You might also be interested in the African art at Galerie Annamel.

**No. 24** has a fine wooden door, but the courtyard beyond is not very interesting. We will take a look at the shops here instead. The first, the **Jardin de Flore**, is an excellent print and engraving gallery. The remarkable doorway was made by the sculptor and jeweler, Jean Filhos. He constructed the frame out of a special acrylic combination that turned out to be poisonous. The work made him quite ill, but he has since recovered, and the results, a fantastic combination of Gothic and Art Nouveau, have repaid his effort if not his illness.

The Jardin de Flore sells all kinds of engravings and illustrated pages of antique manuscripts. This is a shop with excellent taste and knowledgeable service.

The antique shop that was here at no. 24 for many years has closed. You will no doubt see another art gallery here by the time you visit.

This *hôtel*, du maréchal de Geran, does not have so illustrious a history as some of the others, but it did have one famous (or notorious) resident, the wife of the maréchal de France, Duke of Bouffleurs. She was fourteen years old when she was married and quickly became known for her beauty, caustic wit, and number of lovers. This verse was written about her:

> *Quant Bouffleurs parut à cour,*
> *On crut voir la mère d'amour;*
> *Chacun s'empressait à lui plaire*
> *Et chacun l'avait à son tour.**

We are now at the end of one side of the *place*, at the corner where the Rue du Pas de la Mule joins the square. Originally there was a house here, and the street joined the square through the arcades of the house. The marks of the building are reportedly visible on the side of the wall of no. 22, but we have never found them. The building was torn down in 1823, making the northern side of the Place des Vosges a too-well-traveled route for cars headed toward the Bastille and the new Opéra.

Walk east out of the *place* to **no. 6** Rue du Pas de la Mule. This is one of the most fascinating shops in Paris. It is called the **Boucherie,** the "butcher's shop," and it no longer sells meat, but musical instruments. Note above the doorway the metal hooks from which the meat was hung. The tiled walls are original. M. Bissonet comes from a long line of butchers, and this shop was his until his passion for musical instruments gradually won out. He began by hanging violins and trumpets alongside his sausages, but eventually the meat vanished, and now the shop is crammed from floor to ceiling with instruments. His cold-storage room has become a library of books on

---

*When Bouffleurs appeared at court,/You would have thought you were looking at Venus;/Everyone tried to please her/And everyone had her in turn.

the topic, and his workrooms are now his office and a workshop to restore the instruments to their original playing condition. He showed us a silver-etched guitar, a porcelain trumpet, and a tuba made of Venetian glass. He also played for us a Breton bombardon, a flutelike instrument that is only twelve inches long and less than one inch wide but makes an enormous sound. He drew quite a crowd. The store also had a player piano that made the sounds of twenty-nine flutes, a mandolin, and violins in addition to the piano. It was built for a merry-go-round in 1920. He is so agreeable that he will play any instrument in the shop for you.

Return now to the Place des Vosges to continue the walk. On the corner at **no. 22** is **La Chope des Vosges.** This restaurant was once a café. The ground floor was lowered and a balcony installed in order to put in more tables. This is an excellent place for lunch, but get there early or reserve ahead of time; it is a popular neighborhood hangout. There is a table laden with hors d'oeuvres in front of you when you enter; this is the specialty. Their *plat du jour* provides a hearty hot meal at a reasonable price. In winter eat in the restored seventeenth-century building; in summer sit outdoors under the arcades. The recent enlargement and renovation of the restaurant cost the owner 3,000,000 francs (approximately $500,000). The Department of Historical Monuments would normally pay 30 percent of this charge, but the owner got tired of waiting and did it on his own. He is very proud of his restaurant, and justifiably so.

**Place des Vosges, no. 20,** a special gift shop, has replaced Déthy, a camping and ski equipment store there from 1938. It was, in fact, the only thing many Parisians seemed to know about the *place* when we first wrote about this walk in 1981. The Déthy family has now retired.

Mme Claudie Larive and her daughter have created a shop with a theme—the Place des Vosges. Most of the gifts are made to order and reflect the history of the *place*.

Delicious chocolates in the shape of thin squares to represent the cut stones of the façades of the *place* are a delicious example. Note: they keep afternoon hours only, including Sunday but not Monday.

Press the button above the keypad, enter the courtyard, and face the front wall (facing the *place*). It is in the midst of repairs that were halted ten years ago. An architect, known for prefabricated constructions, lived here and wanted to restore the façade. He had wanted to finish a nineteenth-century addition: a glassed-in hall on the first floor and a covered passageway on the second floor. Originally the apartments in these buildings had been built without halls; each room opened on to the following. Halls were added later, by taking space from the original rooms, which were usually large enough for the purpose. In this building, though, these halls were built on to the outside of the building. The architect's plan here was to build a new façade in the original seventeenth-century style that would encompass the hallways and incorporate them into the building. He began construction with hollow bricks, but when the authorities found out, they objected, saying that the original did not have bricks at all but rather plaster painted to resemble bricks. The decision? The building must remain *in statu quo*, that is, the ugly glass balcony and the partially completed work would have to remain as they were. Residents assure us that the work will be done this year, now that the architect has died. Not everyone is as lucky as M. Dhulster of the Auberge des Deux Signes, who was able to finish his excavation before anyone caught on (see pages 56–58). Of course, the Monuments Historiques assures the authenticity and quality of the work it endorses, so perhaps it's better that unauthorized restorations are stopped. But is a building better in indefinite limbo?

The walls here do serve a purpose, however, in their present condition: they give us a good opportunity to see how these buildings were constructed. Look at the window frames on the right and left of this wall as well as the corners. You can see how the large stones were used as a frame, which was then filled in with small stones and rubble and covered with plaster. This is essentially the same *colombage* technique used in the sixteenth century, except that here stone replaces the timber framing.

**No. 18** was the Hôtel de Marguerite de Béthune, the duchesse de Rohan and the daughter of Sully, Henri IV's first minister. Married at the age of nine in 1604, she later had innumerable lovers, many of them residents of the Place Royale. Of her nine children, only one daughter survived her. Today the building has little to offer from the seventeenth century other than a frieze in the Greek key pattern on its façade, which can be seen from the street. A glance at the windows of the apartment on the second floor with their *pans clos* hints at what riches may lie inside. The courtyard has been restored only in the entryway. The walls have been lined with wooden cupboards on the right and with pillars on the left. It is all new and somewhat attractive. The rest of the courtyard has not been touched, but take a look at the bronze statue of the gypsy in the stairwell on the left. She has lost the lantern from her left hand and one earring. The concierge proudly told us that Victor Hugo put the statue there, but we have not found mention of that anywhere else. We do know for a fact, though, that the gypsy was stolen some years ago. A woman resident called the police and got immediate results. The statue was found minutes later at the light on a nearby corner. Her head was sticking out of the back of a pickup truck. She is now firmly attached to her red marble base, which is firmly attached to the floor.

The gallery at **no. 18, Mythes et Legendes,** sells antiquities and archaeological artifacts. The furniture is mainly fifteenth- and sixteenth-century and of remarkable quality. (One desk had secret drawers and was decorated inside with a miniature theater made of inlaid woods.) The archaeological pieces come mainly from

South America; they don't stock pieces from Africa or the South Pacific here because they feel they would become too diversified. The gallery puts out a catalogue every year, and much business is done by mail order. Each sale is accompanied by a certificate of authenticity and the gallery guarantees it will buy back any piece for the original sale price at any time. We asked where they got their merchandise, and they said it came from French sources. Since nothing pre-Columbian can be exported any longer these objects get rarer and more valuable every year. Mexican pieces (Mayan and Aztec), we are told, are the most expensive. But the shop also carries small sculpted fragments, attractively mounted on Plexiglas stands, that are not prohibitively priced. Take a look here; it is like a museum, except that everything is for sale.

**No. 16** was owned in the seventeenth century by a royal counselor named François le Roux, who had the dubious distinction of marrying *"une petit garce qui se donnait pour un quart d'écu"* ("a little bitch who gave herself for a quarter of an *écu*"). That was slightly less than a *livre*, but in those days a *livre* was a day's wages for a manual worker, so Mme Le Roux was not cheap after all. Anyway, she had a lot of amateur competition in this area, as we have seen. Today the courtyard needs restoration, but take a look at its wrought-iron railing and the *mascarons* over the portal and entry.

A most pleasant place for lunch or afternoon tea is **Nectarine**. Lunch is mainly salads and vegetable pies, while a changing array of luscious cakes and tarts will tempt you either for dessert or as an afternoon reenergizer with a cup of tea. A dense chocolate cake is always appropriate; in the summer try their ice creams.

A new gallery of contemporary art, **Galerie Philip**, is also at **no. 16**. Again a gallery replaces a gallery. The exposition here changes every two months. Their main artists are Karskaya (Russian), Music (Yugoslavian), and a sculptor, Parvine Curie (French).

The **Hôtel de l'Abbé de la Rivière, no. 14,** is now one

of the best restored in the *place*. The six arcades have been redone in real brick and the wrought-iron balconies have been cleaned of rust. Notice the balcony and the campanile on the roof, which was added at a later date. Step back from the building to look at the roofline and see the arched back of the façade of the building's entrance on the Rue des Tournelles. Today this is a synagogue, and the half of the building that faces the Place des Vosges is used by the Ashkenazic community (the eastern European Jews who are mostly Yiddish-speaking); the half on the Rue des Tournelles belongs to the Sephardic community (Jews who settled in Spain and Portugal; now most are from North Africa). The doors on the *place* are sometimes locked, but you can always enter on Friday evenings and Saturday mornings when services are being held.

The walls are wood-paneled; the stairs are carpeted with Oriental rugs; plants sit in the entry. The interior resembles a Victorian home. Indeed, this half once was; the Chief Rabbi of France lived here with his five children. There is an art gallery on the third floor, exhibiting Jewish artists. Visitors are welcome.

The Sephardic synagogue on the other side of the building serves the growing Oriental Jewish community. It has a large Moorish sanctuary, the stucco pillars are painted with words and designs, and the ceiling, high above the sanctuary, is rounded in a long arch.

The house takes its name from one of its seventeenth-century owners, the abbé de la Rivière, favorite of the duc d'Orléans, tutor of the duke's children, and himself promoted to duke and bishop of Langres. This son of a tailor, a veritable model of social advancement through the Church, never did realize his dearest ambition, however—to be made a cardinal. The best painters of the era, Le Brun and Mignard, created a fabulous interior that is now in the Hôtel Carnavalet.

When la Rivière died, a poet composed the following verse:

*Ci-gît un très grand personnage*
*Qui fut un illustre lignage*
*Qui posséda mille vertus*
*Qui ne trompa jamais, fut toujours très sage.*
*Je n'en dirai pas plus,*
*C'est trop mentir pour cent écus.**

The *hôtel* was later used as a neighborhood city hall for what was then the eighth section. That role is commemorated by a plaque that is barely legible. Later it was used as a school.

Next door to the synagogue is a school—a public nursery school for children aged two to six. If you are interested you can visit between 3:45 and 4:15.

**Eurydice**, at **no. 10,** serves tasty light meals and a superb chocolate cake.

**No. 8,** as the plaque tells us, was the home of the poet Théophile Gautier, who lent his name to the commercial high school next door.

The **Musée Victor Hugo** is at **no. 6**; it was Hugo's residence from 1832–48. Before Hugo's time it was the *hôtel* of the princesse de Guéménée, Anne de Montbazon. She was the most famous *précieuse* of the *place*. She was married at twelve to her cousin, the prince, and like other premature wives of the day, never settled into monogamy. Anne was mistress of the coadjutor of Retz; of the financier d'Emery; of the count Montmorency-Bouteville, beheaded in 1627 for his famous duel; of the duke Henri II of Montmorency, beheaded in 1632; of the count of Soissons, who died tragically in 1641; and of the counselor of Parliament, Auguste de Thou, beheaded in 1642. She did not bring luck to her lovers, but she herself lived to be eighty-one.

The princess is representative of her kind; the *pré-*

*Here lies a very great person/Who had an illustrious lineage/Who possessed a thousand virtues/Who never deceived, was always well behaved./ I won't say more,/That's too much lying for a hundred *écus.*

*cieuses* were liberated women. They established a literary style and a new standard for excellence of the French language. They were also sexually liberated, conducting their many affairs with the grudging consent of their husbands. They seem to have thrived on this, marrying at puberty and living to a ripe old age.

Marion Delorme may also have lived here in a small pavilion at the back, but most historians feel that it was unlikely that two famous women could peaceably share the same house, if only because of the traffic jam that would have resulted. Marion was a match for Anne in every way, in number of lovers and in the brilliance of her salon. She began her career as courtesan with Jacques Vallée, sieur Desbarreaux, a notorious "epicurean" (read hedonist) and, unforgivable at the time, an avowed atheist. Next came the Marquis de Cinq-Mars, a handsome, stylish courtier who made the mistake of plotting intrigue against Richelieu and lost his head, literally as well as figuratively. (The marquis may have died young, but his place in history and literature is assured as the protagonist of Alfred de Vigny's novel *Cinq-Mars*.)

After the execution of Cinq-Mars, Marion is said to have gone on to a long series of lovers, including George Villiers, the first Duke of Buckingham. (You may remember him in *The Three Musketeers*.) Also Louis II de Bourbon, Prince de Condé (called the great Condé), prince of the blood and the last of the great feudal barons. He was eight years younger than she and a great success with the ladies. Yet this great wencher had his own wife confined for her alleged unfaithfulness (which even the malicious gossips of the day refused to credit) and wrote his last letter to the king to ask that she never be released. Nice fellow. Last but not least, Marion is said to have gotten Cardinal Richelieu himself into her bed. Ironically, it was Richelieu's niece who was Condé's unfortunate wife, so everything was neatly kept in the family.

Marion, unlike the other great courtesans of her day, died early, in 1650, but as with other legendary figures, there were those who refused to believe she was gone. Some said she lived on to 1706, when she would have been ninety-three, or even 1741, when she would have been 128. Victor Hugo wrote a drama called *Marion Delorme*, and G. Bottesini wrote an opera of the same name. In a sense, therefore, she really *has* never died.

The property at no. 6 was large, stretching back to no. 17 Rue des Tournelles, with a discreet rear alley for quick exits, a feature that Hugo often used when visiting his mistresses.

Hugo lived here in a rented apartment one floor up until his disagreements with Louis Napoleon required him to flee into political exile on the isle of Jersey. Today the museum is on the first, second, and third floors of the building. Start at the top with the history of Hugo's life, move down to his drawings and mementos on the second, and then visit a recreation of his apartment on the first. The museum has restored his bedroom, adding his death mask, and the Japanese-style dining room that he built himself in his second home in Guernsey. Be sure to look out on to the *place* before you leave to get a good view of the whole square above the trees. The museum is open from 10 to 6 daily except Mondays and holidays.

At **no. 4, Fanny Liautard** has "created a universe of refined femininity," that is, lingerie that is so refined it can be worn in the house or out—extremely elegant and much of it made by women who sew to order in the back room.

**Marc-Annibal de Coconnas** is the restaurant at **no. 2** Place des Vosges, although its front door opens on to the Rue de Birague around the corner. This restaurant is owned by Claude Terrail, who also owns the Tour d'Argent, and it is no accident that both places provided locales for the movie *Who Is Killing the Great Chefs of Europe?* This restaurant is casual and moderately priced. Meals are *prix fixe*—no à la carte. The specialty is pot-au-feu. The menu no doubt commemorates Henri IV's promise of a "chicken in every pot."

Exit the *place* from the northwest corner by Ma Bourgogne, and turn to the **Rue des Francs-Bourgeois.** An entire chapter could be written on this street alone, but we will be briefer than that. It was first called the Rue des Poulies, named after the pulley, or wheel, on a loom, for the street was a street of weavers. It is still a street of fabrics. In the fourteenth century an almshouse was built here. The poor, too poor to pay taxes, were called "free citizens," *francs-bourgeois.* When we first researched this walk, this street had potential but was still dark and, for the most part, uninteresting. Today it is booming. New stores open daily, and the very narrow sidewalks are crowded with shoppers and gawkers, still mostly French. We are going to give you a brief rundown (you can take that literally if shopping bores you) going back and forth across the street. Watch when you cross.

On the corner of Turenne and Francs-Bourgeois, **no. 27 Rue de Turenne,** is **Pastavino**. If you have the stamina to eat standing up, this is terrific for a quick lunch of hot pasta or cold Italian deli plates. It is always packed with the younger set at lunchtime.

On Francs-Bourgeois itself the latest trend (who knows? maybe it will have already changed by the time you read this) is immediately obvious. The passion is American Western with a little country thrown in and some French chic for seasoning. **No. 3, Upside,** sells men's clothing with the emphasis on American Western. **No. 6, Chevignon Trading Post,** offers Taos-style furniture, Navajo rugs, American Indian crafts, country-style ducks, and other cute things of that ilk. For the French, this is the U.S.A. It's quite a culture shock after being immersed in the seventeenth century.

**No. 5, Monic Bijoux,** is an Ali Baba's cave of costume jewelry. They have drawers and drawers of it, much of it Nina Ricci costume pieces that the department stores carry, but the prices here are lower.

**No. 6** is **Catimini,** an adorable, expensive children's clothing store. Across the street at **no. 7** is **Casa Costanza**. This shoe store for men and women gets its shoes from a factory in Italy, bypassing the middleman in order to give you beautiful, stylish shoes at reasonable prices. **No. 8** is a serious art bookstore called **L'Art en Page**. Inside the courtyard at the same address is **Imex**, taking advantage of the fashion for fake furs. They sell coats and jackets in many styles and colors, including a faux fox boa, head and all. The final store in this building is **Autour du Monde/Country Furnishings/Home**, another American-style store, this one with an overwhelming odor of potpourri.

Across the street at **no. 13** is **Lipsic** for leather clothes, **Et Vous** at **no. 15** with smart Western-style clothing, and at **no. 17** both **Archetype,** an architectural drawings gallery, and the street's old-timer, **Jean Pierre de Castro**. When there were only some musty men's tailoring shops here, savvy French ladies came down here to buy silver by the pound. Flatware, candlesticks, bowls, and serving pieces in hundreds of styles, some famous French and English marks, most of it plated, fill baskets on tables. Lots of fun but a little heavy to carry home.

Crossing the street again is **no. 12, Les Bourgeoises,** a small, dark restaurant that anyone who wants a long, private chat might find just perfect. Up at the corner but still at the same address is the French version of Banana Republic, called **Autour du Monde**.

A shop full of miniature figures, especially animals and Viennese bronzes, is **La Charrue et les Etoiles** at **no. 19**. Bring home a souvenir of the small diorama scenes of Paris peopled with lead figures.

You have now reached the Rue de Sévigné and you will have to make a choice about which way to go. To your right are the Musée Carnavalet, the newly refurbished museum of the history of Paris; the continuation of Francs-Bourgeois to the Archives; or one block north to the Picasso Museum. Both routes lead to the Pompidou Center. These options are described in section 5A below. If you turn left (see section 5B), you can walk past the Hôtel Lamoignon, through the Jewish neighborhood, down to St Antoine and its street market, to a piece of the Philippe Auguste wall, the *hôtels* Sens and Aument, the Memorial to the Unknown Jewish Martyr, one of the oldest houses in Paris, and the Hôtel de Beauvais.

## 5 A

If you need a break before starting in on the Musée Carnavalet, the **Galerie Gourmande,** right across from the museum entrance at **no. 38 Rue de Sévigné**, serves all kinds of teas and cakes made by the owner. The specialty of the house is hot chocolate made from a recipe from 1912. It is the most luscious cup of hot chocolate we have ever tasted—even better than Angelina's on the Rue de Rivoli.

The best consequence of the excesses of the celebration of the bicentennial of the Revolution is the changes that it brought to the **Musée Carnavalet** at **23** Rue de Sévigné. In the last edition of this book we wrote, "The exterior is splendid. . . . The same can't be said of the interior. In the last decade most museums have changed from storehouses for the cognoscenti to educational institutions for the general public. The Carnavalet has not made this transition." Today, happily, it has, and a whole day could be devoted to the treasures displayed within. The museum has doubled in size by incorporating the neighboring *hôtel,* **Le Peletier de Saint Fargeau,** and thereby gaining space for the history of Paris from the Revolution to the twentieth century. Twenty million dollars were spent on the renovations and they were well worth it.

As you enter look at the bas reliefs of the four seasons by the sculptor Jean Goujon and mentally compare them to those in the courtyard of the Hôtel de Sully. Most visitors are interested in seeing the Revolutionary rooms and the Belle Epoque. Both are in the Peletier de Saint Fargeau portion of the museum, and with the help of the map, a chronological path can be traced. The Revolution is displayed in eleven rooms decorated in the style of the day. The exhibits combine paintings and documents with politically relevant porcelain, a model guillotine, and even a model of the Bastille made from the stones of the original.

After the passion and seriousness of the Revolution, the Belle Epoque (missing the equally serious history of the Paris Commune) was like the bubbles in a glass of champagne. With as much of the original furnishings as possible, the Carnavalet has reproduced several rooms from the period. Proust's cork-lined bedroom is there as well as a private dining room from the Café de Paris decorated in mauve with furniture by Louis Majorelle. The jewels that adorned the "Grandes Horizontales," as the *demi-mondaines* of that time were called, were purchased by their wealthy, ardent admirers in Fouquet, magnificently recreated here in all its Alphonse Mucha glory. The final room from the twentieth century was a great discovery to us. We entered and immediately realized we had been in this room before. We were in M. and Mme Maurice de Wendel's Art Deco salon, which was originally in their magnificent *hôtel* on the Quai de New York. The room was decorated by José Maria Sert in 1924 with panels of metal (the Wendel fortune came from iron and steel) painted in crimson and white gold and depicting the Queen of Sheba's journey across the desert to visit King Solomon. The queen is accompanied by an enormous retinue, and her accoutrements include fireworks, a menagerie, and even palm trees to be planted every evening to provide her with an oasis wherever she might be.

The original building of the museum, Mme de Sévigné's beloved home, will exhibit prehistoric, Merovingian, Carolingian, and medieval pieces that have been in storage for years as well as the entire pre-Revolutionary collection. The Orangerie of Le Peletier de Saint Fargeau should also be open by now with the historic collection of pictorial and rebus shop signs. Don't miss it.

Across the Rue des Franc-Bourgeois is the garden and orangerie of the **Hôtel Lamoignon** (see page 245). Note the Art Nouveau panels on what was once a bakery, now Le Garage. They are classified as historical decorations.

**Marais Plus** at **20 Rue Francs-Bourgeois** is a tea-book-gift shop worth looking into. This was the cultural center for the Marais until the city cut funding, and now it is all privately run. There are several specialties in this store. You'll notice the first displayed in the window—the collection of over one hundred teapots in the shape of houses, people, animals, etc. The downstairs is used to display travel and art books, the art books being of exceptional quality, with paintings reproduced so realistically on onionskin paper, that you think you are holding the fresco in your hands. Upstairs the tables and shelves are jammed with baskets and Chinese steamers filled with small toys and objects ranging in price from one to ten dollars. You can lunch on quiche and cakes and tea in a very casual atmosphere at the back of the ground floor. The shop is open until midnight every night.

Also at **no. 20** is **La Chaise Longue**, selling reproductions of the things we took for granted in the 1930s through the 1950s. **No. 29 bis** has a restored façade only.

**No. 31**, the **Hôtel d'Albret**, has recently been restored by the city as offices for the Cultural Affairs of the City of Paris. Originally built at the end of the fifteenth century for the Connetable (supreme commander of the royal army) de Montmorency, it has been repeatedly reworked over the centuries. Today it is a striking combination of preservation of the past and twentieth-century design. Examine the fine decorations of the façade and then enter the courtyard. On the right side were the stables. Today there is a Louis XIII staircase that ends in stone on the top floor. The cellars underneath have been restored for receptions. The left wing is called "the boat" because of the free-standing staircase that looks as if it came from an ocean liner. This wing has been painted the national colors of blue, white, and red to affirm the spirit of the city. Space was lost in this wing because the building started tipping and needed support when a staircase was removed from the entry. There is still an old staircase in the front left side. The wrought-iron railing is especially grand. The sculpture by Bernard Pagès was made for the Bicentennial.

Rue Elzevir on your right will lead you on a small detour to the Picasso Museum. Go one block up to the Place de Thorigny and cross diagonally left to the other side. At **no. 5 Rue Thorigny** the Hôtel Aubert de Fontenay, better known as the **Hôtel Salé,** is the recently restored home to the **Picasso Museum.** This beautiful *hôtel particulier* has been completely renovated to house a collection of works given by Picasso's heirs as a means of paying off their inheritance taxes. The paintings and sculptures, as well as photographs and personal papers, are chronologically displayed in what was a sumptuous private home of the king's tax collector in the seventeenth century. (The tax was on salt, hence the name.) Be sure to look at the main staircase, a forerunner of the majesty of the one at the Opéra.

Return to the Rue des Francs-Bourgeois, where at **no. 33, Valerie Stern** sells "wholesale" women's clothing to individual buyers. The selection leans to the conservative but pretty and the prices are definitely reasonable. Across the street the **Hôtel de Sandreville** at **no. 26** has a Louis XVI façade. In the courtyard, unfortunately, the original ground floor in brick and stone is hidden by "parasite" buildings. Across the street at **no. 35** the **Maison de l'Europe** is now a center for international meetings. This was the **Hôtel de Coulanges** built in the mid-seventeenth century. It was nearly torn down in the sixties, but a media campaign saved it. Enter the courtyard to see the arcaded façade, the *mascarons*, and the wrought-iron staircase on the right.

No. 30, the **Hôtel d'Almeras**, is in the same brick-and-stone pattern as the Place. Push the door button and stand at the grill to see a beautiful courtyard. Henri IV's bust looks down from the third story, and if the light is right (within or without), you will see the beams in the ceilings of the lovely apartments.

The blue store, **Murat and Co.**, has a fine collection of toys at reasonable prices, and is run by very nice people.

At **no. 45** there is an unusual store with an unusual name, **A L'Image du Grenier sur L'Eau** ("the picture of the barn on the water"). Here two brothers have assembled postcards from the last quarter of the nineteenth century to 1945 in hundreds of drawers classified by every possible subject. The cards range in price from a dollar to one hundred dollars. If you can bear to mail them, they make a great change from the typical tourist cards you have already sent home.

At the corner of Francs-Bourgeois and Rue Vieille du Temple you will immediately notice the flamboyant Gothic tower. This is a reconstruction from the manor house of **Hérouët**, which was destroyed by the last German bombing of Paris in August 1944. For years the building was supported by heavy railroad-type buttresses extending out into the street. Two short blocks to the south (toward St Antoine and the Seine) there is the very pleasant and reasonable restaurant **Le Gamin de Paris (no. 51 Rue Vieille du Temple)**, one block to your left. Come here on the early side (before 7:30 and before the lines—people wait in the street) for an excellent bistro-style dinner.

Turn right down Rue Vieille du Temple to **no. 87** and enter the courtyard of the Palais de Rohan. On the wall to your right, you will see the famous and fabulous horses of Apollo riding out of the stone they are sculpted from. The more you look at these horses of the air, the more detail you see.

Back on Francs-Bourgeois, note the elegant discount *parfumerie* on the corner.

One of the most architecturally interesting restaurants in Paris is at **no. 53 bis Rue des Francs-Bourgeois. Le Dômarais** was originally the chapel for the religious order of the Blancs-Manteaux and then was used as the auction room of the municipal pawn bank (the Crédit Municipal or *mont de piété*, colloquially known as *"ma tante"*). The restaurant is behind a very small courtyard past the kitchens. It is a large round room encircled by a high balcony. The ceiling is a glass dome (hence the name) and quite spectacular. On our last visit, we found a new chef and had a superb meal at reasonable prices. If you are cigarette-smoked out of small, cozy restaurants, this is the place for you. The ceiling is so high you will breathe freely regardless of your neighbors. Be sure to visit the clever and pretty WC at the balcony level.

Enter **no. 55,** the courtyard of the Crédit Municipal, the government-run pawn shop. The wall surrounding Paris, begun by Philippe Auguste about 1190 (see the plaque on the wall), cut across this yard. It occupied the space traced on the ground. If you are on the entry side, you would have been outside the boundaries of twelfth-century Paris.

Walk right through the second courtyard to a large tower at the corner of the building. The base is a section of Philippe Auguste's wall, and the building opposite is decorated with *mascarons* of women, lions, and a satyr. Today the building is Munigarde, a storage and security facility for works of art. Turn right toward the street to see a doorway, the remains of a house that once stood there, and an antique column.

The **National Archives** at **no. 67 Rue des Francs-Bourgeois** is the entrance to a large complex extending east-west from Rue Vieille du Temple and Archives to

north-south from the Rue des Quatre Fils to the Rue des Francs-Bourgeois. Within this perimeter are to be found two of the most beautiful *hôtels* of the old regimes, the Palais de Soubise and the Palais de Rohan, both visitable.

Until recently the Palais de Soubise in front of you was used for consultation of the national archives. The great reception rooms that once heard the rustle of silks and the music of dance now heard the whisperings of researchers and the scratching of pens. The oldest construction in the complex is the medieval gate with its two round towers and escutcheons on the walls on the Rue des Archives about 100 yards to your left around the corner. This is all that the Prince de Soubise left from the fourteenth-century fortress that was originally built by Olivier de Clisson. This is a great boon, especially for the residents who have the pleasure of seeing a piece of the Middle Ages illuminated at night.

The Prince de Soubise, who once lived at 13 Place des Vosges, found much wider scope here, as can be seen from this grandest colonnaded courtyard and the large gardens behind and to the side. The most beautiful rooms, decorated by Boffrand, designer-architect, in the rococo style, give on to the interior garden. The sun fills these rooms, painted in pale pastels with white sculpted panels and ceilings covered with scenes of Venus at her toilette and the Education of Love.

The archives have now moved to the Rue des Quatre Fils in an electronically up-to-date building, and the palace is used for receptions—a kind of republican return to royalist elegance.

On the corner is a fascinating shop that sells memories of French history—medals, seals, facsimiles, and the like. They make wonderfully decorative and historic gifts.

At the corner of the Rue des Archives, the Rue des Francs-Bourgeois changes its name to the Rue Rambuteau. This is a market street, and in two fairly long blocks it leads right into the pedestrian zone that comprises the

**Pompidou Center**, commonly known as Beaubourg, the **Place Igor Stravinsky**, and the **Quartier de L'Horloge**. A good part of a day can be devoted to this area alone. The Pompidou Center, after being reviled by everyone in Paris, is now the most visited attraction in the city, surpassing the Eiffel Tower, which also had a history of intense criticism when it was first built. When the Center went up, with all its colored entrails of ducts and pipes (water, gas, air, and electricity) on the outside, the Parisians were horrified. The interior houses a free exhibit area, the largest open-stack library in the city, and the Museum of Modern Art. Be sure to ride the caterpillarlike escalator in the clear tube on the front of the building to the roof-top café. This will give you a bird's-eye view of the musicians, magicians, and fire-eaters (*cracheurs de feu*) in the plaza below and of the city spread out all around you.

The Place Stravinsky is to your left as you exit from the Center. The brightly colored sculptures by Nikki St. Phalle and intricate and mechanical metal automats by Tingley bob in the large rectangular fountain. Surrounded by playing children, this makes a perfect spot for a relaxing, people-watching drink in the sun at any of the tea-shops that border the area.

The Quartier de l'Horloge to the north of the Place Beaubourg is a combination of apartments and shops named for the huge brass clock in the heart of its interior courtyard. The clock, made of hammered and polished lead, was built by Jacques Monestier and inaugurated here in 1979. The sculpture represents a man, The Defender of Time, in his victorious struggle against attacks by a dragon, a crab, and a rooster. They symbolize the earth, the sea, and the sky. Rumblings of the earth, stormy waves, and blustering wind accompany each attacker. At noon, 6, and 10 P.M., the man is attacked by all three. At all other hours he has the easier task of fending off only one of the three, chosen at random. The *automate* weighs one ton and is about 12 feet high. Worth seeing.

For reasons of space we have not detailed all the streets in this area, but that does not mean that you should skip them. They are laced with historical buildings, interesting shops, and restaurants.

The **Hôtel Lamoignon** is on the corner of the Rue Pavée, one of the first paved streets of Paris. Before reaching the corner, look at the lovely garden that is part of the Hôtel Lamoignon. The *hôtel* was originally built in 1555 by Robert de Beauvais, counselor to the king and comptroller general of the city of Paris. He died in 1568, and the property was purchased by Diane de France, duchess of Angoulême. She was the natural daughter of Henri II. It seems her mother, who was Italian, had refused the king's advances. Not deterred, he had her house burned down in order to kidnap her. Diane was legitimized and became one of the important women of her time, "wise in counsel, beautiful, and the finest woman on horseback."

Notice the square-windowed turret at the corner. A few other such turrets can still be found, one at the Hôtel de Sens. They are the last survivors of what was once a popular design that allowed householders to see what was happening in every direction. The initials S.C. carved into the stone on the base of the turret supports mark the limits of the property owned by the Culture of St Catherine, the largest religious settlement on the Right Bank.

In the circular pediment of the entrance wall there are statues of two children. One holds a mirror, Truth, the other, a serpent, Prudence. Today, the *hôtel* has been completely restored and enlarged. The right wing, built as recently as 1968, and in perfect harmony with the original section, houses the library of the City of Paris. Go into the courtyard, turn right up a few steps and left into the reading room, sit down, rest, and admire this beautiful room—its proportions, windows, and view, and the painted beams with Diane in the middle of a back beam. There is always an interesting exhibition here. When you are done browsing, take a look at the mausoleum to your left in the courtyard.

Return to the Rue Pavée. Spot the small antique store with no name on your left. It is crowded with porcelain, glass, prints, and other small objects.

**Rue des Rosiers:** The coming of high fashion on the Rue des Rosiers is a kind of public announcement that the Marais and its beautifully renovated buildings have been discovered. The real estate is now some of the most valuable in Paris. Ten years ago, it was some of the least valuable. **Lolita Lempicka,** a young designer, has opened on both corners of the street, **3** and **2 bis,** one shop for women, and one for younger women. The fashion, although high styled and high priced, is quite wearable. As with many young designers today, the look is Deco. There are always people looking in the windows and people inside buying. Next door, another fashion shop with dresses for special occasions, **Labels,** prints all the designer names on the door. Another bow to fashion is **Apparence,** recently a kosher butcher, now a fake-fur store. Quite a change for this neighborhood.

Across the street was a hammam, a Turkish bath, where the chicest, slimmest ladies came from all over Paris to keep thin and fit, the better to buy the clothes across the street. It has been bought by the owners of the Chevignon stores and will have a restaurant, curiosities, a bookstore, and a trading port. The entire neighborhood mourns the loss of this establishment. The beautifully tiled walls and pool will be dismantled.

None of this, however, reveals the real history of the street. The Rue des Rosiers is the historic home and first stop for Jewish immigrants and refugees. It plays the same role for French Jews as the Lower East Side once did in New York. When Jews were forced to leave Eastern Europe because of pogroms at the end of the nineteenth century, they came here. When Jews fled the Nazis, they again came here. This is also the street the Nazis and the Vichy French marched down in order to drag out 75,000 Jews to concentration camps.

A third wave of immigrants arrived as a result of the French exodus from Algeria. This time the newcomers included both Muslims and Jews, who live side by side in the area. The corner of Rue des Rosiers and Rue Ferdinand Duval, the center of the Jewish quarter, is marked by the restaurant **Goldenberg**, which serves all the typical eastern European Jewish dishes. This was the scene of a terrorist attack in which four people were killed in the summer of 1982. A sign on your right as you enter reads in part: *"on ne cède pas au terrorisme"* ("we don't give in to terrorism"). Goldenberg is not strictly kosher, but other places in the area are. From near Goldenberg's on down, the street is still Jewish, but we wonder for how long. It is dotted with butchers, bakers, fast-food *schwarma* and felafel places, bookstores, stores that sell religious articles, and appetizer stores. One, in particular, is worth the visit. **Finkelsztain**, at **no. 27**, sells the finest breads, cakes, and appetizers. The dark rye bakes so slowly it takes on a caramelized taste. The eggplant is smooth and silky, topped with sesame seeds. Even if food doesn't tempt you, enter the store and look at the photograph above the cheesecake table in the right rear. It shows nineteen children who lived in a home because their parents had been picked up by the Vichy for the Nazis. The picture, taken in 1944, was taken on the eve of their departure to foster homes in the south, because they had reason to believe they would be picked up the next day. A somber reminder of tragedy in the midst of sweets.

Now, return through this crowded street (except on Friday afternoons and Saturdays), to the corner of Pavée and Rosiers. Watch the dramas unfold among the cars that cram and jam and inch forward. Down the Rue Pavée at **no. 10** is the synagogue built in 1913 by the famous Art Nouveau architect of the *métro*, Hector

Guimard. The design recalls the shape of the Ten Com-
mandments tablet.

Walk down to the Rue St Antoine and the *métro* St
Paul. You will find the eighteenth-century church of the
same name. To the right is an entrance to the **Lycée
Charlemagne,** a secondary school. The first thing that
will surprise you is a large marble plaque commemorating the death of its students in the First World War.
There are five hundred names, often two sons from one
family. Turn right into a courtyard and look: it is 1900s,
without any of the charm and with all the inconve-
niences.

Continuing on St Antoine will take you, on the right
side of the street, to a street market. Barrows of fresh food
on the edges of the street are competition for the shops
behind them. A crowd of serious food shoppers blocks
the way with lines and baskets. It outdoes anything we
have at home, matches Buci in the fifth arrondissement
and Belles Feuilles in the sixteenth, but Mouffetard (see
Walk 4) still wins.

**No. 53** Rue St Antoine, M. Bassonis's fish shop, was
recently on television to show off its Art Nouveau ceramic walls. The decorating plans had just been discovered in the Sarreguemines factory that produced the tiles.
The shop is classified, and justly so, as a historical monument.

One block east of the église St Paul, turn right on the
Rue St Paul to the antique shop quarter known as **Le
Village St Paul.** There you will find open, afternoons
only, close to fifty antique stores clustered together, all
offering their specialties—from two hundred to twenty
years ago. It is a friendly place with lots of opportunity
for browsing. The dealers have earned their good reputation.

Take the Rue Charlemagne one block and make a left
to see, on the Rue des Jardins St Paul, the largest remaining piece of the **Philippe Auguste wall,** complete with
the remains of two lookout towers. Today it forms the
wall of the yard of the primary school Charlemagne.

The **Hôtel de Sens, no. 1 Rue du Figuier** (toward the Seine), is one of the oldest buildings in the Marais. It was first a small fortified castle in 1475 for the archbishop of Sens, a religious and military-minded man. In 1605 this became the residence of *"chère Margot"* (see page 125). Be sure to find the hole above the portal that was used for dropping boiling oil on unwelcome visitors.

On the corner to the west is another grand *hôtel*, the Hôtel d'Aumont. Its history goes back to the fifteenth century, ownership passing from one important family to another. It fell, nevertheless, into disrepair, and the city of Paris finally undertook its restoration in 1938. Today it is part of the International City of Arts, next door on the quai. Except for a fine *mascaron* above the heavily sculpted doorway, the hotel has little decoration.

Walk west, past the **Cité des Arts**, to the Rue Geoffroy l'Asnier. At **no. 17 Rue Geoffroy l'Asnier** is the **Memorial to the Unknown Jewish Martyr**, dedicated to the Jews killed in the Holocaust. Downstairs is a large, quietly impressive crypt with a torch burning in memoriam. The upper floors house a museum of documents and pictures of the Holocaust. Turn left onto Rue François Miron.

One of the oldest and most attractive houses in Paris is at **no. 13 Rue François Miron.** Restored in the late sixties, the building has gone from crumbling, filthy plaster with the sign "Aux Frites" painted on the front to a re-creation of its original exterior of exposed beams and plaster and small wood-framed windows. The house next door, no. 11, has also been restored in the same manner.

**Hôtel de Beauvais, no. 68** Rue François Miron, is an elegant mansion built for Kate Bellier (married to Pierre Beauvais) when she was ennobled for service to the queen in 1654. Note the balcony in front for procession watching and the marvelous stone staircase *à vis*, without a central pillar, to your left in the courtyard. Check next door for information about the annual Festival of the

Marais, especially known for its concerts in the courtyard of the Hôtel de Beauvais.

Turn left to the Seine and the Ile St Louis or right to the Rue de Rivoli and a bus ride to the Louvre and the Place de la Concorde.

Paris may be exhausting but the rewards and discoveries are worth the trip.

# Cafés, Restaurants, Hotels, and Shops

## Cafés and Restaurants

The following is a list of restaurants and cafés in or near the areas of the walks. We have divided them into two categories of price, the more expensive first. These are the ones we have frequented, but there are many others for you to discover. See section on restaurants in the Introduction.

### *St Julien le Pauvre*

**La Cour Colbert**, 12 Rue de l'Hôtel Colbert, tel. 43-54-61-99. Classic French cuisine. Restored seventeenth century interior. 230f. and up.

**L'Auberge des Deux Signes**, 46 Rue Galande, tel. 43-25-46-56. Architectural and gastronomic offerings. A must. 220–400f.

**La Bûcherie**, 41 Rue de la Bûcherie, tel. 43-54-24-52. Open from 11 A.M. to 2 P.M. Walls hung with tapestries by Lurçat. 300f.

**Dodin-Bouffant**, 25 Rue Frédéric Sauton, tel. 43-25-25-14. Very fresh shellfish. 350f.

**Le Pactole**, 44 Blvd. St Germain, tel. 43-26-92-28. Reserve ahead. 145–300f.

MODERATE

**Le Petit-Pont**, 1 Rue le Petit-Pont, tel. 43-54-23-81. Pleasant café.

**Le Petit Châtelet**, 39 Rue de la Bûcherie, tel. 46-33-53-40. Traditional French food.

**Les Trois Colonies**, 10 Rue St Julien le Pauvre, tel. 43-54-31-33. Despite the name, the food is French.

**The Tea Caddy**, 14 Rue St Julien le Pauvre, tel. 43-54-15-56. Tea and lemon tart or a light lunch.

**Caveau des Oubliettes**, 52 Rue Galande, tel. 43-54-94-97. Musical nightspot with medieval artifacts.

**La Fourmi Ailée**, 8 Rue du Fouarre, tel. 43-29-40-99. Bookstore and tearoom. Books by and about women.

**Les Trois Mailletz**, 56 Rue Galande, tel. 43-54-00-79. Food and music, 10:30 P.M. to 2:30 A.M.

**Hippopotamus**, 9 Rue Lagrange, tel. 43-54-13-99. French food, with an American touch.

**Chez Maître Albert**, 1 Rue Maître Albert, tel. 46-33-13-78. Romantic and reasonable.

## St Séverin

**Allard**, 41 Rue St André des Arts, tel. 43-26-48-23. Famous bistro. Reserve ahead.

MODERATE

**Caveau de la Huchette**, 5 Rue de la Huchette, tel. 43-26-65-05. Celebrated jazz cabaret.

**Le Latin Mandarin**, 4 Rue St Séverin, tel. 46-33-04-03. Small, good, and inexpensive.

## St Germain des Prés

**L'Hôtel**, 13 Rue des Beaux Arts, tel. 46-33-89-20. Lunch in a garden atmosphere.

**Procope**, 13 Rue de l'Ancienne Comédie, tel. 43-26-89-20. The oldest restaurant in Paris, richly reminiscent of such former guests as Robespierre, Ben Franklin, and Balzac.

**Brasserie Lipp**, 151 Blvd St Germain, tel. 45-48-53-91. Reserve in advance. Restaurant of writers and publishers.

**Vagenende**, 142 Blvd St Germain, tel. 43-26-68-18. Original Art Nouveau setting.

**L'Assiette au Beurre**, 11 Rue St Benoit, tel. 42-60-87-41. Elegant Art Nouveau setting.

**Rôtisserie de L'Abbaye**, 22 Rue Jacob, tel. 43-26-36-26. Medieval spectacle and dinner.

### MODERATE

**L'Assiette au Boeuf**, 11 Rue St Benoit, tel. 42-60-88-44. One popular menu.

**Restaurant des Beaux-Arts**, 11 Rue Bonaparte, tel. 43-26-92-64. Busy bistro. Hearty food.

**Café des Deux Magots**, 170 Blvd. St Germain, and the **Café de Flore** at 172 are the intellectual cafés, made famous by writers like Sartre and Camus.

**Le Drugstore**, 113 Blvd St Germain, tel. 43-25-19-71. Food plus books plus many other things.

**La Grosse Horloge**, 22 Rue Benoit, tel. 45-48-28-12. Eat outside and watch the scene. Good food.

**Petit Zinc**, 25 Rue de Buci, tel. 40-33-79-34. Good bistro. Open until 3 P.M. The heart of a busy market street.

## Mouffetard

**La Truffière**, 4 Rue Blainville, tel. 46-33-29-82. Historic
   building. Food from Perigord.
**Coupe Chou**, 9 Rue de Lanneau, tel. 46-63-68-69. Lively.
   Waiters are often actors. Open until 1:30 A.M.

### MODERATE

**Brasserie Mouffetard**, 116 Rue Mouffetard, tel. 43-31-
   42-50. Homemade pastry and light lunches. Lively.
**Vellu**, 12 Rue Mirbel, tel. 43-31-64-89. Small place, small
   price, good food.
**Jardin de la Mouff**, 75 Rue Mouffetard, tel. 47-07-19-29.
   Known for its Tarte Tatin.
**Baskin-Robbins**, 26 Rue Mouffetard. The best ice cream
   in town.
**Crêperie de la Mouffe**, 9 Rue Mouffetard. Original Breton
   artifacts. Wide choice of crêpes.
**Maison de Corée**, 6 Rue Mouffetard. Try their chicken
   with scallions and garlic.
**Luu Dinh**, 6 Rue Thouin, tel. 43-26-90-01. Vietnamese
   food served by the boss and cooked by the family.

## Place des Vosges

**L'Ambroisie**, 9 Place des Vosges, tel. 42-78-51-45. One
   of the newest three stars and the only one in the
   Marais. High cuisine and, as expected, high price.
**La Guirlande de Julie**, 25 Place des Vosges, tel. 48-87-
   94-07. A bower of flowers and fine French food. Our
   favorite spot for outdoor dining.
**Coconnas**, 2 bis Place des Vosges, tel. 42-72-58-16. Their
   specialty is hearty stews. The owner is Claude Terail
   of La Tour d'Argent.

**Le Dômarais**, Rue Francs-Bourgeois, tel. 42-74-54-17. Elegant domed dining room that was once part of a convent. A gastronomic and architectural visit.

## MODERATE

**La Chope des Vosges**, 22 Place des Vosges, tel. 42-72-64-04. The local lunch spot. Recently redesigned.

**Nectarine**, 16 Place des Vosges, tel. 46-34-68-59. Clever salads and vegetable pies. Dense chocolate cake. Very busy.

**Eurydice**, 10 Place des Vosges, tel. 42-77-77-99. Attractive, light lunch and homemade apple pie.

**Ma Bourgogne**, 19 Place des Vosges, tel. 42-78-44-64. A good café with outdoor tables.

**Galerie Gourmande**, 38 Rue de Sévigné. The best hot chocolate anywhere. Better than Angelina's.

**Le Loir dans la Théière** ("the dormouse in the teapot"), 3 Rue des Rosiers, tel. 42-72-90-61. A homey tea room. Light lunches.

**Goldenberg**, 7 Rue des Rosiers, tel. 42-27-67-74. Jewish, but not Kosher, restaurant and take-out. Eastern European style.

**Finkelsztain**, 27 Rue des Rosiers, tel. 42-72-78-91. Bakery and appetizers, Polish style. Do try something.

**Le Gamin de Paris**, 51 Rue Vieille du Temple. Crowd always waiting outside for good bistro fare. Arrive before 7:30 P.M.

# HOTELS

## *St Julien le Pauvre*

**Hôtel le Colbert**, 7 Rue de l'Hôtel Colbert, tel. 43-25-85-65. Recently redone. TV in every room. Highly recommended.

**Hôtel Esmeralda**, 4 Rue St Julien le Pauvre, tel. 43-54-19-20. Small and wonderful.

## *St Séverin*

**Hôtel Parc St Séverin**, 22 Rue de la Parcheminerie, tel. 43-54-32-17. Pleasant spot. Best in the area.

**Hôtel du Mont Blanc**, 28 Rue de la Huchette, tel. 43-54-49-44. Remodeled. Choose a room in the back.

**Hôtel l'Albe**, 1 Rue de la Harpe, tel. 46-34-07-70. In the middle of the busy Huchette area.

**Hôtel Claude Bernard**, 43 Rue des Ecoles, tel. 43-26-32-52. English spoken. Near Blvd. St Michel.

## *St Germain des Prés*

**L'Hôtel**, 13 Rue des Beaux Arts, tel. 46-33-89-02. An extraordinary hotel with atrium.

**La Villa à St. Germain des Prés**, 29 Rue Jacob, tel. 43-26-60-00. Ultramodern. Elegant.

**St Germain des Prés**, 36 Rue Bonaparte, tel. 43-26-00-19. Modern, waterfall in lobby. Breakfast in garden room.

## MODERATE

**Hôtel Danube**, 58 Rue Jacob, tel. 45-48-42-70. Special arrangements needed for three or four in a room.

**Hôtel d'Angleterre**, 44 Rue Jacob, tel. 42-60-34-72. Breakfast served in quiet, grassy courtyard.

**Hôtel des Deux-Continents**, 25 Rue Jacob, tel. 43-26-72-46. Two connected buildings. Modern.

**Hôtel des Marronniers**, 21 Rue Jacob, tel. 43-25-30-60. Quiet. Rooms face garden.

**Scandinavia**, 27 Rue Tournon, tel. 43-29-67-20. Attractive. Breakfast extra. Very popular.

**Hôtel de Nice et des Beaux-Arts**, 4 bis Rue des Beaux-Arts, tel. 43-26-54-05. Very helpful staff.

**Hôtel du Pas de Calais**, 59 Rue des Sts Pères, tel. 45-48-78-74. Seventeenth-century with modern furnishings.

## Place des Vosges

**Hôtel Pavillon de la Reine**, 28 Place des Vosges, tel. 42-77-63-06. Recently built, but looks and feels Old World.

## MODERATE

**Hôtel de la Place des Vosges**, 12 Rue du Birague, tel. 42-72-60-46. Small, beamed ceilings, near the Place.

**Hôtel du Grand Turenne**, 6 Rue de Turenne, tel. 42-78-43-25. Convenient location.

**Vieux Marais**, 8 Rue du Plâtre, tel. 42-78-47-22. Redecorated.

# HOSTELS

**Acceuil des Jeunes en France** (AJF)—"Welcoming the Young in France." Many residences offer bed and breakfast for a low, government-regulated price in restored residences. You can make reservations on the spot only, and for a maximum of five days in the summer and, if open, eight in the winter. For general information, call 42-77-87-70 or 42-54-95-86.

## *Near Place des Vosges*

**Hôtel du Fauconnier**, 11 Rue des Fauconnier, tel. 42-74-23-45.
**Hôtel de Maubisson**, Rue des Barres, tel. 42-72-72-00.
**Hôtel de Fourcy**, Rue de Fourcy, tel. 42-74-23-45.

## *Near St Germain*

**Foyer Bonaparte**, 24 Rue Bonaparte, tel. 43-26-65-45. July 1–September 30. Women only.
**Foyer Jane Vialle**, 14 Rue Rollin, tel. 40-33-10-11. June 1–October 1. Near Mouffetard.

## *Near Mouffetard*

**Residence Mouffetard**, 80 Rue Mouffetard, tel. 45-35-09-53.

# SHOPS

The following is a selected list of shops you will pass on the walks.

# Cafés, Restaurants, Hotels, and Shops

## St Julien le Pauvre

**Shakespeare and Company**, 41 Rue de la Bûcherie. A treasury of books in English, a haven for talk and lectures.

**Cybelle**, 65 Rue St Julien le Pauvre. Archaeological gallery and bookstore.

**Librairie Gourmande**, 4 Rue Dante. Excellent collection of new and old cookbooks.

**Galerie Urubamba**, 4 Rue de la Bûcherie. Museum-quality American artifacts.

**Rouvray**, 1 Rue Frédéric Sauton. American patchwork quilts.

**L'Objet Trouvé**, 5 Rue Frédéric Sauton. Indian artifacts and jewelry.

**Tortue Electrique**, 7 Rue Frédéric Sauton. Everything about games.

## St Séverin

**Scorpion**, 9 Rue St Séverin. North African jewelry and objects.

**Metamorphoses**, 15 Rue du Petit Pont. Art Deco jewelry.

**Bookstalls** all along the Quai.

**Sartoni-Cerbeau**, 13 Quai St Michel. Engravings.

**Musique, Quai St Michel.** Large selection of sheet music.

**Galeries Michel**, 19 Quai St Michel. Engravings.

**Gibert Jeune**, The Quai and Place St Michel. Several book shops and stationery.

## St Germain

**Librairie le Divan**, 18 Rue de l'Abbaye. Serious book store.

**Claude Maxim**, 16 Rue de l'Abbaye. Chic beauty shop.

**La Hune**, 14 Rue de l'Abbaye. Art gallery.

**Cadeaux du Louvre**, 10 Rue de l'Abbaye. Museum books and posters.

**Manuel Canovas**, 6 bis Rue de l'Abbaye. One of many decorating shops in the area.

**Cipango**, 5 Rue Cardinale. Jewelry from natural materials.

**Boullé**, 28 Rue Jacob. Rare stones and minerals.

**Anaïs**, 23 Rue Jacob. Needlepoint and wool shop.

**Mme Castaing**, 32 Rue Jacob. Antiques.

**Vicky Tiel**, 21 Rue Bonaparte. Her own designer dresses.

**Librairie du Cygne**, 17 Rue Bonaparte. Scholarly art bookshop.

**Paris American Store**, 2 and 4 Rue Bonaparte. Artists' materials, framing, and gallery.

**Librairie Rossignol**, 8 Rue Bonaparte. Antique book store.

**La Porte Etroite**, 10 Rue Bonaparte. A hallway of a bookstore with a title from Gide.

**Roux Devillas**, 12 Rue Bonaparte. Old documents and scientific instruments.

**Boulakia**, 20 Rue Bonaparte. Twentieth-century art.

**Simone de Monbrison**, 22 Rue Bonaparte. Primitive art.

**Galerie Jacob**, 28 Rue Bonaparte. Modern art.

**Le Mur de Nomade**, Rue Jacob. Tapestries.

**Nobilis**, seven stores on Rue Bonaparte between the Rue Jacob and the Rue de l'Abbaye. Wall coverings and materials for the home.

**Fabrice**, 33 Rue Bonaparte. High-fashion accessories.

**Arthus Bertrand**, 6 Place St Germain des Prés. Museum reproductions of jewelry in gold, and medals and swords.

## Mouffetard

Mouffetard is a street of shops, each one worth a stop. We have chosen only a few.

**Fachetti**, 134 Rue Mouffetard. Wide and splendid choice of *charcuterie*.

**Produits de la Nature**, 130 Rue Mouffetard. Natural soaps and cosmetics.

**Evelyne Gray**, 35 Rue Daubenton. Attractive shop with gifts for the home.

**Les Panetons** and **Le Moule à Gateau**, 113 Rue Mouffetard. Eclairs, napoléons, and variations on French bread in the first give way to fruit-based tarts in the second. Worth an early visit.

## Place des Vosges

**Issey Miyake**, 3 Place des Vosges. Five dresses, presented like sculptures, on each rack. Avant-avant-garde.

**Nikki Diana Marquardt Galerie**, 9 Place des Vosges. Huge space, huge sculptures and murals.

**Popi Moreni**, 13 Place des Vosges. Young fashions.

**Galerie des Indépendants**, 17 Place des Vosges. A new gallery replacing an old gallery.

**Paco Funado**, 19 Place des Vosges. Japanese couture.

**Richelieu**, 21 Place des Vosges. For collectors. Specializes in scientific instruments.

**Les Deux Orphelines**, 21 Place des Vosges. 18th- and 19th-century popular art and objects.

**Galerie Medicis**, 23 Place des Vosges. Oldest gallery in the *place*. Watercolors are here, oils at #26.

**Max Spira**, 23 Place des Vosges. Old and new bric-a-brac, twenties-style.

**Jardin de Flore**, 24 Place des Vosges. Engravings and maps.

**Boucherie**, 6 Rue Pas de la Mule. Antique musical instruments.

**No. 20 (Place des Vosges)** is the name and address of this imaginative and history-oriented gift shop.

**Mythes et Legendes**, 18 Place des Vosges. Archaeological artifacts and antiques.

**Galerie Philip**, 16 Place des Vosges. Contemporary art.

**Fanny Liautard**, 4 Place des Vosges. Refined lingerie and home attire.

**Rue Francs-Bourgeois**—the interesting shops here are too numerous to name. Walk slowly and look.

**Lolita Lempicka**, 2 bis and 3 Rue des Rosiers. Young designer clothes.

**Labels**, 5 Rue des Rosiers. High fashion.

**Apparence**, Rue des Rosiers. Fake—but almost undiscernibly so—fur.

**Finkelsztain**, 27 Rue des Rosiers. The finest bread, cake, and appetizers on the street.

**Rue St Antoine**—food stores.

**Le Village St Paul**—antiques.

# Index

# Index

# Index

268

# Index

# *Index*